W9-BVF-070

QUICKBOOKS® 2012
QuickSteps™

THOMAS E. BARICH

New York Chicago San Francisco
Lisbon London Madrid Mexico City
Milan New Delhi San Juan
Seoul Singapore Sydney Toronto

LONGWOOD PUBLIC LIBRARY

The McGraw·Hill Companies

Cataloging-in-Publication Data is on file with the Library of Congress

McGraw-Hill books are available at special quantity discounts to use as premiums and sales promotions, or for use in corporate training programs. To contact a representative, please e-mail us at bulksales@mcgraw-hill.com.

McGraw-Hill, the McGraw-Hill Publishing logo, QuickSteps™, and related trade dress are trademarks or registered trademarks of The McGraw-Hill Companies and/or its affiliates in the United States and other countries and may not be used without written permission. All other trademarks are the property of their respective owners. The McGraw-Hill Companies is not associated with any product or vendor mentioned in this book.

Information has been obtained by McGraw-Hill from sources believed to be reliable. However, because of the possibility of human or mechanical error by our sources, McGraw-Hill, or others, McGraw-Hill does not guarantee the accuracy, adequacy, or completeness of any information and is not responsible for any errors or omissions or the results obtained from the use of such information.

QUICKBOOKS® 2012 QUICKSTEPS™

Copyright © 2012 by Thomas E. Barich. All rights reserved. Printed in the United States of America. Except as permitted under the Copyright Act of 1976, no part of this publication may be reproduced or distributed in any form or by any means, or stored in a database or retrieval system, without the prior written permission of publisher, with the exception that the program listings may be entered, stored, and executed in a computer system, but they may not be reproduced for publication.

1234567890   QDB QDB   10987654321

ISBN   978-0-07-177594-6
MHID   0-07-177594-3

SPONSORING EDITOR / Megg Morin

EDITORIAL SUPERVISOR / Jody McKenzie

PROJECT MANAGER / Tania Andrabi, Cenveo Publisher Services

TECHNICAL EDITOR / Bobbi Sandberg

COPY EDITOR / Lisa McCoy

PROOFREADER / Paul Tyler

INDEXER / Valerie Haynes Perry

PRODUCTION SUPERVISOR / Jean Bodeaux

COMPOSITION / Cenveo Publisher Services

ILLUSTRATION / Cenveo Publisher Services

ART DIRECTOR, COVER / Jeff Weeks

COVER DESIGNER / Pattie Lee

SERIES CREATORS / Marty and Carole Matthews

SERIES DESIGN / Bailey Cunningham

To my good buddies, Zoe and Benjamin, who've been with me through thick
and thin for as long as I care to remember.

About the Author

Thomas E. Barich is a QuickBooks expert, author, and consultant. In addition
to using QuickBooks to maintain his own books for the past 14 years, he has
been providing QuickBooks consulting services to small-business clients and
keeping accountants happy everywhere.

Acknowledgments

Megg Morin, my acquisitions editor, and I have been working together for so many years (on this book and others) that I can't think of anything new and clever to say about her, so I'll repeat what I've already said before. She's great to work with and makes the job (almost) a pleasure.

Bobbi Sandberg is one of the best technical editors I've ever worked with, and I'm so relieved each year when she agrees to edit my book again.

Big thanks go out to Holly Gallup at Intuit, and to Brad White and Michael Cobb at Real World Training for all the help getting beta software issues resolved.

I also want to mention a few people at Intuit who jumped in to help me resolve some last-minute issues. A heartfelt thanks to Tim Teichman, Susmitha Kodamarthi, Vinod More, Apparna Ramadoss, and Varun Nirmal.

Lisa McCoy, my copy editor, makes a difficult job look easy. She always ensures my writing has that polished look (and sound), and for that, I'm eternally grateful.

The production team, working behind the scenes, doesn't get much glory, but they certainly deserve a lot of the credit for the outstanding quality of the final product.

Jody McKenzie is my editorial supervisor, and it's her job to herd this book through the editorial and production processes. With the help of Tania Andrabi she has pulled all the loose ends together and created a work we are all proud of.

Contents at a Glance

Chapter 1 **Stepping into QuickBooks**..1
Install QuickBooks, take the EasyStep Interview, navigate the
Home Page, use the Company Snapshot, configure basic settings

Chapter 2 **Banking with QuickBooks**.................................29
Add bank accounts, make deposits, reconcile bank accounts,
understand the Online Banking Center, download transactions

Chapter 3 **Working with Lists**...............................45
Use numbered accounts; create accounts and subaccounts;
add, edit, and delete list items; manage Price Levels

Chapter 4 **Managing and Invoicing Customers**......................63
Understand the Customer Center, add and merge customers, create
jobs, view transactions, generate invoices, run sales reports

Chapter 5 **Managing Vendors and Paying Bills**......................93
Navigate the Vendor Center; add, edit, and delete vendors; enter
bills and receive items; pay bills; generate vendor reports

Chapter 6 **Tracking Inventory**...............................111
Configure inventory control; add, edit, and delete inventory items;
create subitems; generate purchase orders; adjust inventory

Chapter 7 **Running Payroll**..............................129
Get organized; add employees; enter employee wage, benefit, and
deductions data; configure payroll preferences; run payroll

Chapter 8 **Using QuickBooks Reports**............................157
Use the Report Center, filter reports, change data display, modify
report headers/footers, memorize reports, run multiple reports

Chapter 9 **Performing QuickBooks Maintenance**...............175
Back up and restore the company file, create portable files, rebuild
data, work with the Accountant's Copy, import and export data

Chapter 10 **Customizing QuickBooks**...................................197
Understand QuickBooks preferences, set e-mail defaults, use
multiple currencies, customize templates, use the Layout Designer

Appendix **Budgeting and Planning**......................................211
Prepare for a budget, create budgets, run budget reports,
export budgets, import budgets

Index 223

Contents

Introduction xi

1   Chapter 1   **Stepping into QuickBooks**...................................1
     Understanding QuickBooks Versions...2
     Get Organized 2
       Gather Your Financial Information 2
       Talk to Your Accountant...2
     Installing QuickBooks 3
       Choose a Start Date...3
     Create a New Company...3
       Use the Express Start Wizard 3
       Use the Advanced Setup (EasyStep Interview)....................................4
       Get Started with the QuickBooks Setup Wizard 11
     Use the Quick Start Center 15
       Track Money In...16
       Track Money Out 16
     Convert from Other Software 16
     Get Around in QuickBooks 17
       Understand the Home Page 18
       Use the Icon Bar 18
     Customizing the Icon Bar 19
       Display the Open Window List 19
       View the Company Snapshot..19
       Use the QuickBooks Calendar 21
     Use Access Help and the Intuit Community 23
     Using the Search Feature 24
     Set Basic Operating and Display Options...24
       Configure General Preferences 25
       Set Desktop View Options..27

2   Chapter 2   **Banking with QuickBooks** 29
     Set Up Bank Accounts...29
     Adding a Bank Account..30
       Use the Account Register...30
     Creating a Bounced Check Item 32
       Deal with Bounced Checks..32
     Make Deposits..32
     Using the Make Deposits Window..33
     Reconcile Bank Accounts 33
       View the Discrepancy Report..36
       Undo the Last Reconciliation 37
     Understanding Online Banking Services 38
     Bank Online 38
       Sign Up for Online Banking 38
       Use the Online Banking Center 38

Configuring Online Bank Accounts...39
    Add Downloaded Transactions to QuickBooks 40
    Use Renaming Rules...42
Setting Online Preferences..43
Run Banking Reports 43

Chapter 3   **Working with Lists** 45

Understand the Chart of Accounts...46
    Use Numbered Accounts...46
    Create Accounts...47
    Create Subaccounts...48
Enter List Data Quickly..49
    Customize Add/Edit Multiple List Entries Columns 51
Understanding Item Types..52
Use the Item List 52
    Create Subitems 53
Understand and Use the Class List 53
    Enable Classes 53
Adding Items 54
    Create Classes and Subclasses 54
    Add List Items 55
Understanding Customer and Vendor Profile Lists 56
    Modify and Delete List Items 56
Use Other Lists...57
    Track Assets with the Fixed Asset Item List....................................57
    Adjust Prices with the Price Level List 58
    Manage the Sales Tax Code List..58
Creating Price Levels..59
    Use the Payroll Item List..60
    Work with the Currency List..62

Chapter 4   **Managing and Invoicing Customers** 63

Understand the Customer Center 64
Adding Customers...65
    View the Customers & Jobs Tab...65
    Merge Customers...65
    Create Jobs 67
    Use the Transactions Tab..70
Setting Sales & Customers Preferences...71
Set Payments Preferences 71
Configure Sales Tax 73
Create Invoices and Sales Receipts..74
    Generate Invoices...74
    Memorize Invoices...76
Preparing Customers for Batch Invoicing...77
    Use Batch Invoicing...77
    Use Sales Receipts...79
Send Statements..81
Issuing Credit Memos 82
Receiving Payments 86
Use the Collections Center 86

Run Sales and Customer Reports...88
    View Customers & Receivables Reports...88
    Generate Sales Reports...91

Chapter 5   Managing Vendors and Paying Bills 93

Work in the Vendor Center...93
    Customize the Vendor Center...95
    Add Vendors...96
    Setting Bills Preferences...98
Enter Bills and Receive Items...98
    Enter Bills...98
    Receive Items...100
    Entering Bills for Received Items...101
    Receive Items and Enter Bills...101
    Enter Credits...101
    Entering Recurring Bills...103
Pay Bills...103
    Review and Pay Recorded Bills...103
    Pay Bills as They Arrive...105
Manage Use Tax...107
    Understand Use Tax...107
    Understanding Vendors & Payables Reports...108
    Track Use Tax...108
    Remit Use Tax...109
Run Purchase Reports...109

Chapter 6   Tracking Inventory 111

Configuring Inventory Control...111
    Configuring Inventory Preferences...112
Working with Inventory Items...112
    Add Inventory Items...112
    Understanding Inventory Tracking Basics...114
    Create Subitems...114
    Use the EasySaver Feature...115
    Create Custom Fields...116
    Use Add/Edit Multiple List Entries...117
    Generating Purchase Orders...119
Print the Worksheet...119
    Change the Display Options...119
    Preparing for an Inventory Count...121
    Use Filters on the Inventory Worksheet...121
    Change the Worksheet Appearance...122
    Memorize the Worksheet...122
Take the Physical Count...122
Make Inventory Adjustments...123
    Adjust Inventory Quantity...123
    Adjust Inventory Value...124
Make Special Inventory Adjustments...125
    Track Inventory Giveaways...125
    Understanding Inventory Reports...127
    Manage Damaged Inventory...127

Chapter 7 **Running Payroll** 129

Understand Payroll Service Choices...129
🖉 Getting Organized Before You Start.......................................130
Enable the QuickBooks Payroll Feature 130
Configure QuickBooks Payroll 131
🖥 Activating Manual Payroll 132
🖥 Creating Payroll Items as You Need Them 133
    Enter Wage and Salary Information......................................133
    Add Employee Benefits 134
🖉 Understanding Employee Types 135
    Set Up New Employees 135
🖉 Understanding Payroll Setup Wizard Limitations 138
    Configure Payroll Preferences...138
🖉 Understanding Payroll Preferences.......................................139
Navigate the Employee Center..139
    Add, Edit, and Delete Employees 140
🖉 Setting Employee Preferences..141
    View Employee Transactions 141
🖉 Setting Default Employee Information..................................143
Use Timesheets...143
    Record a Single Activity...144
🖥 Using the Weekly Timesheet 145
Create Payroll Schedules 146
🖥 Assigning Employees to Payroll Schedules 147
Run Payroll 147
🖉 Understanding Payroll Liabilities Payment Options 149
Run Payroll Reports 150
Track Vendors Who Need a 1099..150
🖥 Configuring 1099 Vendors 151
    Configure 1099 Tracking 151
    Prepare and File 1099 Forms 151

Chapter 8 **Using QuickBooks Reports** 157

Navigate the Report Center..157
🖉 Understanding the Report Center Views 159
🖉 Selecting a Report Tab 160
Configure Report Preferences...160
🖉 Understanding Basic QuickBooks Reports 162
Customize Reports 162
    Filter Reports 163
    Change Data Display...165
🖥 Setting Display Tab Options in Summary Reports...............167
    Change Header/Footer Settings..167
    Configure Fonts & Numbers Tab Options 170
🖥 Memorizing Reports..171
🖥 Running Multiple Reports..172
Export Report Data...172

Chapter 9 **Performing QuickBooks Maintenance**.......... 175

Manage Housekeeping Chores...175
    Back Up Your Data..176

7

8

9

Scheduling Regular Backups...178
Use QuickBooks Data Utilities...179
    Verify Data 179
Restoring a Backup 180
Creating a Portable Company File 181
    Rebuild Data 181
Getting Ready to Rebuild Data 182
    Condense Data 182
Create an Accountant's Copy...184
Working with the Accountant's Copy 185
Importing Your Accountant's Changes 186
Import and Export 186
    Use the File Import Utilities 186
Exporting Addresses to Text Files 189
    Export List Files...189
Understanding IIF Files 190
Understand Document Management 190
    Attach and Retrieve Documents...192
Understanding Password Protection 193
Maintain Security..193
Configuring Credit Card Protection 194
    Add Users 194

Chapter 10 **Customizing QuickBooks** 197
Add the Favorites Menu...197
Understanding QuickBooks Preferences..198
Configure Reminders 199
Using Multiple Currencies 200
Set Spell-Checking Options 201
Setting E-mail Defaults 202
Configuring Web Mail..203
Customize Templates 203
    Perform Basic Customization...203
    Use Additional Customization 205
Understanding Form Elements..207
Use the Layout Designer 207
    Customize Templates 207
Using Form Actions 209

Appendix **Budgeting and Planning** 211
Understand QuickBooks Budgets 211
Preparing for a Budget...212
Build a Profit And Loss Budget 212
    Set Up Budgets Window Basics..214
    Handy Set Up Budgets Window Tools 215
Creating Profit And Loss Budgets with Additional Criteria 217
Run Budget Reports 217
    Budget Overview Report...218
Exporting Your Budgets 221
Importing Budgets into QuickBooks 222

Index 223

Introduction

QuickSteps books are recipe books for computer users. They answer the question "How do I...?" by providing quick sets of steps to accomplish the most common tasks in a particular program. The sets of steps are the central focus of the book. QuickSteps sidebars show you how to quickly do many small functions or tasks that support the primary functions. Notes, Tips, and Cautions augment the steps, yet they are presented in such a manner as to not interrupt the flow of the steps. The brief introductions are minimal rather than narrative, and numerous illustrations and figures, many with callouts, support the steps.

QuickSteps books are organized by function and the tasks needed to perform that function. Each function is a chapter. Each task, or "How To," contains the steps needed for accomplishing the function, along with relevant Notes, Tips, Cautions, and screenshots. Tasks will be easy to find through

- The table of contents, which lists the functional areas (chapters) and tasks in the order they are presented

- A How-To list of tasks on the opening page of each chapter

- The index with its alphabetical list of terms used in describing the functions and tasks

- Color-coded tabs for each chapter or functional area, with an index to the tabs just before the table of contents

Conventions Used in This Book

QuickBooks 2012 QuickSteps uses several conventions designed to make the book easier for you to follow. Among these are

- A ⊘ in the table of contents or the How-To list references a QuickFacts sidebar in a chapter.

- A ⊙ in the table of contents or the How-To list references a QuickSteps sidebar in a chapter.

- **Bold type** is used for words on the screen that you are to do something with, such as click **Save As** or **Open**.

- *Italic* type is used for a word or phrase that is being defined or otherwise deserves special emphasis.

- Underlined type is used for text that you are to type from the keyboard. SMALL CAPITAL LETTERS are used for keys on the keyboard such as **ENTER** and **SHIFT**.

- When you are expected to enter a command, you are told to press the key(s). If you are to enter text or numbers, you are told to type them. Specific letters or numbers to be entered will be underlined.

- When you need to perform a menu command, you will be told, "Click File | Open."

How to...

- *Understanding QuickBooks Versions*
- *Gather Your Financial Information*
- *Talk to Your Accountant*
- *Installing QuickBooks*
- *Choose a Start Date*
- *Use the Express Start Wizard*
- *Use the Advanced Setup (EasyStep Interview)*
- *Get Started with the QuickBooks Setup Wizard*
- *Track Money In*
- *Track Money Out*
- *Understand the Home Page*
- *Use the Icon Bar*
- *Customizing the Icon Bar*
- *Display the Open Window List*
- *View the Company Snapshot*
- *Use the QuickBooks Calendar*
- *Using the Search Feature*
- *Configure General Preferences*
- *Set Desktop View Options*

Chapter 1
Stepping into QuickBooks

For the non-accountant, there is no accounting software more powerful and easier to use than QuickBooks. If getting your business finances in order is a top priority, QuickBooks is the right program for you. QuickBooks enables you to manage everything from invoicing your customers, to paying your bills, to generating sophisticated financial reports and graphs. When used properly, it can even cut down significantly on your accountant's fees. However, harnessing all the power that QuickBooks has to offer does have its price—a certain amount of preparation, patience, and effort on your part. Nevertheless, the time and energy you invest in QuickBooks will be amply rewarded with a clearer picture of your business finances as well as a more efficient, and hopefully a more profitable, business.

QUICK**FACTS**

UNDERSTANDING QUICKBOOKS VERSIONS

Intuit offers three versions of QuickBooks:

- **QuickBooks Pro** Pro is the most popular version, and the one that is used as the basis for this book. It offers a wide range of features suitable for most small to midsize businesses.

- **QuickBooks Premier** This is an enhanced version of QuickBooks Pro that offers additional features as well as several customized versions for different business types. It comes in an Accountant Edition, a Contractor Edition, a Retail Edition, and several other industry-specific editions. This book, *QuickBooks 2012 QuickSteps*, covers all the basics, as well as the majority of features found in QuickBooks Premier Editions.

- **QuickBooks Enterprise** This edition is aimed at the accounting departments of large organizations. This book covers many, but not all, of the features found in the QuickBooks Enterprise Edition.

In this chapter we're going to cover the basics of the latest QuickBooks release, QuickBooks 2012. To make sure you get started on the right foot, we'll cover installing the software, creating a new company, preparing your data for entry into QuickBooks, getting around in the software, and a lot more.

Get Organized

Remember, QuickBooks, like any other piece of software, is only a tool. How you use that tool determines the results of your labor. If you're familiar with the old acronym GIGO (Garbage In, Garbage Out), be advised that it applies here. If you input full, accurate financial information into QuickBooks, you will be rewarded with great results. If, on the other hand, you enter partial or inaccurate information, the results are going to reflect that. Therefore, it is imperative that you collect and organize your data before even cracking open the QuickBooks 2012 CD.

Gather Your Financial Information

The first thing to do is get all the current information for your bank accounts, customers, vendors, employees, assets, and anything else you plan to track in QuickBooks. Whether it's stored in filing cabinets, Microsoft Excel spreadsheets, or on scraps of paper in shoeboxes, now is the time to gather it all together so you have it at your fingertips when you need it.

Talk to Your Accountant

While the basic accounting rules are fairly straightforward, there are different ways of applying them. Therefore, it's important to consult with your accountant before configuring QuickBooks. The most important areas in which your accountant's input will be invaluable are opening balances, the Chart of

QUICKSTEPS

INSTALLING QUICKBOOKS

1. Insert the CD in the CD drive.

2. The installation procedure should start automatically, displaying the Welcome To QuickBooks installation wizard screen. Make sure all your Windows programs are closed, and then click **Next** to view the license agreement.

3. Click **I Accept The Terms Of The License Agreement**, and then click **Next** to display the Choose Installation Type screen.

4. Unless you have a reason to change the default settings, choose **Express (Recommended)**, and click **Next** to display the License And Product Numbers screen. The Custom And Network Options selection allows you to change the default installation folder and other advanced settings.

5. Enter your license number and product number, which should be included with the CD. After you enter the required numbers, click **Next** to view the Ready To Install screen.

6. This is your last chance to change any of the installation options you selected. To make changes, simply click the **Back** button until you reach the option you want to change. When you're satisfied, click **Install** to begin the QuickBooks installation.

7. When the installation is complete, the Congratulations! screen appears to let you know the installation has been successful. The screen includes two options—one to open QuickBooks, and the other to display help on getting started. Set these options to your liking, and click **Finish** to end the installation process.

Accounts, and payroll (if you use it). If you don't get these things right from the beginning, either you or your accountant will have a lot of cleaning up to do later on.

Choose a Start Date

The start date is the point at which you begin using QuickBooks to track all your transactions. If you're installing QuickBooks on the first day of January, this is an easy decision. As you get further into the year, the decision becomes a little trickier. The reason is that to get the most out of QuickBooks, you should still use January 1 as your start date and enter all the individual transactions that occurred between January 1 and the date you're installing QuickBooks. You can enter some historical data as cumulative totals, but you'll lose the detail information for that entire period.

Create a New Company

Unless you're upgrading QuickBooks from a previous version, your first job is to create a new company file. QuickBooks offers two ways to accomplish this task. You can use either the simplified Express Start wizard or the EasyStep Interview, which holds your hand through the setup process.

Use the Express Start Wizard

The first time you open QuickBooks after installation, the QuickBooks Setup dialog shown in Figure 1-1 appears.

As you can see, it contains a large Express Start button, an Advanced Setup button, and an Other Options button. The easiest method for creating a new company is the Express Start wizard. It contains two screens and only three mandatory fields. If you want to get up and running in just a few minutes, click the **Express Start** button.

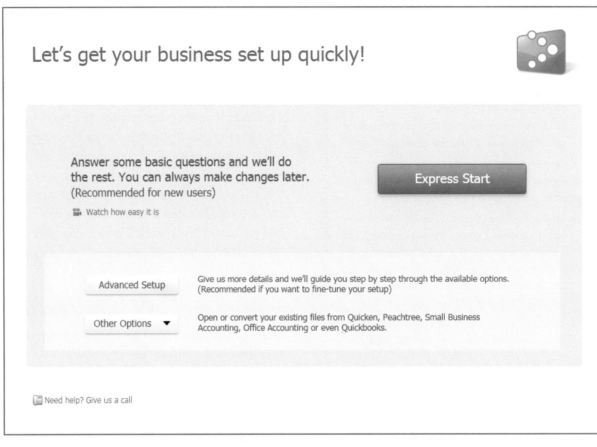

Figure 1-1: *The QuickBooks Setup dialog offers several ways to start a new company.*

Use the Advanced Setup (EasyStep Interview)

If you have a little time on your hands and want to enable all the features you'll probably need, you'll want to opt for the Advanced Setup, which opens the EasyStep Interview (see Figure 1-2).

1. Click the **Advanced Setup** button to launch the EasyStep Interview and open the company information screen.

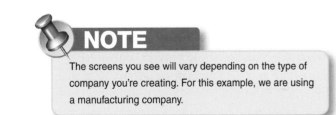

NOTE

The screens you see will vary depending on the type of company you're creating. For this example, we are using a manufacturing company.

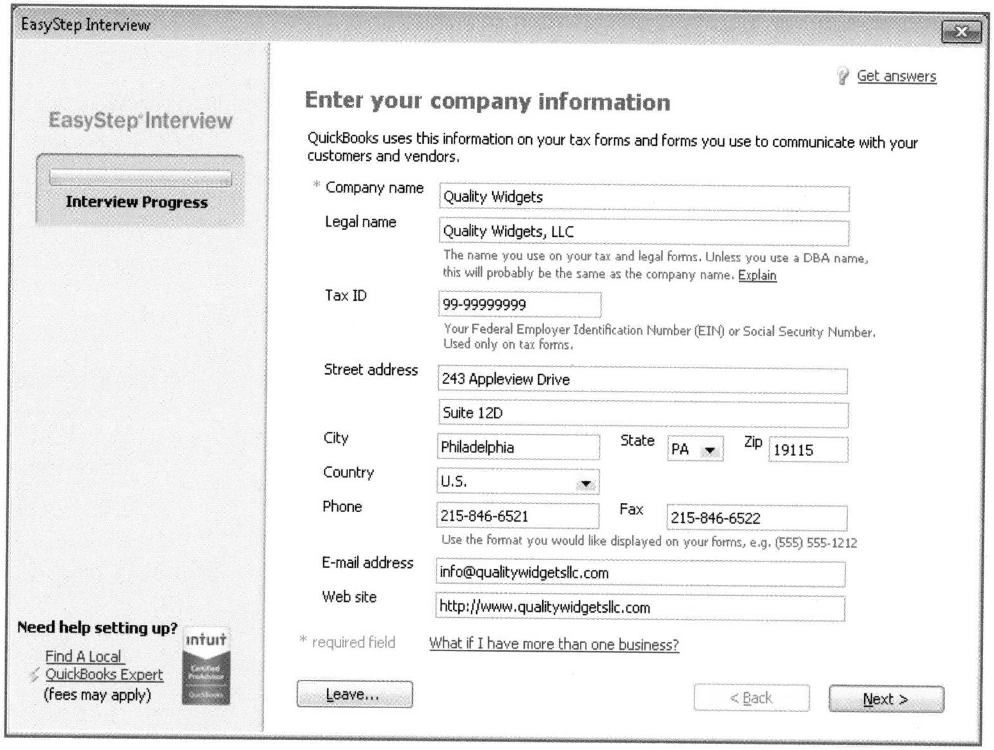

Figure 1-2: *The EasyStep Interview offers lots of guidance in setting up your company file.*

2. After you enter your company name, you can enter as much or as little information as you want. Anything you skip now, you can always add later.

3. Click **Next** and choose your industry type from the Industry list on the next screen. If your industry doesn't appear on the list, choose one that's close or one of the "General" industry types.

4. Once you've made your selection, click **Next** to view the company organization screen seen in Figure 1-3. Select the type of business entity that is appropriate for your company. If you're not sure, it's best to select **Other/None** and consult with your accountant. You can return at a later time and enter the correct information.

5. Click **Next** to choose the first month of your fiscal year. This may or may not be the same as the calendar year. This is your income tax year, so if you're not sure, check with your accountant.

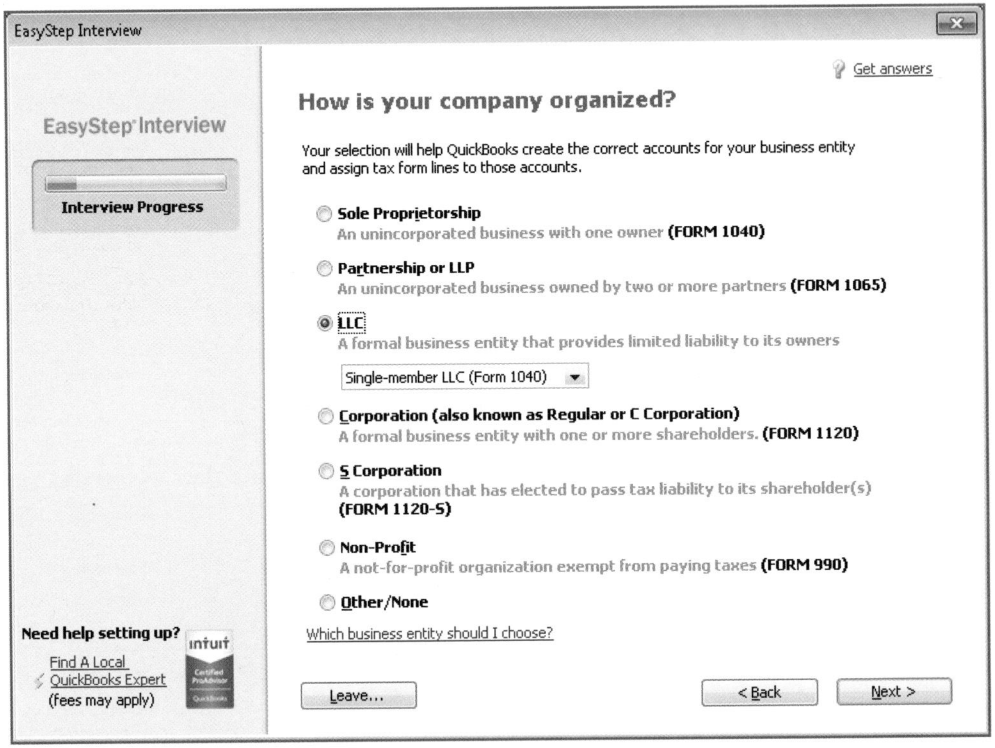

Figure 1-3: Selecting the correct business entity ensures that QuickBooks uses the proper tax forms for your company.

TIP

When choosing passwords, be sure to avoid easily guessed passwords, such as birthdays, street addresses, phone numbers, and the like. Also, make sure you write them down and put them in a secure place.

6. Clicking **Next** takes you to the administrator password screen. To ensure your financial data is secure, enter a password. Enter the password a second time, and then click **Next** to save the password and move to the Create Your Company File screen. If you don't want to assign a password, leave both fields blank and click **Next**.

7. If you're satisfied with your choices thus far, click **Next** to create the company file. If you want to make any changes, click the **Back** button until you reach the option(s) you want to modify.

8. In the Filename For New Company dialog box that opens, select a folder in which to place the company file, give the file an appropriate name, and click **Save**. For most users, accepting the default location and filename is adequate.

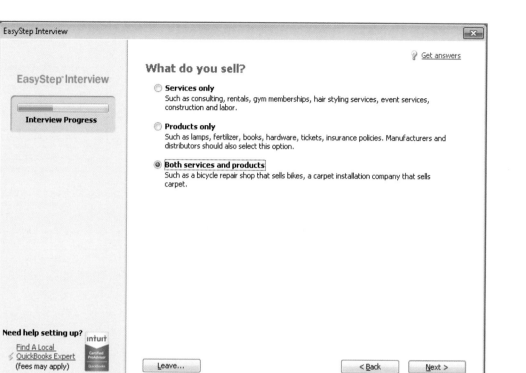

Figure 1-4: *The choice you make here will help determine the features that are enabled in QuickBooks.*

NOTE

In most cases, the choices you make during the EasyStep Interview are not etched in stone. You can usually change these settings later by modifying the QuickBooks Preferences.

9. Once the file has been created, the EasyStep Interview continues. The next screen that appears explains that the customization process is about to begin. Click **Next** to proceed to the What Do You Sell? screen shown in Figure 1-4.

10. When you click **Next**, the sales tax screen appears, asking if you charge sales tax. Choose the appropriate response, and click **Next** to view the estimates screen.

11. If your business is a retail business, you probably won't need estimates. However, if you're a contractor, manufacturer, or service provider, QuickBooks estimates might prove useful. Make the correct selection, and click **Next** to view the Using Statements In QuickBooks screen (Figure 1-5).

12. If you regularly invoice your customers, you will most likely want to turn on statements so you can periodically update customers on the status of their accounts. Select **Yes** to turn on billing statements or **No** to keep them off, and then click **Next**.

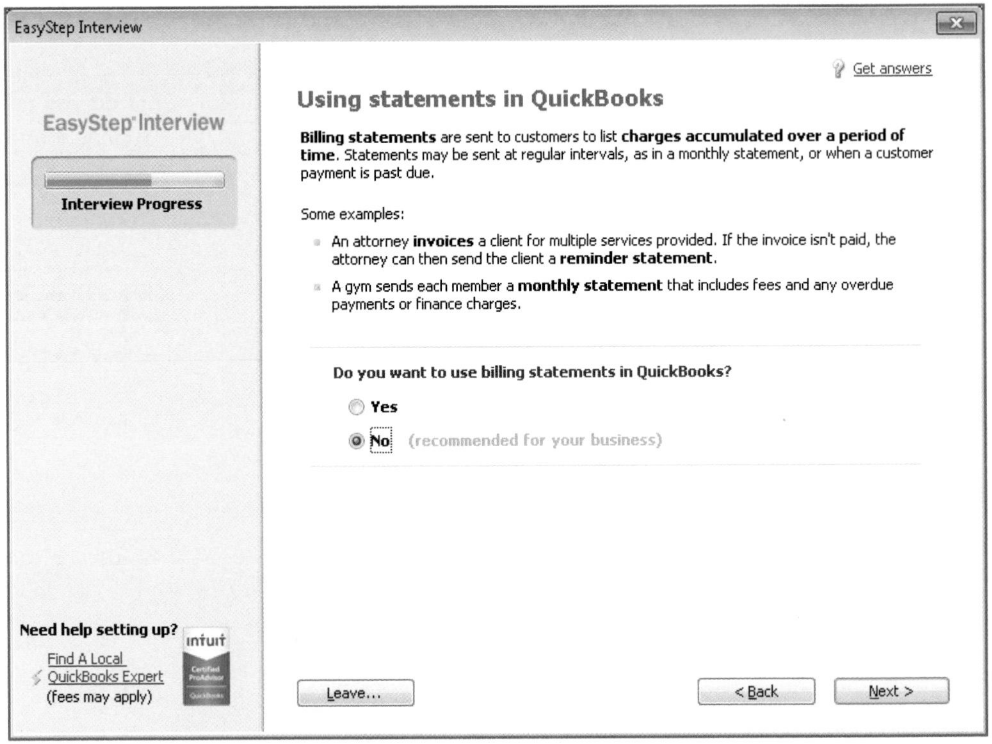

Figure 1-5: ***Statements are handy for reminding your customers about outstanding balances due, or for billing regularly recurring charges.***

13. What you see here depends on your selection in the earlier estimates screen. If you said no to estimates, this screen asks if you want to enable invoicing. Unless all your sales are paid for at the time the sale is made, you should turn invoicing on. If you said yes to estimates, invoicing was automatically enabled, and this screen asks if you want to enable progress invoicing (invoicing on partially completed jobs). Make the appropriate selection(s) for invoicing and/or progress invoicing, and click **Next**.

14. The bill tracking screen appears next. If your vendors bill you for inventory, services, and supplies, you'll want to turn on bill tracking so you can keep an eye on all your accounts-payable transactions. After you make your choice, click **Next** to move to the inventory tracking screen shown in Figure 1-6.

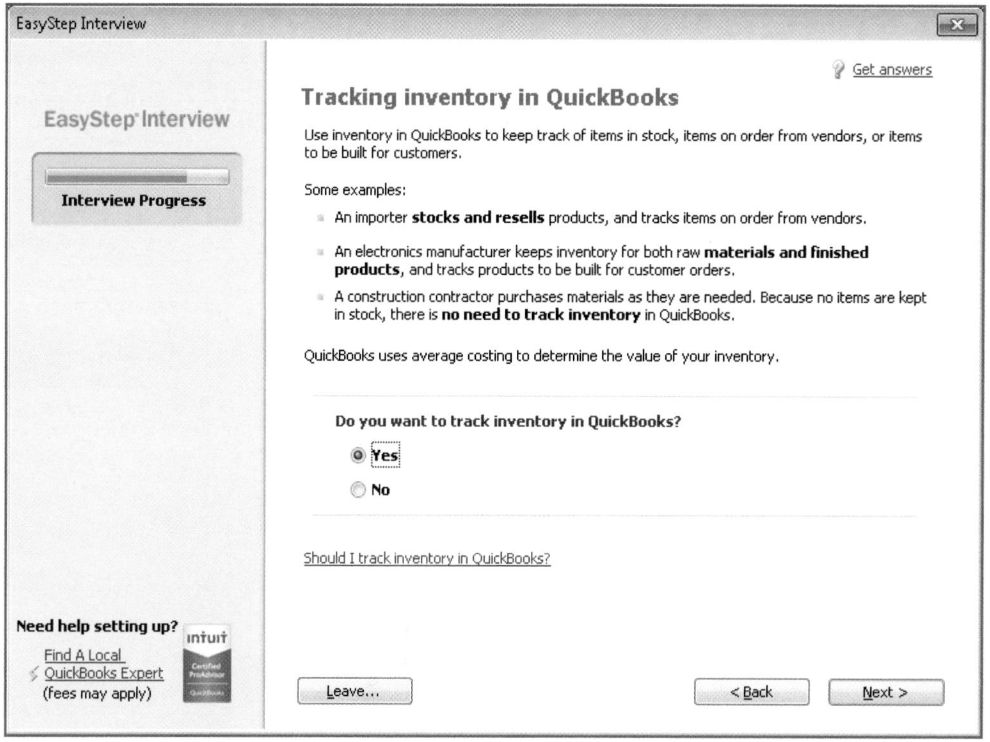

Figure 1-6: **QuickBooks is a great tool for managing your inventory.**

15. Inventory tracking is an invaluable tool if you buy or manufacture products for resale. If your company carries inventory (not supplies that you use for your business) for resale, you should turn on the inventory feature. Once you've made your selection, click **Next** to set the time-tracking option.

16. If you bill clients for time spent on projects or pay employees for time worked, time tracking will come in handy. To turn it on, select **Yes**; to turn it off, select **No**. Then click **Next** to move to the employees screen (see Figure 1-7).

17. If you have regular employees for whom you withhold taxes and pay benefits, select **Yes** and check the **We Have W-2 Employees** option. If you use independent contractors for whom you have no tax or benefit liabilities, check the **We Have 1099 Contractors** option. Of course, if you don't have employees of any type, click **No**. After you make your selection(s) click **Next** to start the process of setting up your Chart of Accounts.

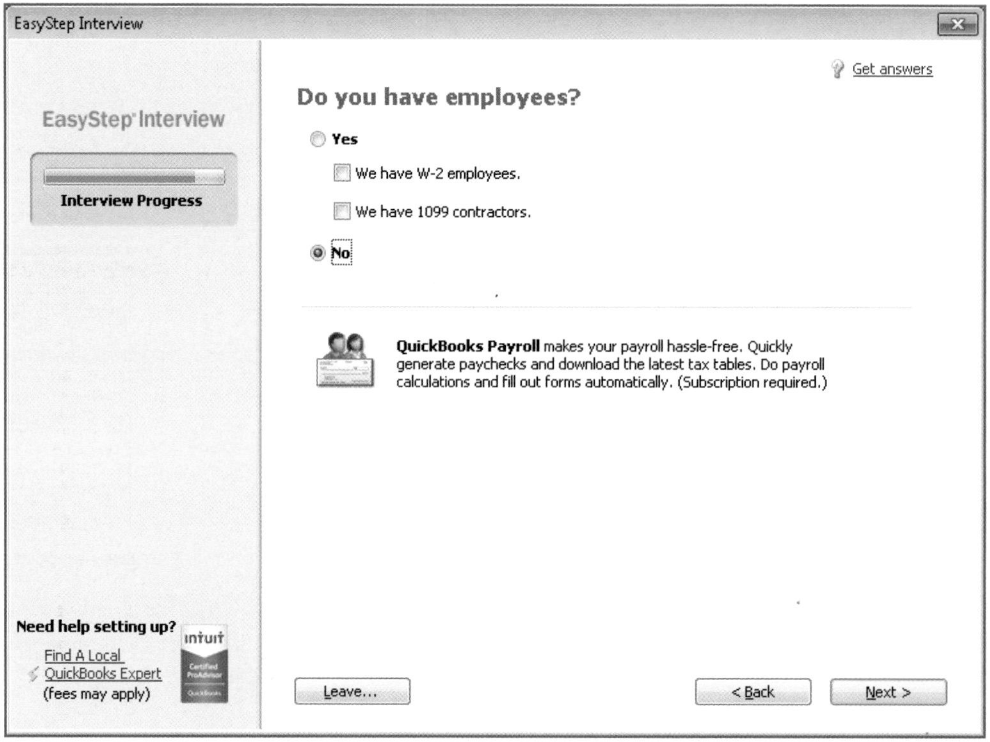

*Figure 1-7: **QuickBooks handles both regular employees and contractors.***

NOTE

For the most accurate record-keeping, you should choose the first day of the current fiscal year and then enter all the detailed transactions that have occurred between the first of the year and the date that you are setting up QuickBooks. Choosing any other date means you'll have to maintain two sets of books (your pre-QuickBooks system and QuickBooks) for the year. If you're at all unsure, you should check with your accountant.

18. The next screen is informational only, so click **Next** to begin setting up your Chart of Accounts by choosing a QuickBooks start date. Your choices are the first day of the current year or a specific date (i.e., today, the first day of the month, the first day of the quarter). Set the start date, and click **Next** to review the income and expense accounts QuickBooks has determined are appropriate for your business (see Figure 1-8).

19. Unless your accountant has suggested different accounts, the recommended list is a good starting place for most businesses. You can select or deselect accounts as you wish. When you're satisfied with the list, click **Next** to accept it and move to the final screen (whew, finally!).

The last screen is nothing more than a notification that you've completed the EasyStep Interview. Click **Go To Setup** to close the interview and begin using QuickBooks.

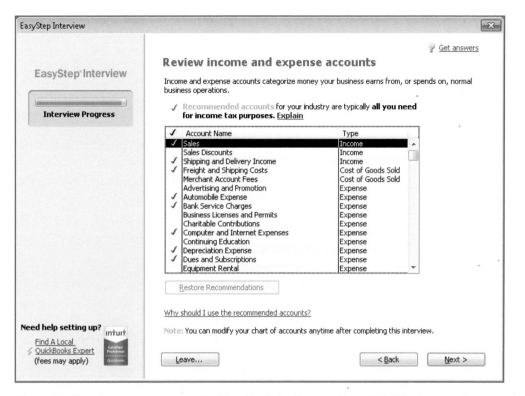

Figure 1-8: *Based on your answers to the EasyStep Interview questions, QuickBooks generates a basic Chart of Accounts for your business.*

Get Started with the QuickBooks Setup Wizard

As soon as you finish the EasyStep Interview, QuickBooks launches the QuickBooks Setup wizard (see Figure 1-9) to help you get up and running quickly. The wizard offers tools to add people you deal with (customers, vendors, and employees), products and services you offer, and bank accounts to QuickBooks.

ADD CUSTOMERS, VENDORS, AND EMPLOYEES

Adding the people you deal with is essential to maintaining your financial records. Therefore, it should be one of the first tasks you undertake. Fortunately, the QuickBooks Setup wizard makes it pretty easy. Click the **Add** button in

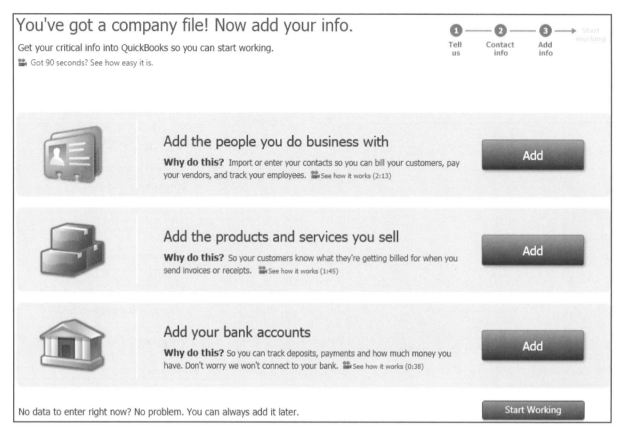

Figure 1-9: *Use the QuickBooks Setup wizard to enter essential information.*

the Add The People You Do Business With section to display your options for inputting customers, vendors, and employees.

Import from Outlook   This is a great little tool if you already have your customers, vendors, and/or employees in an Outlook contact folder.

1. Select **Import From Outlook** to display a drop-down list of Outlook contact folders.

2. Choose the Outlook contact folder to use, and click **Continue** to view a table with all the contacts from the folder (see Figure 1-10).

NOTE

The wizard offers you the opportunity to add opening balances at this point. However, it's better to wait and enter detailed information after you've imported your contacts.

3. Make a selection in one of the first four columns for each contact. Choose **Skip** to exclude the contact from QuickBooks, **Customer** to add it to the customer list, **Vendor** to add it to the vendors list, or **Employee** to add it to the Employee list.

4. Once you've assigned a category to all of the contacts, click **Continue** to review your selections.

5. Once you're satisfied with your choices, click **Continue** to add the contacts to QuickBooks.

You're immediately returned to the QuickBooks Setup wizard where the number of imported contacts is displayed. If you have additional contacts in a web mail address book or an Excel spreadsheet, you can click the **Add More** button to use a different import method.

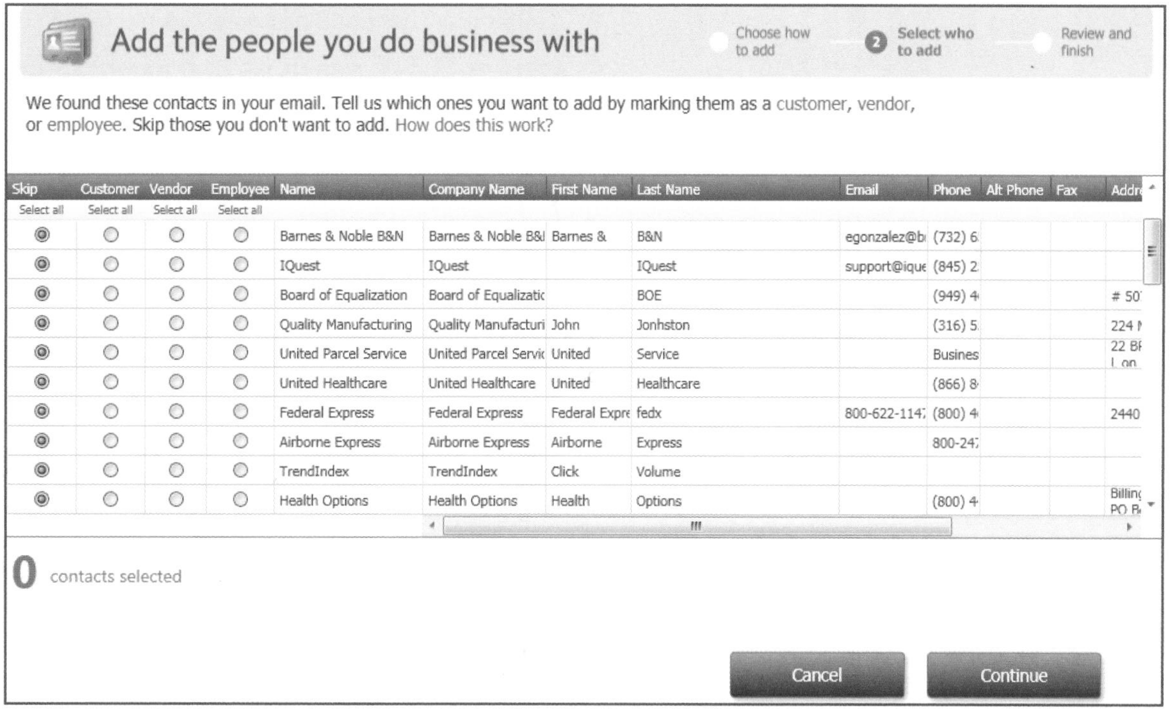

Add the people you do business with

Choose how to add — 2 Select who to add — Review and finish

We found these contacts in your email. Tell us which ones you want to add by marking them as a customer, vendor, or employee. Skip those you don't want to add. How does this work?

Skip	Customer	Vendor	Employee	Name	Company Name	First Name	Last Name	Email	Phone	Alt Phone	Fax	Addre
Select all	Select all	Select all	Select all									
◉	○	○	○	Barnes & Noble B&N	Barnes & Noble B&J	Barnes &	B&N	egonzalez@bı	(732) 6			
◉	○	○	○	IQuest	IQuest		IQuest	support@ique	(845) 2			
◉	○	○	○	Board of Equalization	Board of Equalizatic		BOE		(949) 4			# 50
◉	○	○	○	Quality Manufacturing	Quality Manufacturi	John	Jonhston		(316) 5			224 M
◉	○	○	○	United Parcel Service	United Parcel Servic	United	Service		Busines			22 BF Lon
◉	○	○	○	United Healthcare	United Healthcare	United	Healthcare		(866) 8			
◉	○	○	○	Federal Express	Federal Express	Federal Expre	fedx	800-622-1147	(800) 4			2440
◉	○	○	○	Airborne Express	Airborne Express	Airborne	Express		800-247			
◉	○	○	○	TrendIndex	TrendIndex	Click	Volume					
◉	○	○	○	Health Options	Health Options	Health	Options		(800) 4			Billing PO Bı

0 contacts selected

Cancel   Continue

*Figure 1-10: **Importing Outlook contacts is a breeze.***

Import from Web Mail Address Books When you click the **Add** button (or the **Add More** button if you've already used one import method) in the Add The People You Do Business With section, you'll see that there are two options to import contacts from Yahoo! and Gmail. Select either option, and click **Continue** to connect to a login page for the selected mail service. Log in and follow the instructions to import your contacts into QuickBooks.

Paste from Excel or Enter Manually The final import option lets you enter contact information directly into the table or copy and paste it from an Excel worksheet. Select the option and click **Continue** to view a blank table. To enter information, click in a cell and type the appropriate data. Then press the TAB key to move to the next field.

If you're going to copy and paste contact information from an Excel worksheet, it's best to copy and paste one column of data at a time.

ADD PRODUCTS, SERVICES, AND BANK ACCOUNTS

The next two sections of the QuickBooks Setup wizard allow you to manually enter product, service, and bank account information that is then imported into QuickBooks.

To enter product or service data, click the **Add** button in the Add The Products And Services You Sell section. Next, select the item type you want to add (Service, Non-Inventory Part, or Inventory Part), and click the **Continue** button. The next screen provides a blank table into which you can enter basic information about the selected item. When you're done entering data, click **Continue** to review your entries. When you're satisfied with your entries, click **Continue** to add them to QuickBooks.

Upon returning to the main screen of the QuickBooks Setup wizard, you can opt to enter more products or services by clicking the **Add More** button in the Add The Products And Services You Sell section, or you can add your bank account(s) by clicking the **Add** button in the Add Your Bank Accounts section.

If you decide to add your bank accounts, the process is even simpler. As soon as you click the **Add** button, an empty table appears with fields for entering basic account information. Enter your data, review the information, and import it into QuickBooks.

When you're done, click the **Start Working** button at the bottom of the window to open the Quick Start Center.

Use the Quick Start Center

The Quick Start Center offers a jumping-off point for getting right to work. As you can see in Figure 1-11, the Quick Start Center is divided into two sections: Track Money In and Track Money Out. To access the Quick Start Center from within QuickBooks, click the **Quick Start Center** button on the Home Page.

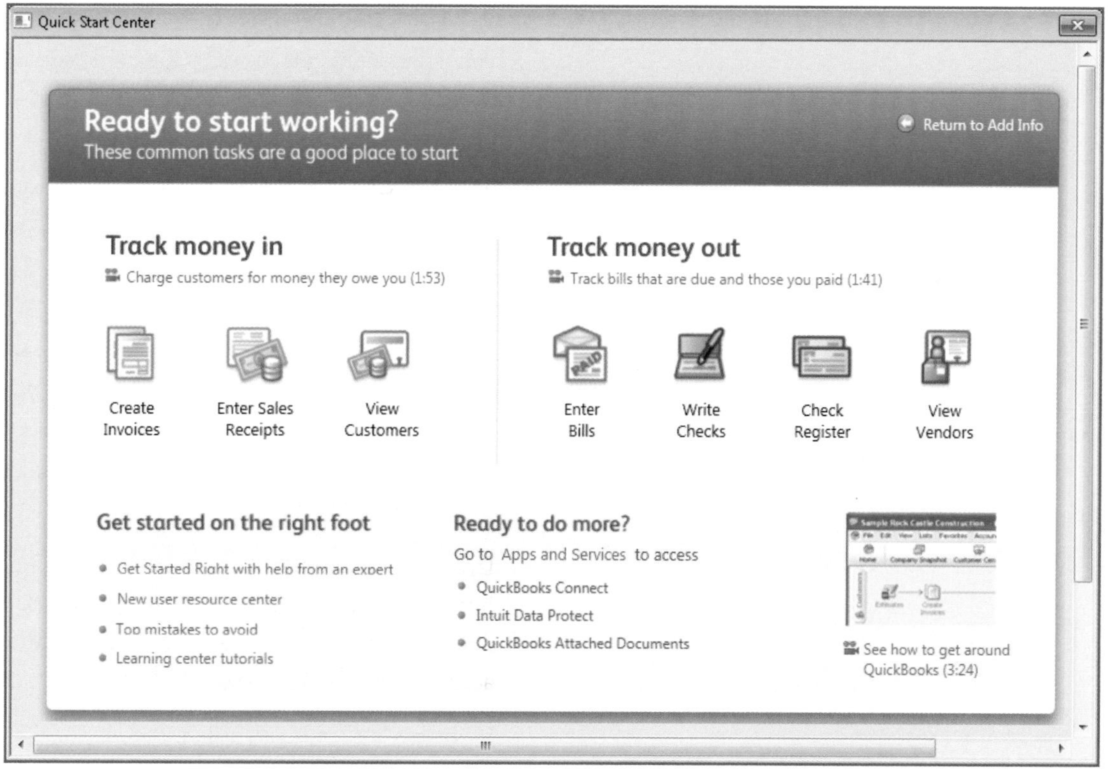

Figure 1-11: *The Quick Start Center offers ready access to some of the most commonly used QuickBooks features.*

Track Money In

This is where you'll find the features you'll need to deal with customers and customer charges. If you've already entered or imported your contacts into QuickBooks, you can start working immediately by clicking one of the icons in this section. Click the **Create Invoices** icon to open the Create Invoices window. To create a sales receipt for a customer, click the **Enter Sales Receipts** icon. Finally, to open the Customer Center where you can add new customers, edit existing customers, and view all customer-related transactions, click the **View Customers** icon.

Track Money Out

The second section deals with vendors and vendor-related transactions. Here you'll discover icons to access the Enter Bills and Write Checks windows, as well as one to open an account check register, and another to display the Vendor Center.

In addition to providing icons for accessing common features, the Quick Start Center offers a number of helpful links to related videos and webpages.

Convert from Other Software

If you've been keeping your financial data in Quicken, Peachtree, Microsoft Small Business Accounting, or Microsoft Office Accounting, you can utilize the QuickBooks conversion utility to import some or all of that information. To access the conversion utility, click **File | Utilities | Convert** and select the appropriate software from the list that appears. For anything other than Quicken, you will have to go online and download a special conversion tool.

It is beyond the scope of this book to discuss the conversion process in detail. Therefore, you should read the documentation and help file information on completing the conversion.

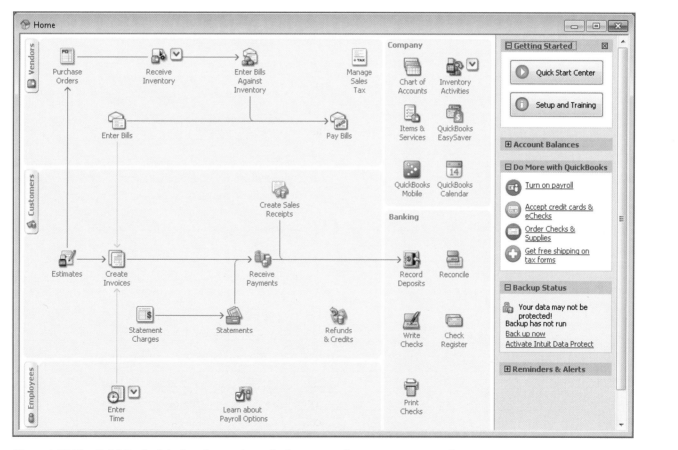

Get Around in QuickBooks

QuickBooks has a wide range of features, which means that you'll need to learn how to navigate the software so you can find the features you need, when you need them. Fortunately, the QuickBooks interface is user-friendly and offers a variety of ways to access features, including a comprehensive menu and toolbar (Icon Bar) system, as well as a handy Home Page (see Figure 1-12).

Figure 1-12: **The QuickBooks interface is easy to navigate once you learn your way around.**

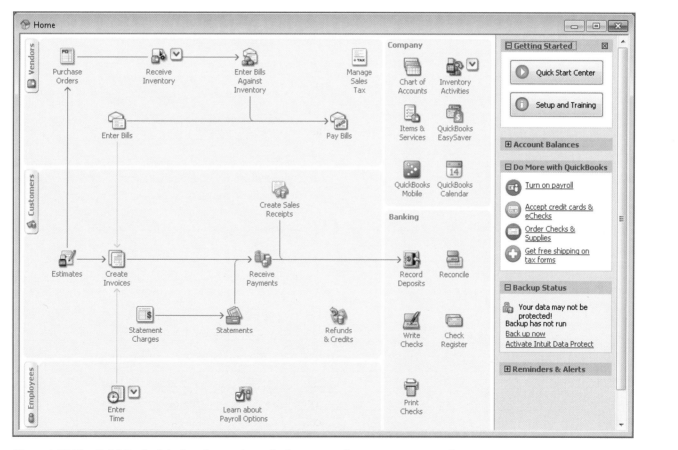

Understand the Home Page

The Home Page is really an interactive flow chart that lists the main QuickBooks features you've enabled. For example, Figure 1-12 displays the Home Page for a business that has inventory, estimates, and time tracking turned on. As you can see, it contains five main sections plus the QuickBooks Coach pane:

- **Vendors** In this section you'll find icons for common vendor-related tasks, such as creating purchase orders, receiving inventory, and entering and paying bills. To access the feature, simply click the icon.

- **Customers** The Customers section provides quick access to estimates, invoicing, statements, refunds, and more.

- **Employees** If you have employees and are running payroll, the Employees section contains icons for entering time and processing payroll.

- **Company** Here you'll find icons for the Chart of Accounts, the Item List, the inventory adjustment form, and information about Intuit online services.

- **Banking** Icons for recording deposits, writing checks, working with account registers, and more can be found here.

- **Getting Started** Clicking the Quick Start Center button launches the Quick Start Center, where you can quickly access customer and vendor functions. The Setup And Training button opens an Intuit webpage offering access to QuickBooks experts who will provide telephone support.

As you're perusing the Home Page, you'll notice that there are vertical icons along the left side of the Home Page (Vendors, Customers, Employees). Clicking these icons will take you to the associated center (Vendor Center, Customer Center, Employee Center). Spend a little time familiarizing yourself with the Home Page, and you'll see just how easy it is to access basic features using the Home Page icons.

NOTE

In theory, you can customize the Home Page. However, to hide most (not all) of the icons that appear, you have to turn off the features associated with them. If you need a feature, you certainly can't turn it off just to customize the Home Page. Therefore, the ability to customize the Home Page is limited to removing a couple of minor icons and deciding when to display it.

Use the Icon Bar

The Icon Bar (referred to in most other Windows programs as the toolbar) is a handy navigation tool—especially since it can be modified to include the icons you use most frequently. Using the Icon Bar is easy: just click an icon to access the associated feature.

QUICKSTEPS

CUSTOMIZING THE ICON BAR

Being able to add, remove, and edit the icons on the Icon Bar makes it an invaluable tool.

1. Right-click anywhere on the Icon Bar, and select **Customize Icon Bar** to open the Customize Icon Bar dialog box.

2. The first thing to do is remove any icons that you don't need or want by selecting the item in the Icon Bar Content list and then clicking the **Delete** button. Don't worry—you're just "deleting" it from the Icon Bar.

3. To add an icon to the Icon Bar, select an existing item in the Icon Bar Content list, and click the **Add** button to display the Add Icon Bar Item dialog box. The new icon appears below the selected item in the list and to the right of it on the Icon Bar.

4. In the Add Icon Bar Item dialog box, click a QuickBooks feature in the left pane, select an icon from the Icon List, accept or change the text for the Label and the Description fields, and click **OK** to return to the Customize Icon Bar dialog box.

5. To modify an existing icon, select the item from the Icon Bar Content list in the Customize Icon Bar dialog box, and click the **Edit** button to display the Edit Icon Bar Item dialog box.

6. Now, select a new icon, change the label text, and/or change the description text. When you're done, click **OK** to return to the Customize Icon Bar dialog box.

Continued . . .

Display the Open Window List

If you're one of those folks who like their windows maximized, you may frequently find that you have no idea just how many windows you currently have open. It's easy to open a window and then move on to another task without closing the original window. Fortunately, QuickBooks offers a simple way to keep track of what's open and to quickly move between all your open windows. It's the Open Window List.

To display the Open Window List, select **View | Open Window List** from the menu bar.

To display any window, simply click the window name in the Open Window List. To close the list, click the **X** in the upper-right corner of the Open Window List pane.

View the Company Snapshot

The name pretty much says it all. As you can see in Figure 1-13, this handy tool provides a quick view of many facets of your business finances. You'll also note that the Company Snapshot has three tabs: Company, Payments, and Customer.

Each of the three tabs offers a variety of graphs and brief reports that give you a quick overview of your financial situation at any given moment:

- **Company tab** Here you'll find an Income And Expense Trend graph, a listing of account balances, another of customer balances, and some previous-year comparison graphs.

CUSTOMIZING THE ICON BAR
(Continued)

To make the Icon Bar even more functional, you can group icons (e.g., all customer-related icons) by arranging them and placing separator bars between groups. This requires two steps: moving the icons into place and adding separator bars.

7. To move an icon, click the item in the Icon Bar Content list, and drag it (by the diamond on the left) up or down. Moving an item up moves the icon to the left on the Icon Bar. Moving it down moves it to the right.

8. Once you've arranged your items in the Icon Bar Content list, select the last item in the group you want to create, and click the **Add Separator** button. This places a vertical separator bar to the right of the last icon in the group. In the dialog box, the separator is listed as "(space)."

9. By default, both the icons and their descriptive text (labels) are shown. However, if you can easily recognize the icons and want to fit more on the Icon Bar, select **Show Icons Only** from the Display Options section.

10. If you like having a Search box in the Icon Bar, check the **Show Search Box In Icon Bar** option.

11. When you're through customizing the Icon Bar, click **OK** to save your changes and return to QuickBooks.

- **Payments tab**   The Payments tab offers a set of links to payment-related features, such as receiving payments and creating sales receipts, credits, and refunds. You'll also see an A/R aging report, a listing of customer balances, and more.

- **Customer tab**   This is where you can get a close look at the performance of a single customer. Select a name from the Customer drop-down list, and you can see a summary of sales, a listing of recent invoices, a sales history in graph form, and quite a bit more.

Not only does the Company Snapshot provide an overview of your business, it also allows you to drill down beyond the surface by double-clicking various elements. As you move your mouse pointer over the page, you'll notice that in certain places the cursor turns into a magnifying glass with a Z (for Zoom). Whenever you see this magnifying glass cursor, you can double-click to see more detail. For example, double-clicking one of the month bars on the graph displays a detailed report for that particular month. If you double-click an account listing, it opens the account register.

There are even a few customizations you can make to the Company Snapshot if you're so inclined:

- **Date range drop-down lists**   All the graphs include a date range field from which you can select a different time period for the displayed graph data.

- **Account drop-down lists**   Many of the graphs that display account information provide a drop-down list to select the account(s) for which you want information shown.

- **Links**   Some of the lists found in the Company Snapshot include links to view or change the source of the list. For example, the Account Balances list offers two links: one to choose the accounts to display in the list (see Figure 1-14), and the other to open the Chart of Accounts list.

In addition to these customization options, the Company Snapshot provides an Add Content button in the upper-left corner that allows you to preview and add views to the snapshot window. To remove a view from the window, simply click the **X** in the upper-right corner of the view window.

Figure 1-13: *A regular review of the Company Snapshot will keep you informed about your company's financial health.*

Figure 1-14: *You decide which accounts to display in the Account Balances section of the Company Snapshot.*

Use the QuickBooks Calendar

The QuickBooks Calendar, seen in Figure 1-15, is a new addition that gives you a quick overview of your transactions in a daily, weekly, or monthly format.

As you can see, the Calendar consists of three distinct areas—the calendar itself, a detail pane below, and a past due pane to the right:

- **Calendar** The Calendar displays a single day's worth of transactions, a week's worth, or a month's worth, depending on which view you select. The three buttons to the right of the Today button at the top of the window let you select the different views. The Daily view offers a complete listing of all transactions for the day. The Weekly view offers five days' worth of daily listings (seven, if you expand the calendar). The Monthly view offers a calendar graphic with totals listed for each day, and a daily view for the selected date, in the pane below the calendar.

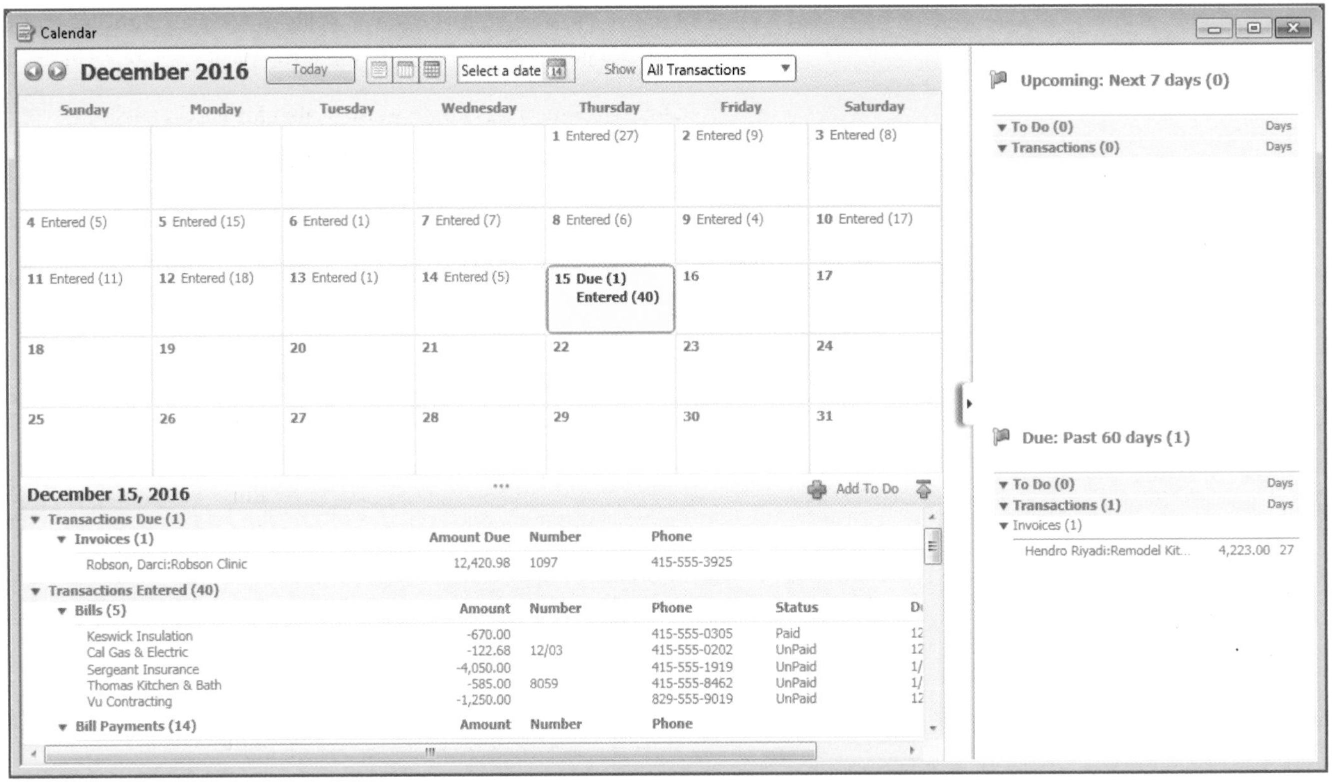

Figure 1-15: *Use the Calendar to see the status of your QuickBooks transactions.*

- **Detail pane** This is actually the Daily view for the selected day in either the Weekly or Monthly view. If you select the Daily view, this pane disappears and the list of transactions for the day fills both the Calendar area and the Detail pane.

- **Past Due pane** Here you'll find a list of any transactions that are overdue as of today's date, regardless of the date you select on the calendar.

Using the Calendar is fairly straightforward. The buttons and fields along the top of the window allow you to change the view, the date, and even determine the type of transactions you want displayed. You can view a transaction by double-clicking its listing in the Daily view, the Weekly view, or in the Detail pane.

One last thing you can do in the Calendar is add to-do items to the To Do List. In either the Weekly view or the Monthly view, click the **Add To Do** icon found on the right side of the Detail pane.

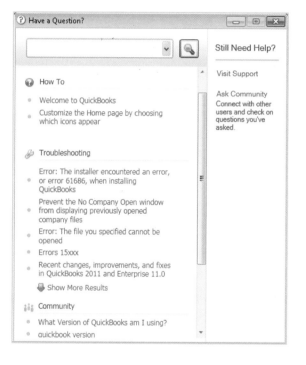

Use Access Help and the Intuit Community

When you find yourself in the middle of a task and realize that you need some help, don't panic—reach for QuickBooks Help. The help system in QuickBooks 2012 has changed somewhat from previous versions. Gone is the Help Viewer that used to appear on the right side of the QuickBooks window. You now have to access help by pressing the F1 key, selecting **Help | QuickBooks Help** from the menu bar, or by enabling the Help search box on the Icon Bar.

Pressing F1 or selecting **Help | QuickBooks Help** brings up a free-floating Have A Question? dialog into which you can enter your search words or phrases. By default, the dialog will be populated with topics related to the currently open window in QuickBooks.

Once you enter a search term and press ENTER (or click the magnifying glass icon), related help topics appear in one of three categories: How To, Troubleshooting, or Community. How To links are to standard QuickBooks help topics. Troubleshooting links open online articles from the Intuit support site, and Community links open topic discussions from the online Intuit Community (formerly Live Community). No matter which type of link you click, a new window opens with the help information. Both help windows remain in the forefront until you close them. If you want to access the Intuit Community directly, click the **Ask Community** link on the right side of the Have A Question? dialog.

CAUTION

While the Intuit Community offers a wealth of QuickBooks information, it also, unfortunately, offers a lot of misinformation. Therefore, be sure to verify any information you glean from the online community. It is best to check with your accountant before implementing any accounting advice you find here—even advice from the experts or the Intuit employees.

QUICKSTEPS

USING THE SEARCH FEATURE

The QuickBooks search feature enables you to perform a comprehensive, company-wide search that even includes menu commands.

1. Select **Edit | Search** from the menu bar to display the Search dialog box.

2. Enter the term(s) on which you want to search.

3. To ensure that all transactions are included in the search, click the **Update Search Information** link. QuickBooks will scour your file for any new transactions and display a confirmation dialog box. Click **OK** to continue.

4. To narrow your search, use the advanced search features and set the following filters:

   a. **Show Results From** This is a listing of transactions and other items found containing the search term(s). It even includes menus that contain the search term. Click a specific listing to display the results from that category.

Continued . . .

If you prefer to access help from the Icon Bar, you can add a Help search box. Right-click anywhere on the Icon Bar, and select **Customize Icon Bar** to display the Customize Icon Bar dialog box. At the bottom of the box you'll find a Show Search Box In Icon Bar option. Enable it and click **OK** to return to working in QuickBooks. You'll now find a Search Company Or Help search box on the right side of the Icon Bar. Enter your search query, click the down arrow to the right, choose **Help** from the menu that appears, and click the magnifying glass icon to the right.

Search Company or Help

Set Basic Operating and Display Options

As good as QuickBooks may be right out of the box, it can be even better with a little tweaking. A couple of things you'll probably want to customize before you get started are the way QuickBooks interacts with you and the way the QuickBooks Desktop is configured.

To change the way QuickBooks works, choose **Edit | Preferences** from the menu bar to open the Preferences dialog box shown in Figure 1-16.

The first thing to notice is that the Preferences dialog box consists of three parts: a category pane to the left, a My Preferences tab, and a Company Preferences tab. When you select a category on the left, the options are shown in the two tabs. The My Preferences tab is for user-specific options. Each person who uses the active company file on this computer can set his or her preferences in this tab without affecting any of the other users. The options in the Company Preferences tab are company-wide options that apply to all users who access this company file through this (or any other) computer.

QUICKSTEPS

USING THE SEARCH FEATURE

(Continued)

b. Amount Filter   Searching for a transaction is a lot easier if you eliminate those transactions that are either over or under the amount of the transaction you're searching for. Even if you don't know the exact amount, you can still narrow the search if you know the approximate amount. You can use Exactly, Greater Than, or Less Than operators.

c. Date Filters   If you scroll down in the Search box you'll find a Date Range filter consisting of a From field and a To field, both containing pop-up calendars. Set your date range, and click **Go**.

5. To view specific items, hover your mouse over the search results, and click the appropriate icon that appears.

One last thing. You can customize the Search feature by opening the Search preferences (**Edit | Preferences | Search | Company Preferences**). Here you can set an automatic search update and determine the frequency of the updates.

NOTE

All users can access and modify the options on the My Preferences tab. However, only the QuickBooks administrator or an External Accountant user can change the Company Preferences options.

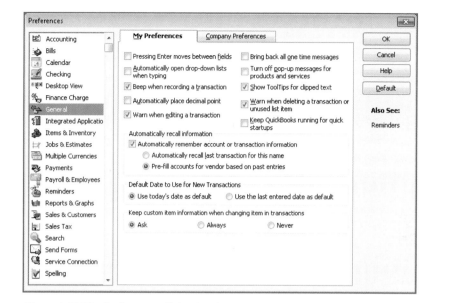

Figure 1-16: **The Preferences dialog box is the control center for QuickBooks customizations.**

Configure General Preferences

Customizing general preferences is the first order of business.

1. Click the **General** category in the left pane.

2. Click the **My Preferences** tab to display the user-specific General options.

3. Enable or disable the following options as needed:

- **Pressing Enter Moves Between Fields**   By default, the TAB key moves the cursor between fields and the ENTER key saves the transaction. If you like using the ENTER key for moving between fields as well, check this option.

- **Automatically Open Drop-Down Lists When Typing**   When you encounter a field that contains a drop-down list in a QuickBooks form, enabling this option will cause the list to open automatically when you begin typing in the field.

- **Beep When Recording A Transaction**   If you like audio feedback, this option's for you. When it's enabled, QuickBooks plays a sound each time you record a transaction.

- **Automatically Place Decimal Point**   Some people love it; some hate it. When this option is checked, QuickBooks automatically inserts a decimal point as you enter numbers. It uses two decimal places. In other words, if you enter 22, it becomes .22. If you enter 2200, it becomes 22.00.

- **Warn When Editing A Transaction**   This is a good option to enable since it alerts you when you try to leave a transaction after editing it but without saving it. When the option is disabled, the edit is discarded without warning.

- **Bring Back All One Time Messages**   Most QuickBooks warning messages include an option to turn the messages off in the future. That's a great option, because sometimes you just want to ignore the warning/advice. However, you can check this option if you want to reactivate all those messages you've turned off.

- **Turn Off Pop-Up Messages For Products And Services**   This is another great option. If you don't want to receive a barrage of advertising messages from Intuit (buy checks, sign up for services, and so on), check this option.

- **Show ToolTips For Clipped Text**   This is a handy option that shows the complete text when a field is too long to display the text entirely. When you hover your mouse over the field, all the text appears in a ToolTip.

- **Warn When Deleting A Transaction Or Unused List Item**   Another safety feature, this option gives you the chance to reconsider when deleting either a transaction or unused list item (you can never delete an item that has been used in a transaction).

- **Keep QuickBooks Running For Quick Startups**   This is one of those options that's great in theory, but not so hot in practice. The idea is to keep QuickBooks running in the background after you close it down so that you can start it up quickly when you need it. While it works as advertised, it also sucks up a lot of valuable memory that could be better used elsewhere. So, unless you're constantly opening and closing QuickBooks (in which case you might as well leave it open all the time), there's really no good reason to enable this option.

- **Automatically Recall Information**   This option, which is an autofill option, has two parts. After you enable it, you can have QuickBooks fill in a new transaction form with information from the last transaction completed for that person or with the accounts most frequently used for the individual.

- **Default Date To Use For New Transactions**   You can elect to have QuickBooks automatically use today's date or the last date (other than today's) that you entered in a transaction. This comes in handy if you regularly enter transactions on one day but with a different transaction date (i.e., entering invoices today, but with the last day of the month as the invoice date).

- **Keep Custom Item Information When Changing Items In Transactions** If you enter a custom description and/or price for an item in a transaction and then change the item, you can still use the custom description and/or price for the new item, depending on how you set this option. If you choose **Ask**, QuickBooks gives you the choice to use or discard the custom data. If you set this to **Always**, QuickBooks automatically retains the custom data. If you select **Never**, QuickBooks automatically discards the custom data.

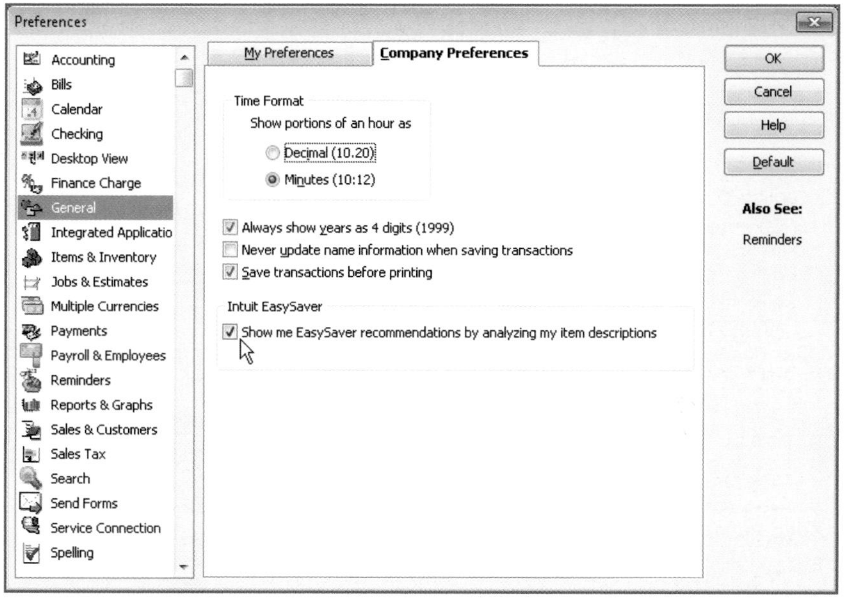

4. Now click the **Company Preferences** tab to display the company-wide options shown in Figure 1-17.

5. Set the **Time Format** option to display partial hours as decimals or as minutes.

6. Enable or disable the remaining options as needed:

   - **Always Show Years As 4 Digits (1999)** There's not much more to say about this option except that if you deselect it, the year will appear as two digits (99).

   - **Never Update Name Information When Saving Transactions** By default, QuickBooks asks if you want to save changes you make to names (customer, vendor, employee) in the course of a transaction. If you check this option, QuickBooks will automatically discard any changes made during a transaction.

   - **Save Transactions Before Printing** This option should always be enabled to minimize the possibility of fraud. When this option is enabled, the user must save a transaction before being allowed to print it. If you deselect this option, a user could create a transaction such as a packing slip to send merchandise to a friend or relative without having any record of the transaction.

Figure 1-17: There are only a handful of options on the Company Preferences tab.

Set Desktop View Options

The next set of options that you should review and customize if necessary is the Desktop View options shown in Figure 1-18.

Since the Company Preferences tab only contains Home Page settings (and not much in the way of true customization options), we're going to only cover the

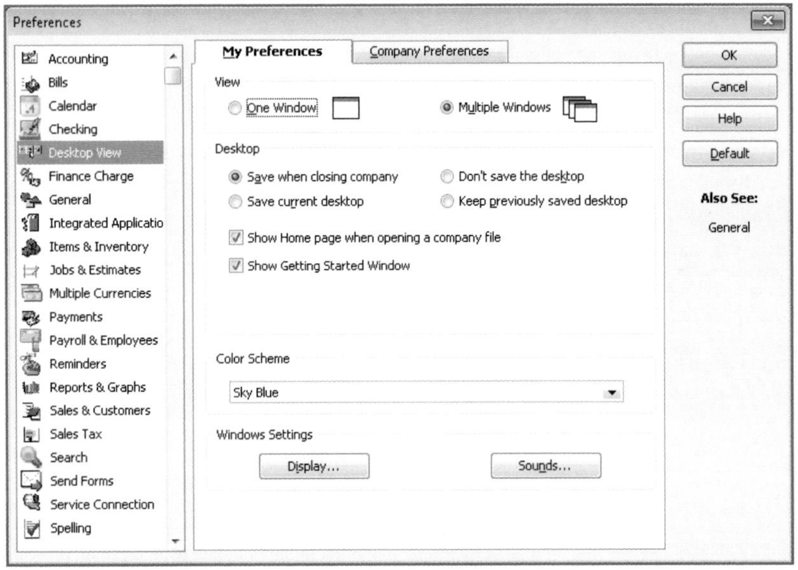

Figure 1-18: **Desktop View options let you customize the way QuickBooks opens and displays windows.**

My Preferences tab here. The following options can be used to customize the QuickBooks desktop:

- **View** If you like to tile or cascade multiple windows so you can see and use them easily, check the **Multiple Windows** option. If you prefer to have only a single, maximized window visible at any given time, check the **One Window** option. Either way, you can have multiple windows open at the same time. This is just a matter of viewing preference.

- **Save When Closing Company** The QuickBooks desktop is really the state of the open windows in QuickBooks. Choosing this option means that whatever windows are open when you close the company file will automatically be reopened the next time you access this company file.

- **Save Current Desktop** If you've got the desktop set just the way you want it, select this option. Once you set this option, QuickBooks always starts with the same windows that were open at the time this option was set, regardless of the windows open at closing.

- **Don't Save The Desktop** Choose this option to start QuickBooks with no open windows. Keep in mind, however, that the Show options (Show Home Page, Show Getting Started Window) found on this page supersede this option and will display, when checked, even if this option is enabled.

- **Keep Previously Saved Desktop** Once you use the Save Current Desktop option, this option is automatically selected. Therefore, the next time you open the Desktop View preferences, you will have the option to use the Save Current Desktop option again, in case you want to save the desktop with a different set of windows than before.

- **Show Home Page When Opening A Company File** Regardless of which Desktop option you selected previously, checking this option ensures that the Home Page displays when you open QuickBooks.

- **Show Getting Started Window** Like the preceding option, this one, when enabled, forces the display of the Getting Started pane that includes the Quick Start Center button and the Get Started Right button, regardless of any other desktop options you have set.

- **Color Scheme** If you want to dress up (or down) the QuickBooks environment, choose a different color scheme from this drop-down list.

- **Windows Settings** This section contains two buttons that will open the associated Windows applets—Display and Sounds. Just remember that changes made here affect all Windows programs, not just QuickBooks.

How to...

- ⚙ *Adding a Bank Account*
- • *Use the Account Register*
- ⚙ *Creating a Bounced Check Item*
- • *Deal with Bounced Checks*
- ⚙ *Using the Make Deposits Window*
- • *View the Discrepancy Report*
- • *Undo the Last Reconciliation*
- ⚙ *Understanding Online Banking Services*
- • *Sign Up for Online Banking*
- • *Use the Online Banking Center*
- ⚙ *Configuring Online Bank Accounts*
- • *Add Downloaded Transactions to QuickBooks*
- • *Use Renaming Rules*
- ⚙ *Setting Online Preferences*

Chapter 2
Banking with QuickBooks

One of the most important functions QuickBooks performs is managing your bank accounts. Today, that means more than simply keeping your checkbook balanced. With online banking fast becoming the norm, you have unprecedented opportunities for taking complete control over all your banking functions. Fortunately, QuickBooks provides you with all the tools needed to do just that.

Set Up Bank Accounts

If you used the EasyStep Interview to configure QuickBooks, you were offered the opportunity to create a new bank account. In this section you're going to learn how to create a new bank account any time you need one, without returning to the interview.

QUICKSTEPS

ADDING A BANK ACCOUNT

In order to manage your bank accounts, you must, of course, first add them to QuickBooks.

1. Press **CTRL+A** to open the Chart of Accounts window.

2. Press **CTRL+N** to display the Choose Account Type dialog box.

3. Choose **Bank** as the account type to create, and then click **Continue** to open the Add New Account dialog box.

4. Enter an appropriate account name (i.e., Operating Account, 1st National Checking Account, Payroll Account, and so on). If you're using numbered accounts, enter the number as well.

5. You can enter a description if you want, but it's entirely optional.

6. While you don't have to enter any additional information, you probably should fill in the **Bank Acct. No.** field now if you plan to use this account with online banking.

7. Once again, if you're going to use this account online, it might be a good idea to enter the routing number now in the **Routing Number** field. You'll find the routing number on the lower-left corner of your checks. It's the nine-digit number that appears to the left of the account number.

8. The Tax-Line Mapping field, which appears next, is useful if you plan to export your tax information to tax preparation software. Otherwise, there's no need to use the line. As always, if you're in doubt, check with your accountant.

Continued . . .

Use the Account Register

Once the bank account is added, you can begin entering transactions immediately. The account register can be used to enter historical data or to enter manually written checks. In either case, you first must open the account register by pressing **CTRL+R** to display the Use Register dialog box.

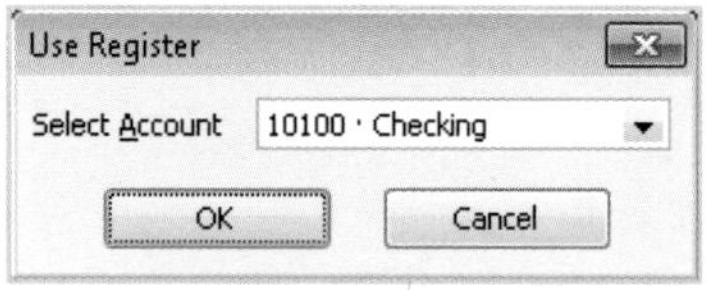

In the Use Register dialog box, select the appropriate account from the **Select Account** drop-down list, and click **OK** to display the account register (see Figure 2-1).

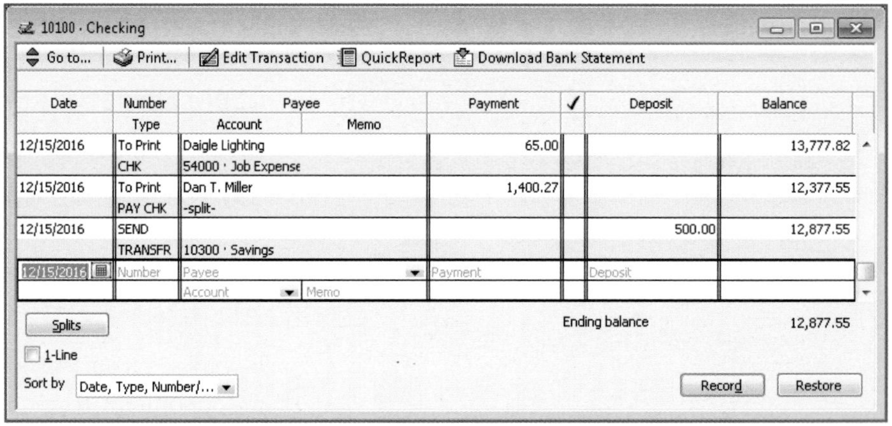

Figure 2-1: **The QuickBooks account register resembles the checkbook register that comes with a regular checkbook.**

QUICKSTEPS

ADDING A BANK ACCOUNT *(Continued)*

9. Save yourself time and aggravation and do *not* enter any information in the Enter Opening Balance field. The opening balance should be created by entering detailed historical information into the account register. This is another area in which the advice of your accountant can be invaluable.

10. If you want to set a reminder to ensure you don't run out of checks, enter the number of the check that you want to use as the trigger for the reminder in the **Remind Me To Order Checks When I Reach Check Number** field.

11. If you check the **Order Checks I Can Print From QuickBooks** option, QuickBooks will open a browser window and take you to the Intuit website (if you have an active Internet connection) as soon as you save and close the Add New Account dialog box. You can order QuickBooks-compatible checks directly from Intuit at this website.

12. When you're done, click **Save & Close** to save the new account and return to the Chart of Accounts. If you want to add more accounts, click **Save & New** to save the account and open a new Add New Account dialog.

NOTE

If you happen to be in the Chart of Accounts with an account selected, pressing **CTRL+R** bypasses the Use Register dialog and automatically opens the register for the selected account.

Entering information in the register is fairly straightforward, but there are a couple of things that you should be aware of:

- **Check Number** QuickBooks automatically assigns the next available check number.
- **Payee** You can select a payee from the Payee drop-down list or add a new one by clicking the **<Add New>** item in the list. The drop-down list includes all customers, jobs, vendors, and employees, as well as Other Names list entries.
- **Account** As with the Payee field, you can either select an account from the Account drop-down list or add a new one by clicking the **<Add New>** item on the list.

The register also features a handy button called Splits. It is great for assigning a transaction to multiple accounts. For example, if part of your phone bill is for internal use and part of it is for calls made on behalf of clients, you can use the Splits button to assign one portion to the Utilities account and the other portion to the Reimbursable Expenses account.

To use the feature, click the **Splits** button to display the splits window shown in Figure 2-2.

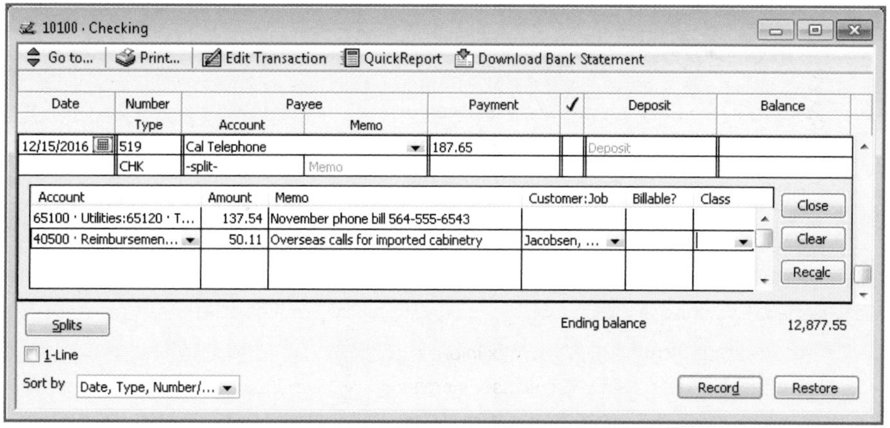

*Figure 2-2: **Not all transactions are assigned to only one account.***

QUICKSTEPS

CREATING A BOUNCED CHECK ITEM

The first step is to create a special item in the Item List to which you can assign the amount of the bad check.

1. Select **Lists | Item List** from the menu bar to display the Item List window.

2. Press **CTRL+N** to open the New Item dialog box.

3. Select **Other Charge** from the Type drop-down list.

4. Enter an appropriate name (i.e., <u>ISF</u> for insufficient funds, or <u>NSF</u> for nonsufficient funds).

5. The Description field is optional, so enter as much or as little as you want.

6. Leave the **Amount Or %** field blank.

7. Select **Non** from the Tax Code drop-down list.

8. From the **Account** drop-down list, choose the bank account into which customer checks are deposited.

9. Click **OK** to save the new item and return to QuickBooks.

NOTE

If you order special deposit slips from Intuit or another provider, you can print deposit slips directly from the Make Deposits window. If you don't have special deposit slips for printing, you can still print a deposit summary that will help in filling out your regular deposit slip. To print a summary, click the **Print** button at the top of the Make Deposits window, select **Deposit Summary**, and click **OK**.

Enter the payee and payment information, and then click the **Splits** button. In the window that appears, enter the first account and change the **Amount** field to reflect the amount you want assigned to this account. QuickBooks automatically recalculates and enters the balance in the Amount field of the second line. Keep entering as many accounts as you need, changing the **Amount** field each time. For the final account, just enter the account and leave the amount as-is.

When you're done entering the transaction, click the **Record** button to save the transaction details and move to the next entry.

Deal with Bounced Checks

When a customer's check is returned by the bank, you have to make sure your records correctly reflect not only the returned check, but also any charges associated with it.

After you create the insufficient funds item, you have one more item to add—a bank service charge item for the service charge levied by the bank. The steps are basically the same for creating this item. Like the insufficient funds item, this is also an Other Charge item. To minimize confusion with other bank charges, give this one a name that indicates it's only for bounced checks. For example, you might name it ISFsvcChg or NSFBankChg. If that's not going to be clear enough, you can add a clarification in the Description field.

Make Deposits

Whether you've received payments from customers, refunds from vendors, or capital that you're putting into the business, you've got to get it into the bank and let QuickBooks know about it. That's where the Make Deposits window, seen in Figure 2-3, comes in.

QUICKSTEPS

USING THE MAKE DEPOSITS WINDOW

The Make Deposits window enables you to deposit customer payments already received in QuickBooks, as well as any other miscellaneous deposits you haven't yet recorded.

1. Choose **Banking | Make Deposits** from the menu bar to open the Make Deposits window.

2. If you have any customer payments that have been received but not deposited, the Payments To Deposit window opens automatically.

3. In the Payments To Deposit window, click (place a check mark to the left of) each payment you want to include in this deposit. To include all the available payments, click the **Select All** button.

4. After you've made your selection(s) click **OK** to move to the Make Deposits window, where you'll find the selected payments listed.

5. From the **Deposit To** drop-down list, select the bank account into which you want the money deposited.

6. Set the date to the actual date the deposit is being made. For example, if you're filling out the deposit information today but going to the bank tomorrow, use tomorrow's date.

7. To deposit money or checks not found in the Payments To Deposit window, move to the next blank line and click in the **Received From** field to display a drop-down list of customers, vendors, employees, and other names.

8. Either select a name from the list or click **<Add New>** at the top of the list to create a new name.

9. Move your cursor to the **From Account** field, and click to display your Chart of Accounts list. Either select an existing account or use the **<Add New>** item to create a new account.

Continued . . .

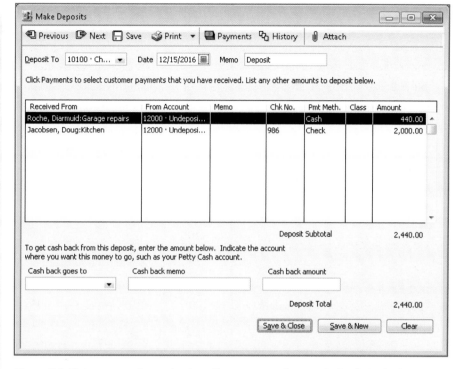

Figure 2-3: Enter payments received or other sources of money to be deposited.

Reconcile Bank Accounts

Reconciling bank accounts is one of those jobs that all too many people like to put off for another day. Unfortunately, it's one of those critical tasks that can come back to bite you if you don't keep up with it. Finding simple mistakes (yours or the bank's) in a timely fashion can save you money, time, and aggravation. So, grab your statement and let's begin.

QUICKSTEPS

USING THE MAKE DEPOSITS
WINDOW (Continued)

10. Add a note to the **Memo** field so you don't later wonder where the money came from.

11. If you're depositing a check, enter the number in the **Chk No.** field; otherwise, leave it blank.

12. From the drop-down list in the **Pmt. Meth.** field, select the type of payment.

13. Repeat for all other monies you want to deposit.

14. If you're depositing checks and getting money back (usually not allowed with a business account), use the **Cash Back Goes To** drop-down list to indicate the account to which the money back should be assigned.

15. If you are getting money back, you should probably make a note in the **Cash Back Memo** field so you don't forget the circumstances.

16. Enter the amount of money you want back in the **Cash Back Amount** field.

17. Click **Save & Close** to finish, or click **Save & New** to save this deposit information and create another deposit.

TIP

If the beginning balances don't match, someone probably modified, voided, or deleted a previously cleared transaction, or erroneously cleared or uncleared a transaction. If you can't find the problem by reviewing the account register, click the **Locate Discrepancies** button and run a Discrepancy Report.

1. From the menu bar, select **Banking | Reconcile** to open the Begin Reconciliation window.

2. From the **Account** drop-down list, select the bank account to reconcile.

3. Enter the date of the paper statement against which you're reconciling the account.

4. Double-check that the Beginning Balance field matches the beginning balance listed on the statement.

5. In the **Ending Balance** field, enter the ending balance on the statement.

6. Finally, enter service charges and interest earned amounts.

7. When you've entered the necessary information, click **Continue** to open the Reconcile window, seen in Figure 2-4, and begin the reconciliation process.

8. To simplify the process, check the **Hide Transactions After The Statement's End Date** option. This (temporarily) eliminates those transactions that could not possibly appear on the statement, since they were created after the statement was issued. If your account does not reconcile, disable this option in case you inadvertently entered an incorrect date in a transaction.

9. In the Reconcile window, check off (click once) each item that appears on the bank statement.

With any luck, when you're finished, the Difference amount will equal 0, meaning that you and the bank agree. If it doesn't, you've got to root out the problem, which may fall into one of the following categories:

- Transactions with incorrect amounts

NOTE

Service charges are only those bank charges for maintaining your account (i.e., monthly service charges). Do not include overdraft, bounced check, ATM, or even check purchase charges here.

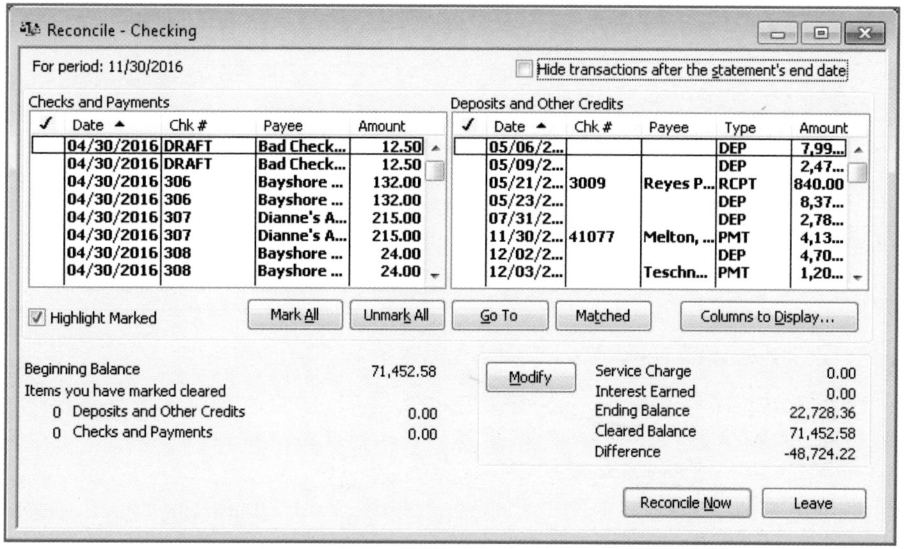

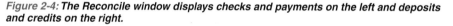

Figure 2-4: *The Reconcile window displays checks and payments on the left and deposits and credits on the right.*

- Transactions with transposed numbers (if the Difference amount is divisible by 9, a transposed number is probably the culprit)
- Payments entered as deposits, or vice versa

10. When the Difference amount equals 0, click the **Reconcile Now** button to finish the reconciliation and display the Select Reconciliation Report dialog.

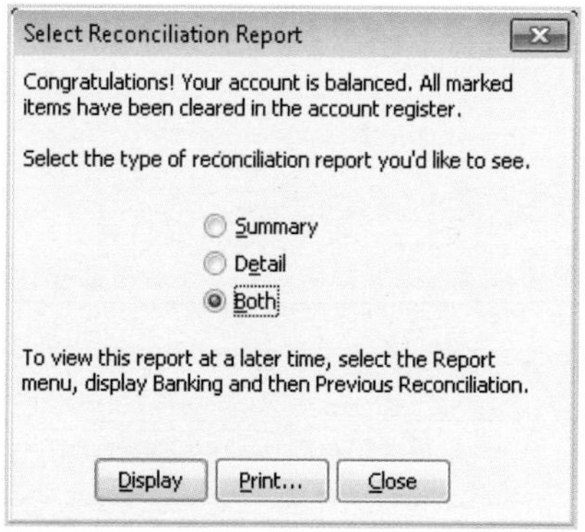

11. Make your choice and click **Display** to see the report(s) on-screen, or click **Print** to open the Print Reports dialog box, where you can set your printing options and print hard copies.

12. If the Difference amount does not equal 0 and you can't find the problem, you can force a reconciliation by clicking the **Reconcile Now** button.

13. In the Reconcile Adjustment window that appears, click the **Enter Adjustment** button to finish the reconciliation and create a journal entry for the adjustment. The Select Reconciliation Report dialog box then appears, from which you can choose the reports you want printed or displayed.

If you force the reconciliation and later find the source of the problem, you (or your accountant) can create another journal entry to transfer the adjustment amount to the appropriate account.

View the Discrepancy Report

QuickBooks has a handy little feature, called the Discrepancy Report, that can help find discrepancies resulting from changes to previously cleared transactions.

1. In the Begin Reconciliation dialog box, click the **Locate Discrepancies** button to show the Locate Discrepancies window seen in Figure 2-5.

2. The Account field displays the bank account listed in the Begin Reconciliation dialog box. If, for some reason, you want to view a Discrepancy Report for another account, select that account from the drop-down list.

3. Click the **Discrepancy Report** button to generate the report, which displays modified transactions, along with the type of change made. QuickBooks only uses three types of changes:

- **Amount**   Amount is listed as the type of change for both voided transactions and transactions with amount changes. Therefore, you'll have to drill down in the report to discover whether the listed transaction was voided or had its amount changed.

- **Uncleared**   If a previously cleared check has been uncleared, that's what you see in the Type Of Change column.

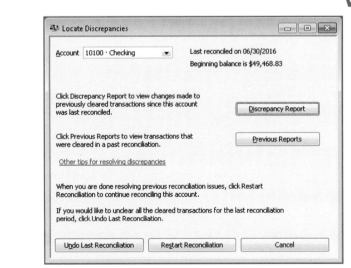

Figure 2-5: *You can run a new Discrepancy Report or view previous reports.*

TIP

You can also run the Discrepancy Report by selecting
Reports | Banking | Reconciliation Discrepancy from
the menu bar. A small dialog box appears with a single
field—Specify Account. Select the account for which you
want to run the report, and click **OK** to generate the report.

- **Deleted**   Deleted transactions are identified clearly in the Type Of Change column by the use of the word "Deleted."

There are few modifications you can make to the report, with the exception of adding and removing columns. If several transactions are listed, you might want to print a hard copy to use while finishing the reconciliation.

Undo the Last Reconciliation

If you're having a difficult time reconciling your account and you believe the problem may be related to the previous reconciliation, you can reset the cleared status of all transactions changed during the last reconciliation by using the Undo Last Reconciliation feature.

1. Select **Banking | Reconcile** to open the Begin Reconciliation dialog box.
2. From the **Account** drop-down list, choose the bank account for which you want to undo the last reconciliation.
3. Click the **Undo Last Reconciliation** button to display the Undo Previous Reconciliation dialog.
4. If you're sure you want to reset the last reconciliation, click **Continue**; otherwise, click **Cancel** to return to the Begin Reconciliation dialog box.

A notification dialog appears letting you know that the process is finished and that service charges, interest earned, and adjustments have *not* been removed. When you click **OK**, you are returned to the Begin Reconciliation dialog box. If you want to start the reconciliation process anew, do not reenter service charges and interest earned amounts, but *do* delete the adjustment following these steps.

1. Press **CTRL+R** to open the Use Register dialog box.
2. From the **Select Account** drop-down list, choose the account containing the adjustment transaction you want to delete.
3. Click **OK** to open the associated register.
4. Right-click the adjustment transaction you want to delete, and select **Delete General Journal** from the shortcut menu that appears.

That's all there is to it. You're now ready to start your reconciliation with a clean slate.

QUICK**FACTS**

UNDERSTANDING ONLINE BANKING SERVICES

The online banking services many banks offer fall into two categories—those accessible through a web browser and those accessible through QuickBooks. Most banks allow users to view their accounts online, make transfers between accounts, and pay bills online, all with an Internet connection and a web browser. Most banks also offer one or more of the following QuickBooks-related services:

- **Web Connect**   With Web Connect, you can log on to your bank's website through QuickBooks and download a QuickBooks-compatible file that contains your account transactions. You can then import the transactions directly into QuickBooks.

- **Direct Connect**   If your bank offers Direct Connect, you can download transactions from your bank's website directly into QuickBooks. This eliminates the two-step process of downloading a file and then importing it into QuickBooks. Since this service requires the bank to install special software on its servers, it's not as common as the Web Connect service, and usually incurs an extra fee.

- **Bill Pay**   These days, most banks offer a bill-paying service that you can use through your web browser. If you're lucky, they'll also offer a bill-paying service that can be accessed through QuickBooks. If they don't, there's still another alternative—the QuickBooks Bill Pay service. For a fee, you can sign up for the service and pay your vendors through QuickBooks.

Bank Online

For convenience and speed, nothing beats online banking. If your bank offers the services, you can check your account balances, transfer money between accounts, download transactions, and communicate directly with the bank. All you need is QuickBooks and an Internet connection.

Sign Up for Online Banking

The first thing to do is find out which, if any, of the services your bank offers and then sign up for them (if you've already signed up, skip to the "Configuring Online Bank Accounts" QuickSteps). Be sure you have an active Internet connection before starting.

1. Select **Banking | Online Banking | Participating Financial Institutions** to launch the QuickBooks web browser, which displays the Financial Institutions Directory.

2. Scroll through the list of financial institutions until you find yours.

3. Click your bank's listing to be taken to a webpage listing the services they offer, the supported QuickBooks transaction download method, and an Apply Now button that opens an online application form, a page with instructions on how to apply, or just takes you to the bank's home page.

4. Click the **Apply Now** button, locate the application form, fill it out, and submit it.

That's all you can do for the moment. You have to wait for your online banking kit to arrive from the bank with instructions as well as your login information.

Use the Online Banking Center

Once your accounts are configured for online access, you can use the QuickBooks Online Banking Center to view your account balances, download transactions, and even send transactions and messages (if you have Direct Connect) to your bank.

To open the Online Banking Center, select **Banking | Online Banking | Online Banking Center** from the menu bar. The Online Banking Center provides an overview of your online accounts, including balances, items ready to send (Direct Connect only), and items received.

QUICKSTEPS

CONFIGURING ONLINE BANK ACCOUNTS

Once you've signed up for online banking with your banking institution, the next step is to set up your QuickBooks bank account(s) to work with the online services.

1. Make sure you have a live Internet connection.

2. Select **Banking | Online Banking | Set Up Account For Online Services** from the menu bar to launch the setup wizard.

3. From the **Select Your QuickBooks Account** drop-down list, choose the existing account you want to set up, or click **<Add New>** to create a new account. Then click **Next**.

4. From the **Enter The Name Of Your Financial Institution** drop-down list, select the financial institution that you want associated with the account, and click **Next**.

5. If your bank only offers Web Connect, the next page instructs you to download a statement for your bank's website into QuickBooks to complete the setup process. Click the **Go To My Bank's Web Site** button to launch the QuickBooks browser and visit your bank's website, where you can download a transaction file. Depending on your bank's site structure, you might find it under Statements, Transactions, Download Transactions, or something similar.

6. If your bank offers both, you have two choices on the next page:

   a. **Direct Connect**   Select **Direct Connect** and click **Next**. QuickBooks asks if you've activated the account. If your answer is yes, choose

   Continued . . .

USE WEB CONNECT

Start by clicking the **Receive Transactions** button to launch the QuickBooks web browser and go to the bank's website.

After you log in, locate the transaction download page, enter the parameters (dates, file type, and so on), and start the download. The Microsoft Windows download dialog box appears.

If you click **Save**, the Save As dialog box appears and you can select the folder into which you want the file saved. If you click **Open**, the QuickBooks dialog box appears, offering the option to automatically import the new transactions or save them to a file to be imported later.

QUICKSTEPS

CONFIGURING ONLINE BANK ACCOUNTS *(Continued)*

that option and click Next to enter your login information and sign in. If you haven't activated your account, select the option to view your bank's contact information.

b. Web Connect Choose this option and click the **Go To My Bank's Web Site** button to launch the QuickBooks browser. When you get there, log in and download a statement.

7. After you log in and download the transactions (Direct Connect) or statement (Web Connect), click **Finish** to open the Online Banking Center.

Once you've completed the initial download and import (if necessary), the account will be configured for online access.

NOTE

The first time you start a download from the Online Banking Center, you may see an Update Branding Files dialog. Don't worry—QuickBooks is just updating its bank-related data.

NOTE

The first time you import a Web Connect file, you'll have to link it to a QuickBooks Bank account.

If you always want the data imported automatically, deselect the **Always Give Me The Option Of Saving To A File When I Download Web Connect Data** option. Click **OK** to either import the data or save the file. If you elect to import the file, QuickBooks does so immediately and informs you when the process is complete. If you choose to save the data to a file, QuickBooks opens the Save Web Connect File For Later Import dialog box. Select a location and filename, and click **Save**.

When you're ready to import saved data, select **Banking | Online Banking | Import Web Connect File** from the menu bar to display the Open Online Data File dialog box. Locate and select the file, and then click **Open** to start the import process. When the import is complete, QuickBooks displays a dialog box informing you that the data has been successfully imported.

USE DIRECT CONNECT

The Direct Connect process is much simpler. As soon as you click the **Send/Receive Transactions** button, QuickBooks displays the Access To *<Name of Bank>* dialog. When you enter your PIN and click **OK**, QuickBooks automatically downloads the new transactions.

Add Downloaded Transactions to QuickBooks

After you download (and import, if necessary) new transactions, the next step is to add them to the account register.

ADD MATCHED TRANSACTIONS

QuickBooks attempts to match all downloaded transactions against existing transactions in the account register using check numbers, amounts, payees, and dates to determine matching transactions. If it finds any matches, it makes a note at the top of the left pane of how many matches it found and hides the details for those transactions. To see the details, click the **Show** link next to the matched transaction(s) listing.

1. Click the **Add Transactions To QuickBooks** button, and select the account to which the transactions should be added.

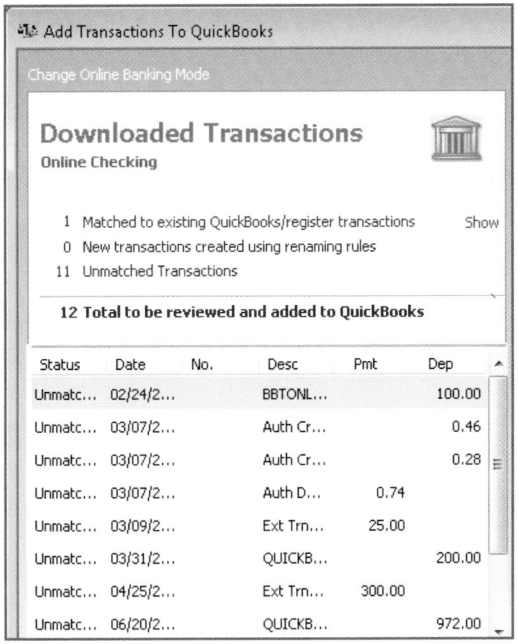

Add Transactions To QuickBooks

Change Online Banking Mode

Downloaded Transactions

Online Checking

1	Matched to existing QuickBooks/register transactions	Show
0	New transactions created using renaming rules	
11	Unmatched Transactions	

12 Total to be reviewed and added to QuickBooks

Status	Date	No.	Desc	Pmt	Dep
Unmatc...	02/24/2...		BBTONL...		100.00
Unmatc...	03/07/2...		Auth Cr...		0.46
Unmatc...	03/07/2...		Auth Cr...		0.28
Unmatc...	03/07/2...		Auth D...	0.74	
Unmatc...	03/09/2...		Ext Trn...	25.00	
Unmatc...	03/31/2...		QUICKB...		200.00
Unmatc...	04/25/2...		Ext Trn...	300.00	
Unmatc...	06/20/2...		QUICKB...		972.00

Figure 2-6: **By default, QuickBooks displays details for unmatched transactions only.**

2. A Temporarily Close All Windows dialog appears, informing you that QuickBooks must close all windows before proceeding. Click **Yes** to open the Add Transactions To QuickBooks window seen in Figure 2-6.

3. Click the **Show** link to display the details of each matched transaction.

4. Select the first matched transaction to display the Confirm Match window in the right pane. The right pane shows the existing transaction in the account register.

5. If the transactions are truly a match, click the **Confirm This Match** button to clear the transaction (QuickBooks adds a lightning bolt symbol to the Cleared column in the register).

6. If the transactions are not a match (i.e., the amount may be the same but the payee is different), click the **Not A Match** button to mark the transaction as Unmatched.

7. Complete the process for all matched transactions.

ADD UNMATCHED TRANSACTIONS

Any transaction for which there is no existing transaction with the same check number, payee, amount, or date is marked Unmatched. Once you open the Add Transactions To QuickBooks window, you can either add the transaction to the register or delete the transaction if it has already been entered and cleared.

As soon as you click the first unmatched transaction, one of two windows appears in the right pane:

- **Record A QuickBooks Deposit**   This window appears only when the unmatched transaction is a deposit. This includes an incoming transfer from another account.

- **Record An Expense**   If the unmatched transaction is a payment or an outgoing transfer, the Record An Expense window is displayed in the right pane.

If the transaction is a deposit, the Record A QuickBooks Deposit window appears with one or both of two tabs—Undeposited Funds and/or Open Invoices. The tabs appear only if there are uncleared transactions in the Undeposited Funds account or if there are open invoices. Select the appropriate tab, and match the downloaded transaction to either an Undeposited Funds transaction or an open invoice. If the deposit does not appear in either list, you can enter the transaction in the Deposit List section of the right pane.

If the unmatched transaction is a payment rather than a deposit, the Record An Expense window appears in the right pane.

First, select the transaction's payee from the Payee drop-down list. Then, from the Account drop-down list, choose the account to which the transaction should be assigned. If the transaction is a payment for a vendor bill in QuickBooks, click the **More Matching Options** link in the upper-right corner to display additional matching options. Choose the **Select Open Bills To Pay In QuickBooks** option, which displays the Record A Bill Payment window in which you select open vendor bills to pay with the unmatched transaction.

Use Renaming Rules

Sometimes the name the bank uses for a payment or deposit does not match the name you use in QuickBooks. When this happens, it appears that there's no way to match the transaction without creating a new name in QuickBooks. While that is one way to handle the problem, the better way is to take advantage of the Renaming Rules in QuickBooks.

This handy feature enables you to assign an alias to a downloaded transaction name so every time QuickBooks sees it, it knows that it should match it up with the real name in QuickBooks. For example, if your bank records a payment to

1
3
4
5
6
7
8
9
10

QUICKSTEPS

SETTING ONLINE PREFERENCES

QuickBooks provides several options that enable you to control how some of the online features work.

1. Select **Edit | Preferences** from the menu bar to open the Preferences dialog box.

2. Click the **Service Connection** listing in the left pane.

3. Click the **Company Preferences** tab, and set the following options:

- **Automatically Connect Without Asking For A Password** With this option selected, anyone who has access to your computer can log on to online services without having to enter a password. Unless you're the only person with access to this computer, it's best not to enable this option.

- **Always Ask For A Password Before Connecting** If others have access to this computer, you will probably want to enable this option so that everyone who tries to access online services will be required to enter a password.

- **Allow Background Downloading Of Service Message** Enabling this option allows QuickBooks to download service updates in the background while you're working.

4. Click the **My Preferences** tab, and set the following options:

- **Give Me The Option Of Saving A File Whenever I Download Web Connect Data** When you download transactions from your bank (and choose Open), or when opening a downloaded file, QuickBooks asks if you want to import the data or save it to a file

Continued . . .

American Express but you have the vendor listed as Amex, you can create a Renaming Rule that matches American Express to Amex.

In reality, you can't create a Renaming Rule; you have to let QuickBooks do it for you when you're matching transactions. Using the previous example, you would select the American Express payment in the left pane and select **Amex** from the Payee drop-down list in the Record An Expense pane on the right. After you enter the appropriate account and click the **Add To QuickBooks** button, the Renaming Rule Created dialog appears.

In the future, all downloaded transactions from American Express will automatically be matched with existing Amex transactions. If you want to modify or delete the Renaming Rule, you can click the **Renaming Rules** link in the upper-right corner to open the Edit Renaming Rules dialog box.

Run Banking Reports

QuickBooks banking reports let you easily track your banking activities, and also assist in troubleshooting reconciliation problems. In all, five banking reports are available in QuickBooks. The following banking reports can be accessed by selecting **Reports | Banking** from the menu bar:

- **Deposit Detail** You can run this report for a listing of some or all of your deposits. By default, it lists deposits for all bank accounts for the current month. You can change the date range, add or remove columns, and apply a variety of filters to customize the report to suit your needs.

- **Check Detail** This is similar to the Deposit Detail report, except that it displays checks instead of deposits. The same customizing options are available for this report as well.

- **Missing Checks** The Missing Checks report provides a complete listing of checks sorted by check number. In addition, it alerts you to check numbers that are not in the register by inserting "***Missing numbers here***" wherever the sequence is broken. By default, it only shows checks for a single account. However, you can use the filter options to display checks for multiple accounts or for all accounts.

Understand the Chart of Accounts

The Chart of Accounts is the heart of your accounting system. It is the listing of accounts that is generally referred to as the general ledger. Each account is used to classify and record all related financial transactions. The Chart of Accounts is sometimes likened to a filing system, with each account representing a file into which you put associated transactions. For example, you would put all the bills and payments for the phone company into a phone expenses file. In your Chart of Accounts, you create a phone expenses account and assign all bills and payments for the phone company to that account.

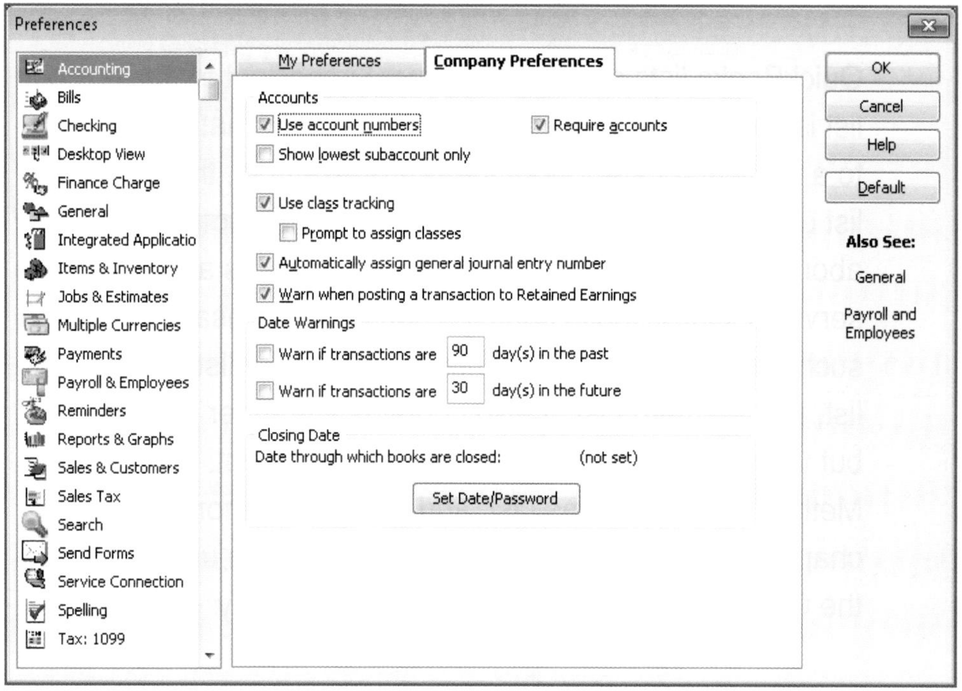

Use Numbered Accounts

By default, QuickBooks does not assign numbers to accounts in the Chart of Accounts. However, it is highly recommended that you turn on account numbering and number all of your accounts. The reason is simple. Numbered accounts are much easier to organize than name-only accounts. If you use name-only accounts, they are sorted alphabetically, which means you'll have to use a very creative naming scheme to ensure the accounts line up the way you want them to.

You can turn on account numbering in the QuickBooks Preferences.

1. From the menu bar, select **Edit | Preferences** to open the Preferences dialog box.

2. Click the **Accounting** category in the left pane, and then click the **Company Preferences** tab to display the company-wide accounting options shown in Figure 3-1.

Figure 3-1: *In addition to account numbering, QuickBooks offers various accounting-related options.*

NOTE

In QuickBooks, you can have accounts with subaccounts, which in turn, can have subaccounts, which in turn, can have subaccounts, and so on. This provides great flexibility, but also potentially unwieldy account names. The Show Lowest Subaccount Only option tells QuickBooks to display only the last subaccount name when displaying the account name in transactions.

NOTE

Unless all of your accounts are numbered, you will get an error message that you cannot enable the Show Lowest Subaccount Only option with blank account numbers. In that case, deselect the option, click **OK** to close the Preferences dialog box, assign account numbers to all of your accounts, and return to the Accounting Preferences and enable the option.

3. Check the **Use Account Numbers** option to turn on account numbering. Enabling this option also makes the Show Lowest Subaccount Only option available.

4. Check the **Show Lowest Subaccount Only** option so that only the last subaccount is displayed in transaction windows.

5. If you want to ensure that all transactions have accounts assigned to them (generally, a good idea), check the **Require Accounts** option. With this option enabled, QuickBooks will not allow you to save a transaction until it has been assigned to an account.

6. Click **OK** to save your preferences and return to QuickBooks.

If you are using a prebuilt Chart of Accounts from QuickBooks, all the accounts will be numbered automatically when you turn on the Use Account Numbers option. Any new accounts that you created will not be numbered. Even if all your accounts are numbered, you might want to check with your accountant to see if he or she has a preferred numbering system that is different from the one QuickBooks uses.

Create Accounts

Even though the standard QuickBooks Chart of Accounts provides a good foundation, it is probably not going to contain all the accounts you need. Therefore, at some point, you're going to have to add new accounts.

1. Press **CTRL+A** to open the Chart of Accounts.

2. Right-click anywhere in the Chart Of Accounts dialog box, and from the shortcut menu that appears, select **New** to open the Add New Account: Choose Account Type dialog seen in Figure 3-2.

3. Select the account type, and click **Continue** to display the Add New Account dialog (see Figure 3-3). If you're unsure about the account type you need, choose a type and review the description in the right pane to ensure it is the appropriate type.

4. The Account Type field reflects the choice you made in the previous dialog box. If you wish to change it, make a new selection from the drop-down list. Depending on the account type selected, the fields may vary. An Expense account is used for this exercise, so if you choose a different account type, the steps will be a little different.

Add New Account: Choose Account Type

Choose **one** account type and click Continue.

Categorize money your business earns or spends

- ○ **I**ncome
- ● **E**xpense

Or, track the value of your assets and liabilities

- ○ Fixed **A**sset (major purchases)
- ○ Ban**k**
- ○ Loa**n**
- ○ Credit Car**d**
- ○ E**q**uity

○ **Other Account Types**   `<select>` ▾

Expense Account

Categorizes money spent in the course of normal business operations, such as:

- • Advertising and promotion
- • Office supplies
- • Insurance
- • Legal fees
- • Charitable contributions
- • Rent

More...

Help me choose the right account type.

[Continue] [Cancel]

Figure 3-2: You have a variety of account types to choose from.

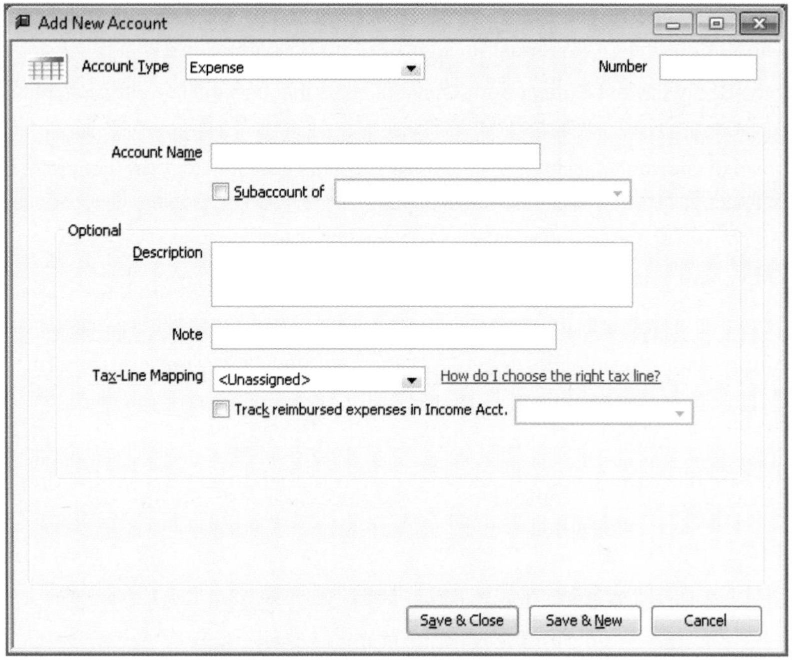

Figure 3-3: *Selecting the correct account type is important.*

5. If you've turned on account numbering, be sure to enter an account in the Number field.

6. Enter an account name.

7. If you want to create a subaccount of an existing account, such as a Telephone subaccount of the Utilities account, check the **Subaccount Of** option, and select the parent account from the drop-down list to the right.

8. Both the Description and Note fields are optional. Fill them in if you have additional information that will eliminate confusion about how the account is to be used.

9. Use the **Tax-Line Mapping** field to link the account to a specific line in an IRS tax form. If you use TurboTax to do your taxes, this facilitates importing tax data directly from QuickBooks. If you don't use TurboTax, you can still print tax reports that you can use to fill in your tax forms.

10. Once all the fields are filled in as needed, click **Save & New** to open a new form, or click **Save & Close** to save the new account and return to QuickBooks.

As noted earlier, the fields you encounter may be different depending on the account type you select.

Create Subaccounts

Subaccounts are very useful for tracking your financial information more precisely. While you can have a single account for sales, it is not going to give you the detailed information you need to analyze your business. For example, if you have a sporting goods store and only one sales account, you'll have no idea which departments are doing well and which need some improvement. However, if you have subaccounts for Tennis, Golf, Baseball, and so on, you'll know at a glance how the different departments are faring.

To create a subaccount, simply follow the steps in the previous section for creating an account, and check the **Subaccount Of** option. Then, from the drop-down list to the right, select the parent account. After that, just fill in the remaining fields and click **Save & Close** or **Save & New**.

TIP

If you don't know the correct number to assign, you can check the **Subaccount Of** option and open the drop-down list to the right to see the current list of accounts of the type selected. Once you determine the correct account number, deselect the check box (unless you're actually creating a subaccount) and continue.

TIP

One of the pitfalls many companies encounter is a lack of consistency in account naming. All too often, a Chart of Accounts ends up with multiple accounts for the same thing, all with similar, but not identical, names. When an employee can't find the account he's looking for, he simply creates a new one using the name that seems logical. For example, you may find an expense account called Postage, another called Delivery and Postage, and possibly a third called Stamps. Be sure to implement (and enforce) a standardized naming convention for accounts.

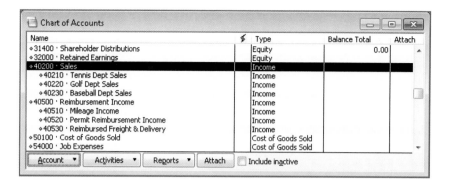

Figure 3-4: Subaccounts are easily identified in the Chart of Accounts.

TIP

When creating accounts that have an opening balance field, do *not* fill it in. Opening balances should be determined by entering historical data and transactions for each account. If you have any questions or concerns, check with your accountant first.

NOTE

The tax lines available are determined by your selection in the Income Tax Form Used field of the Company Information dialog. To view or change it, select **Company | Company Information** from the menu bar.

As you can see in Figure 3-4, subaccounts appear indented under the parent account.

If, for some reason, you don't like having the subaccounts indented, you can change the view so all accounts and subaccounts appear on the same level. Click the **Account** button on the bottom of the Chart Of Accounts window, and select **Flat View** from the menu that appears. To change it back, click the **Account** button again, and select **Hierarchical View** from the menu.

Enter List Data Quickly

Entering list items can be a time-consuming process, especially when you have a lot of items to add all at once. It's even worse when you only want to add a limited amount of information for each item. For example, if you have a lot of new customers to add and only want to include the customer name, address, phone number, customer type, and account number, you have to open a new customer record, add information to three different tabs, and click **Next** to open another new record and start again.

TIP

To clear the Add/Edit Multiple List Entries window so you have a blank screen to work with, select **Unsaved <*List Items*>** from the View drop-down list.

TIP

If you want to enter item data for a limited number of fields, you can customize the Add/Edit Multiple List Entries window to include only those fields for which you have data. See the section "Customize Add/Edit Multiple List Entries Columns" for detailed instructions.

Fortunately, QuickBooks offers a feature that will dramatically speed up the process. It's called Add/Edit Multiple List Entries, and it can be found at the bottom of the Lists menu.

1. Select **Lists | Add/Edit Multiple List Entries** to open the Add/Edit Multiple List Entries window shown in Figure 3-5.

2. From the List drop-down menu, select the QuickBooks list to which you want to add new items.

3. If you're adding new items, you can scroll to the bottom of the list and start entering items in the first blank line you encounter.

4. You can now begin entering new items line by line.

5. Starting at the first blank line, enter the data for each item field for which you have data, using the TAB key to move from field to field.

6. When you've finished entering all the new item records, you need to click **Save Changes** to store the new records and close the window.

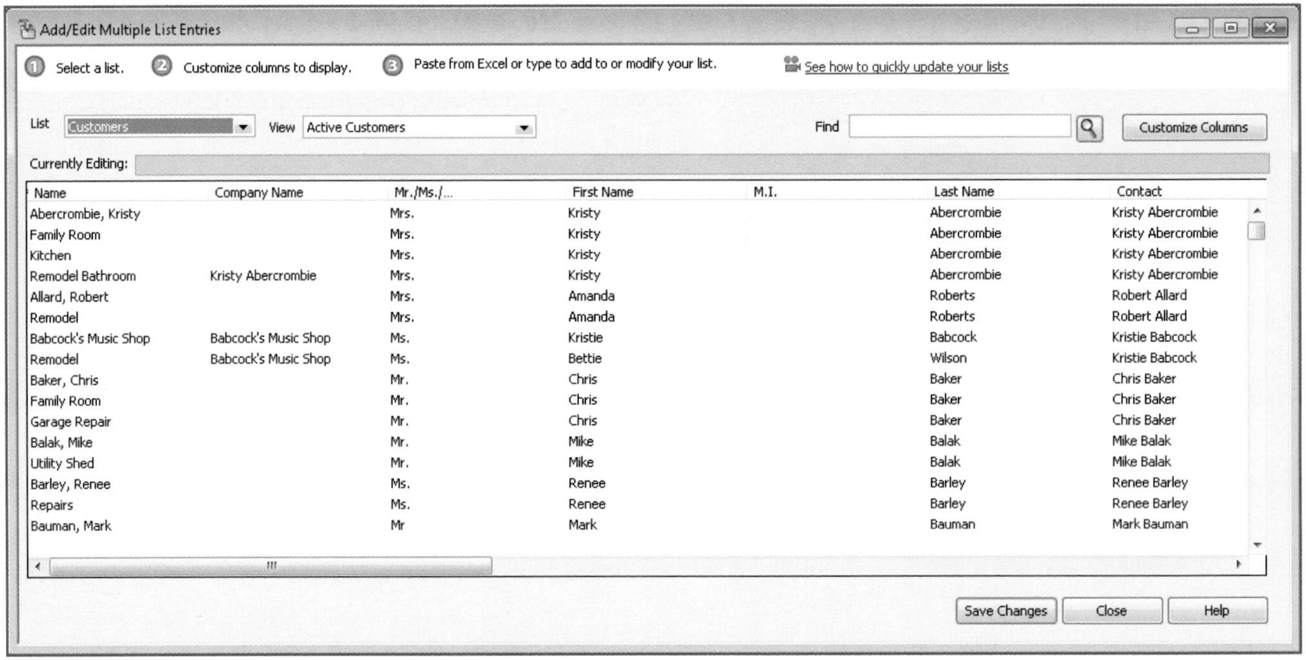

Figure 3-5: *Now it's easier than ever to enter multiple list items.*

TIP

If you are entering multiple items that have a field in common (i.e., customers with the same Customer Type, Terms, or Rep), you can enter the data for the first customer and leave the field blank for the others that share the same data. When you enter all items sharing the common field, right-click the field containing the shared data, and choose **Copy Down** to automatically fill in the common field in the other records with the same text.

NOTE

You cannot remove the first column (Name) in the Add/Edit Multiple List Entries window. However, you can reduce it to only a couple of characters in width by dragging the right side of the column header to the left. Actually, you can resize any column by dragging the sides of the header.

The Add/Edit Multiple List Entries window is also ideal for editing QuickBooks lists. After you open the list, use the **View** drop-down menu to filter out the records you don't want to modify, or use the **Find** field to locate specific records that you want to change. If you have a lot of records to change, you can use the Customize Columns dialog box to display only those fields that need to be edited. If you need to re-sort the list by a particular field, simply click the column header once for an ascending sort (A–Z) and a second time for a descending sort (Z–A).

One last thing. You'll also find an Add/Edit Multiple <List Items> command on the shortcut menu that appears when you right-click in a QuickBooks list that supports the feature.

Customize Add/Edit Multiple List Entries Columns

When you want to edit or add information to a limited number of fields, the most efficient method is to display only those fields (columns) that you need to work with.

1. Select **Lists | Add/Edit Multiple List Entries** to open the Add/Edit Multiple List Entries window.

2. From the **List** drop-down menu, select the QuickBooks list that you want to modify.

3. Click the **Customize Columns** button to display the Customize Columns dialog box. Only the columns in the right pane (Chosen Columns) appear in the Add/Edit Multiple List Entries window.

UNDERSTANDING ITEM TYPES

Since the various item types offered by QuickBooks enable you to keep track of the specific services and goods you sell, sales taxes you collect, and a number of other critical items, it's important to understand how they should be used:

- **Service**   For each different type of service you offer, you create a separate Service item. Service items are usually an hourly rate or a job fee. For example, a computer consultant might have one fee (or hourly rate) for network setup, another for programming, and a third for training. Each of these would be a separate Service item.

- **Inventory Part**   This item type is only available if you have enabled inventory in QuickBooks (see Chapter 6). If you buy and resell merchandise, each item you place into inventory is an Inventory Part item.

- **Non-Inventory Part**   Use this item type for items you stock but do not resell (such as supplies) and for special items you buy and resell but do not stock.

- **Other Charge**   Shipping charges, setup fees, and other line-item charges that do not fall under Service or Inventory Part items.

- **Subtotal**   This is a handy little item for providing a line-item subtotal for all items appearing above it on the transaction form. Great for providing discounts or markups to some, but not all, of the items on the form.

- **Group**   The Group item is a great timesaver for adding items that frequently appear together. For example, a dive shop package that includes a snorkel, a mask, and a pair of fins would be an ideal candidate for a Group item. Instead of adding each item separately, you add the Group item, and all items in the group appear on the transaction.

Continued . . .

4. In the Chosen Columns pane select a column you want to eliminate from the Add/Edit Multiple List Entries window, and click the **Remove** button. Don't worry—you're only removing it from the list. Any time you want to put it back you can select it from the Available Columns list and add it to the window again.

5. Repeat this process for all columns you want to remove from the list.

6. Now, move to the Available Columns pane on the left, and select a column that you want to add to the Add/Edit Multiple List Entries window. Click the **Add** button to move the selected column into the Chosen Columns list.

7. Repeat this process for all the columns you want to add to the list. New columns are automatically added to the bottom of the Chosen Columns list, which puts them all the way to the right in the Add/Edit Multiple List Entries window.

8. To move a column to the left in the Add/Edit Multiple List Entries window, move it up in the Chosen Columns list by highlighting the column name and clicking the **Move Up** button until the column is where you want it.

9. To move a column to the right in the Add/Edit Multiple List Entries window, move it down in the Chosen Columns pane. Highlight the column name, and click the **Move Down** button until the column is in the appropriate place.

10. When you've added, removed, and repositioned the columns to your satisfaction, click **OK** to return to the Add/Edit Multiple List Entries window.

With the columns properly situated you no longer have to scroll and hunt to make the necessary changes. All the fields are at your fingertips.

Use the Item List

The QuickBooks Item List is where you'll find (or create) all the basic items necessary for filling out your transaction forms. In addition to such essentials as Service and Inventory items (if you have inventory enabled), you'll find items for sales tax tracking, adding subtotals, giving discounts, and more.

QUICK**FACTS**

UNDERSTANDING ITEM TYPES
(Continued)

- **Discount** Everybody eventually gives discounts for one reason or another—good customers, overstock, sales, and so on. You can create Discount items for each discount you offer. For example, you could have a good-customer discount of 10 percent and a volume discount of 20 percent.

- **Payment** If you accept partial payments, you will need to create a Payment item to record them.

- **Sales Tax Item** The name says it all. Create one for each type of sales tax you collect (i.e., state, county, city, local, and so on).

- **Sales Tax Group** If you have to collect more than one type of sales tax, create a group and include all the different taxes. Each sales tax included in the group appears on the transaction form.

Create Subitems

Using subitems allows you to fine-tune your inventory so that you can generate a detailed analysis of your sales. For example, if your sporting goods store sells baseball gloves, it's not enough to just know how many gloves you sold. You need to know how many catcher's mitts, how many first-base mitts, how many infielder's mitts, and so on. While you could create a different item for each type, using subitems achieves the same purpose, but with the added ability to run sales reports that display both individual items and category totals.

Creating subitems is essentially the same as creating an item. However, not all items can have subitems. Subtotals, Groups, Payments, Sales Tax Items, and Sales Tax Groups cannot have subitems. For all other item types, use the steps in the previous section to create the subitem. The only difference is that you must check the **Subitem Of** option and select a parent account from the drop-down list.

Understand and Use the Class List

If you have different locations or different business types (wholesale and retail), you might want to consider using classes to create reports that break down your business by those divisions. If, for example, you have four different stores, you could create a different class for each one, such as East, West, North, and South. When you run your sales report, you can display report columns by class, and you can filter the report by classes as well.

Enable Classes

Before you can create or use classes, you must first turn on the class-tracking feature.

1. Open the Preferences dialog box by selecting **Edit I Preferences** from the menu bar.

2. Click the **Accounting** icon in the left pane, and then click **Company Preferences** to view the accounting options seen in Figure 3-6.

3. Check the **Use Class Tracking** option to turn the feature on.

Now that you understand the different items available to you, the next step is to add them.

1. Open the Item List by selecting **Lists | Item List** from the menu bar.

2. Press **CTRL+N** to open a New Item dialog box.

3. From the **Type** drop-down list, select the item type you want to create. The item type you select determines the available fields. For this exercise, we'll create an Inventory Part item, since it is one of the more complex items.

4. Fill in the fields as needed. Some fields, such as Item Name/Number, are self-explanatory, while others need a little more explanation. Those are the ones we'll cover here:

- **Description On Purchase Transactions** The text you enter here appears on purchase orders.

- **Description On Sales Transactions** Enter the item description that you want to appear on invoices, estimates, and sales receipts.

- **Cost** This is the last price you paid (or the current price, if you have the item on order). Keep in mind that QuickBooks ignores this cost when posting to the Cost of Goods (COGS) account, and uses an average cost calculated from your purchases and inventory adjustments.

- **COGS Account** Since QuickBooks automatically creates a COGS account when you enable inventory, this field should be filled in. If not, select the appropriate Cost of Goods account.

- **Sales Price** This is the price you're charging for the item.

Continued . . .

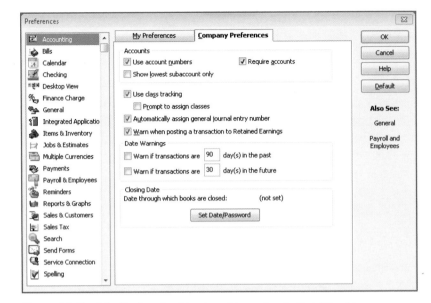

Figure 3-6: By default, class tracking is not turned on in QuickBooks.

4. If you want QuickBooks to remind you to assign classes in transactions, check the **Prompt To Assign Classes** option also. With this option enabled, QuickBooks will display a reminder every time you try to save a transaction without first assigning items to a class.

5. Click **OK** to save your changes and return to QuickBooks.

You'll now find the Class List on the Lists menu, and you will be able to create new classes and subclasses.

Create Classes and Subclasses

Classes are most useful when limited to one specific function. Whether it's location, business type, or some other classification, don't try to combine them.

UICKSTEPS

ADDING ITEMS *(Continued)*

- **Tax Code** Is the item taxable or non-taxable?

- **Income Account** Choose the income account to which sales of the item are assigned. Depending on how you set up your new company, QuickBooks may have already created one for you.

- **Asset Account** This is another field that should already be populated, since QuickBooks automatically creates an Asset account for you when you enable inventory tracking.

- **Reorder Point** When the On Hand (field) quantity reaches this number, QuickBooks will remind you that it's time to reorder (as long as the Inventory To Reorder option is enabled in the Reminders Company Preferences).

- **On Hand** You can use this field to enter the number of units you currently have in stock, but your accountant will probably appreciate it if you leave the field blank and add the on-hand quantity by using an inventory adjustment.

- **Total Value** This field will be calculated when you make the inventory adjustment to add your current stock, and then again as you receive new shipments into stock.

- **As Of** The only time this date is important is if you're converting a Non-Inventory or Other Charge item into an Inventory item. In that case, it must be after the last date on which the item was used in a transaction.

5. Click **OK** to save the new item and return to the Item List, or click **Next** to save the item and create another new item.

It won't work. Once you've decided on your class structure, you can create the classes you need.

1. Select **Lists | Class List** from the menu bar to open the Class List.

2. Press **CTRL+N** to open the New Class dialog box.

3. Enter a unique name in the Class Name field.

4. If you want to make this a subclass of an existing class, check the **Subclass Of** option, and select the parent class from the drop-down list located below.

5. Do not select the Class Is Inactive option unless you want to hide the class in the Class List and on transaction forms.

6. Click **OK** to save the new class and return to QuickBooks, or click **Next** to save the class and create another one.

If you faithfully assign classes to transactions, you'll find that you can produce extremely helpful reports broken down by class.

Add List Items

Adding list items is simple and pretty much the same for all lists.

1. Open the list by selecting **Lists** from the menu bar to display the menu of lists.

2. Then, from the menu (or submenu), select the list to which you want to add items.

3. Once the list is open, press **CTRL+N** to open a new item form.

Depending on the item type you choose, the number and type of fields available will vary. Fill in the fields, and click **OK** to save the new item.

QUICK**FACTS**

UNDERSTANDING CUSTOMER AND VENDOR PROFILE LISTS

While the major QuickBooks lists, such as the Chart of Accounts, Item List, Customer & Jobs, and Vendors, do the heavy lifting, there are a number of smaller lists without which QuickBooks would be a lot less effective. Among those miscellaneous lists is the group called the Customer & Vendor Profile Lists:

- **Sales Rep List** Use this list to associate sales reps, which can be employees, vendors, or people from the Other Names List, with sales. You assign each sales rep up to five initials, which then appear in the Sales Rep drop-down list on sales forms. It's great if you pay your sales people commissions, or if you want to track their performance.

- **Customer Type List** Do you have wholesale and retail customers? Maybe you have walk-ins and mail-order customers. However you break down your customer base, you can create a list of customer types and assign one to each customer. You can then run sales reports broken down by customer type.

- **Vendor Type List** The Vendor Type List allows you to create and assign a special vendor type to each vendor with whom you deal.

- **Job Type List** For more precise reporting, assign a job type to each of your jobs. When it comes time to analyze your business, you can run reports broken down by job type to see which kinds of jobs are most profitable.

- **Terms List** If you sell on credit, you'll want to create a list of the terms that are acceptable that you can apply to your invoices. For example, one

Continued . . .

Modify and Delete List Items

Editing existing items is easy. Simply open the list containing the item, select the item to edit, right-click, and choose **Edit <item name>** to display the Edit <item name> dialog box (see Figure 3-7).

Just move to the field(s) you want to change, make the edit(s), and click **OK** to save the change(s).

Deleting list items is even easier. Open the list containing the item you want to delete, select the item, right-click, and choose **Delete <item name>** from the shortcut menu that appears. However, keep in mind that items and accounts previously used in transactions cannot be deleted, only made inactive. If you try

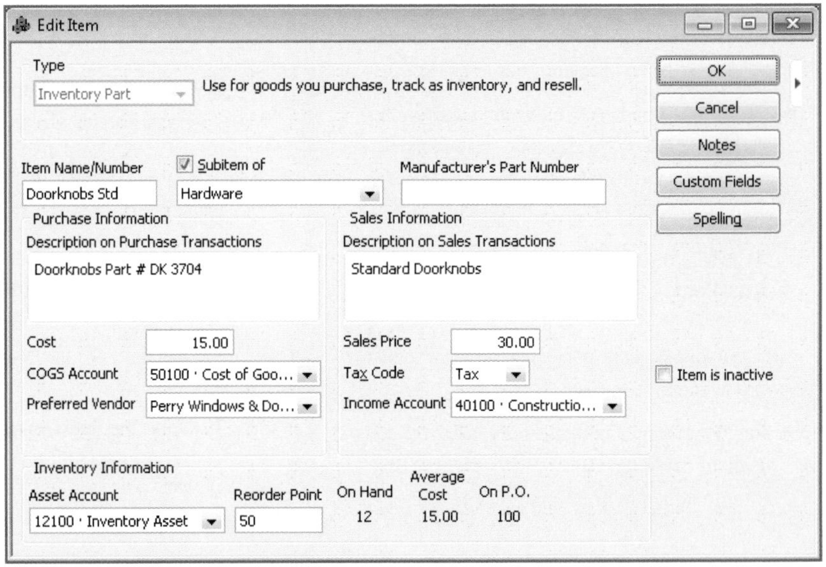

Figure 3-7: The Edit <item name> dialog box is, in most cases, identical to the New <item name> dialog box.

of the more popular terms is "Due on receipt," which, of course, means send the money now! Whatever your terms are, you must let your customers know to prevent confusion.

- **Customer Message List** If you like adding a brief message at the end of a sales receipt or invoice, you can create a variety of them in the Customer Message List. For example, you might say "We appreciate your business" or "Pay up or else!" Here you can create as many different messages as you like.

- **Payment Method List** Keeping track of customer payments is easier if you identify the payment type. By default, QuickBooks populates this list with common payment types, such as Cash, Check, VISA, and so on. You can create additional payment methods as you need them.

- **Ship Via List** Use this list to store the various shipping methods you use. When you create a sales transaction, you can select the method to use for that particular shipment. You can add as many shippers as you need.

- **Vehicle List** If you want to track mileage for your company vehicles, you must first enter them in this list.

to delete such an item, QuickBooks will display a message informing you that you cannot do this.

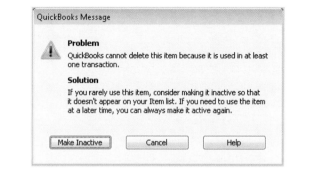

If the item can be deleted, QuickBooks asks for confirmation.

Use Other Lists

In addition to the lists covered in previous sections, QuickBooks has several other lists that provide added flexibility and record-keeping capabilities.

Track Assets with the Fixed Asset Item List

The Fixed Asset Item List provides a handy place to record some basic information about your fixed assets (buildings, vehicles, and so on). While it's a convenient place to store information on the assets, keep in mind that it is nothing more than that. No financial data from QuickBooks is linked to the Fixed Asset Item List, and no calculations are performed using the information in the list. It's only a catalog of fixed assets.

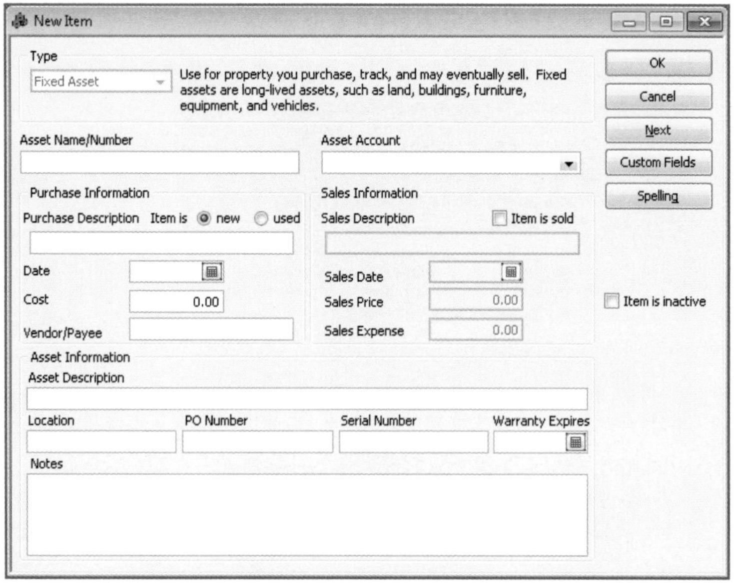

Figure 3-8: *You can record a lot of information about fixed assets.*

Select **Lists | Fixed Asset Item List** from the menu bar to open the Fixed Asset Item List window. To create a new item, press **CTRL+N** to display the New Item dialog seen in Figure 3-8.

You must enter a name, an asset account, a purchase description, and a purchase date. The other fields are optional. When you're done, click **OK** to return to QuickBooks, or click **Next** to add another fixed asset to the list.

Adjust Prices with the Price Level List

The Price Level List enables you to create your own pricing structure and offer special pricing to different customers. The most obvious use of this feature would be for wholesale and retail customers, who, based on purchasing volume, would warrant different prices. The beauty of the feature is that you can associate price levels with individual customers, thereby eliminating the need to apply a discount each time the customer makes a purchase.

If you don't see the Price Level List on the Lists menu, it's because you haven't enabled the feature.

1. Choose **Edit I Preferences** from the menu bar to open the Preferences dialog box.
2. Click the **Sales & Customers** icon in the left pane, and then click the **Company Preferences** tab to display the options shown in Figure 3-9.
3. Check the **Use Price Levels** option.
4. Click **OK** to save your changes and return to the QuickBooks window in which you were working.

Now if you open the Lists menu, you should see a Price Level List item on the menu.

Manage the Sales Tax Code List

Sales tax codes should not be confused with sales tax items. The codes indicate the tax status of either a customer or an item. They do not contain sales tax rates.

TIP

The one place that the items on the Fixed Asset Item List show up that could present a problem is in the Item drop-down lists on transaction forms. Therefore, it is possible that someone could attempt to sell a fixed asset or enter one into inventory. If this isn't caught, it could create a little confusion. One way to eliminate fixed assets from appearing in transaction form drop-down lists is to make them inactive.

NOTE

If you have QuickBooks Premier or Enterprise Edition, you can also associate price levels with individual items, which is handy for discounting overstocked items or items on which you got a great deal that you want to pass on to your customers.

QUICKSTEPS

CREATING PRICE LEVELS

After you enable the Price Levels feature, the next task is to create one or more price levels, depending on your needs.

1. Select **Lists | Price Level List** to display the Price Level List window.

2. Press **CTRL+N** to open a New Price Level dialog.

3. Enter an appropriate name for the new price level (i.e., Wholesale, Retail, Preferred Customer, and so on).

4. Choose the price level type. Depending on your version of QuickBooks, you will have either one or both of the following options:

   ● **Fixed %** All versions of QuickBooks offer the Fixed % option. With this option, the price level you create is assigned to specific customers and applies to all items and services purchased by those customers.

   ● **Per Item** This option, which is available only to QuickBooks Premier and Enterprise Edition users, allows you to create a price level that you can apply to individual items, regardless of which customer is making the purchase. It also lets you make the adjustment based on the price, cost (for markups), or the current custom price, if you've previously applied a price level to the item.

5. From the This Price Level Will drop-down list, choose **Decrease** to create a discount or **Increase** to create a markup.

6. Next, enter the percentage of the discount or markup. If you're running QuickBooks Premier or Enterprise Edition and you selected Per Item for

Continued . . .

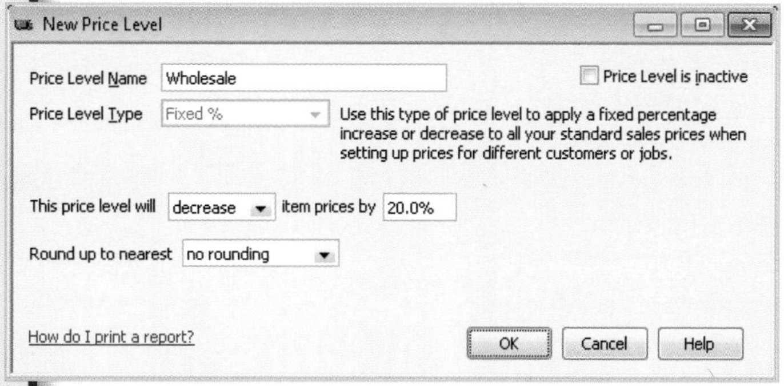

That's the job of sales tax items. By default, QuickBooks creates two basic sales tax codes—Tax for taxable sales and Non for non-taxable sales. These two may be enough for you. However, if you find that you need more, you can create them in the Sales Tax Code List. For example, you might want special

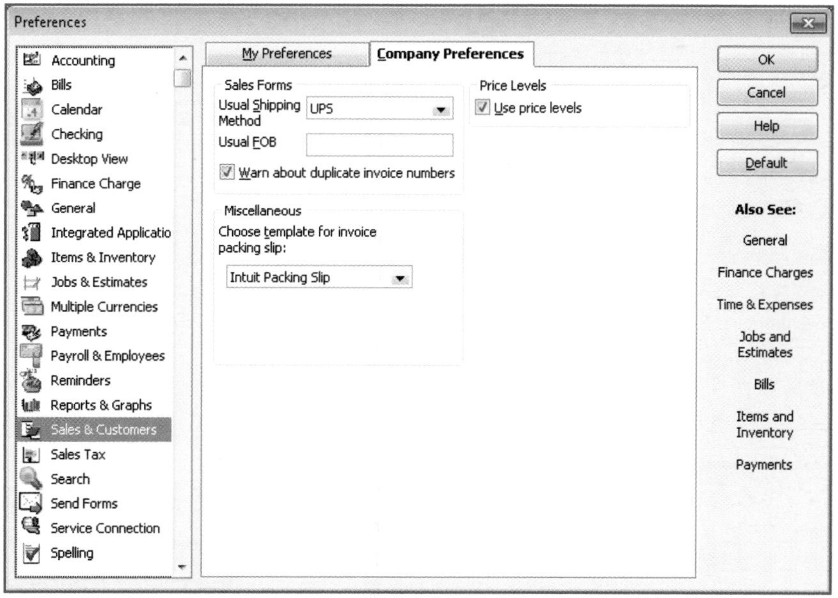

Figure 3-9: Price Levels must be turned on before you can use them.

CREATING PRICE LEVELS (Continued)

the price level, a list of your items appears, from which you can choose the items to be assigned the new price level. Then indicate the amount, whether it's an increase or decrease, and to what the adjustment should be applied—the cost, the price, or a previously applied price-level price.

7. Now, indicate if you want the results to be rounded and, if so, how. You can even create your own rounding scheme by selecting **User Defined** from the Round Up To Nearest drop-down list.

8. Finally, click **OK** to save the new price level and return to the Price Level List.

If you created a Fixed % price level, the next step is to assign it to those customers you want it applied to. Go to the Customer Center, and edit each customer record. On the Additional Info tab, you'll find a Price Level field. Select the appropriate price level, and click **OK** to save the record.

If you created a Per Item price level, you can select the price level from the Rate field drop-down list on sales transaction forms.

non-taxable codes for nonprofit organizations (NPF) or for wholesalers who buy to resell (WHO). Creating tax codes is easy.

1. Select **Lists | Sales Tax Code List** from the menu bar to open the Sales Tax Code List.

2. Press **CTRL+N** to display the New Sales Tax Code dialog box.

3. Enter a three-letter tax code. Actually, the code can include letters, numbers, or even punctuation.

4. Since you only have three characters to name the code, it's a good idea to add a description that will help you and other users remember exactly what the code is for.

5. Select **Taxable** or **Non-Taxable** as needed.

6. Click **OK** to save the new code and return to the list, or click **Next** to create another sales tax code.

You'll find the new tax code is available on transaction forms and customer records, as well as most item forms.

Use the Payroll Item List

If you have enabled payroll in the QuickBooks Preferences and have a subscription to a payroll service, you'll find the Payroll Item List on your Lists menu. If you have enabled payroll in the QuickBooks Preferences but do not have a payroll

NOTE

If you don't see the Sales Tax Code List on the Lists menu, it's because you haven't turned on sales tax tracking. To do so, choose **Edit I Preferences** to open the Preferences dialog box. Next, click **Sales Tax** in the left pane, then **Company Preferences** in the right pane. Select **Yes** for the Do You Charge Sales Tax? option.

subscription, the Payroll Item List does not appear until you turn on manual payroll (see Chapter 7 for more on this).

If you have only a couple of employees with simple pay rates and deductions, manually calculating the payroll is not difficult. However, if you have a lot of employees with complex rates and deductions, you should consider either a payroll subscription from Intuit or an outside payroll service.

To use the Payroll Item List seen in Figure 3-10, choose **Lists | Payroll Item List** from the menu bar. Here, you can view, edit, or delete the payroll items that QuickBooks automatically creates, and you can create new items as you need them.

To create new payroll items, press **CTRL+N** to launch the Add New Payroll Item wizard. Creating payroll items is covered in Chapter 7.

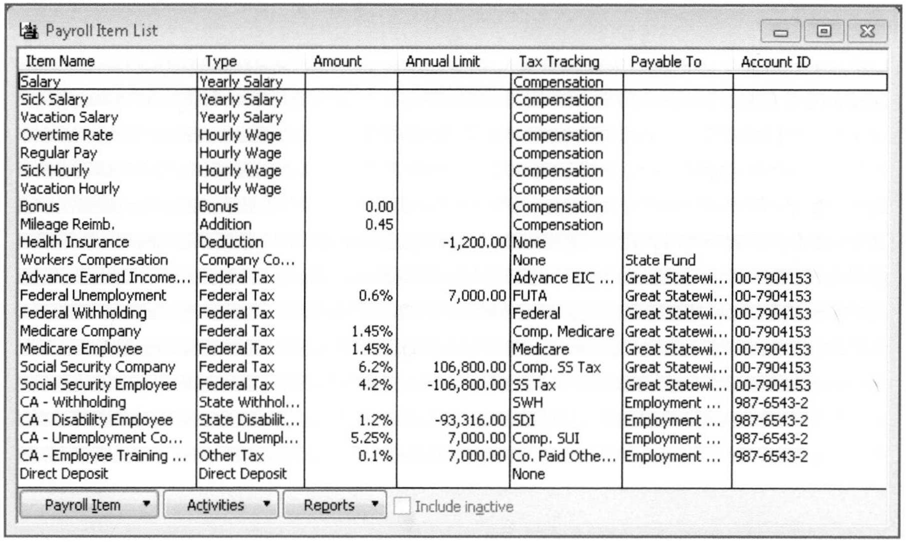

Item Name	Type	Amount	Annual Limit	Tax Tracking	Payable To	Account ID
Salary	Yearly Salary			Compensation		
Sick Salary	Yearly Salary			Compensation		
Vacation Salary	Yearly Salary			Compensation		
Overtime Rate	Hourly Wage			Compensation		
Regular Pay	Hourly Wage			Compensation		
Sick Hourly	Hourly Wage			Compensation		
Vacation Hourly	Hourly Wage			Compensation		
Bonus	Bonus	0.00		Compensation		
Mileage Reimb.	Addition	0.45		Compensation		
Health Insurance	Deduction		-1,200.00	None		
Workers Compensation	Company Co...			None	State Fund	
Advance Earned Income...	Federal Tax			Advance EIC ...	Great Statewi...	00-7904153
Federal Unemployment	Federal Tax	0.6%	7,000.00	FUTA	Great Statewi...	00-7904153
Federal Withholding	Federal Tax			Federal	Great Statewi...	00-7904153
Medicare Company	Federal Tax	1.45%		Comp. Medicare	Great Statewi...	00-7904153
Medicare Employee	Federal Tax	1.45%		Medicare	Great Statewi...	00-7904153
Social Security Company	Federal Tax	6.2%	106,800.00	Comp. SS Tax	Great Statewi...	00-7904153
Social Security Employee	Federal Tax	4.2%	-106,800.00	SS Tax	Great Statewi...	00-7904153
CA - Withholding	State Withhol...			SWH	Employment ...	987-6543-2
CA - Disability Employee	State Disabilit...	1.2%	-93,316.00	SDI	Employment ...	987-6543-2
CA - Unemployment Co...	State Unempl...	5.25%	7,000.00	Comp. SUI	Employment ...	987-6543-2
CA - Employee Training ...	Other Tax	0.1%	7,000.00	Co. Paid Othe...	Employment ...	987-6543-2
Direct Deposit	Direct Deposit			None		

Payroll Item ▼   Activities ▼   Reports ▼   ☐ Include inactive

*Figure 3-10: **The Payroll Item List keeps track of your wage rates and payroll deductions.***

CAUTION

If all your transactions are completed using the U.S. dollar, there's no benefit to enabling the Multiple Currencies feature. It will only clutter up your forms with a currency field that is of no value to you. In addition, the Multiple Currencies feature cannot be turned off. Once it's enabled, it's on for good.

Work with the Currency List

The Currency List only appears if you have enabled multiple currencies in the QuickBooks Preferences. This option is great if you deal with vendors or customers from countries using a currency other than the U.S. dollar.

If you've decided to enable the Multiple Currencies feature, you can use the Currency List to keep an up-to-date list of exchange rates. The QuickBooks list already contains all the major world currencies available at the time the software was published.

In the event you have to add a new currency, simply choose **Lists | Currency List** to open the Currency List. Then press **CTRL+N** to open the New Currency dialog box. Enter the name and the ISO-4217 code, both of which you can find by doing a search on the Internet. Use the **Change Format** button to modify the manner in which the currency is presented. Finally, enter the exchange rate and the date as of which the exchange rate was confirmed.

By default, only the U.S. dollar, the Euro, the Canadian dollar, and the Japanese yen are active currencies. All the rest are inactive. To download exchange rates, the currency must be marked active. Therefore, the first thing to do is open the list and click (to remove) the X to the left of each currency you want to activate. Then connect to the Internet. Finally, click the **Activities** button, and select **Download Latest Exchange Rates** from the drop-down menu that appears. QuickBooks will download the most recent exchange rates for all the active currencies on the list.

How to...

- Adding Customers
- View the Customers & Jobs Tab
- Merge Customers
- Create Jobs
- Use the Transactions Tab
- Setting Sales & Customers Preferences
- Generate Invoices
- Memorize Invoices
- Preparing Customers for Batch Invoicing
- Use Batch Invoicing
- Use Sales Receipts
- Issuing Credit Memos
- Receiving Payments
- View Customers & Receivables Reports
- Generate Sales Reports

Chapter 4

Managing and Invoicing Customers

Whether you love 'em or hate 'em, customers are the reason you're in business. Therefore, keeping track of them and the business you do with them is one of the primary functions of QuickBooks. This chapter deals with the many tools that QuickBooks provides to help you track your customer-related transactions. Coverage includes the Customer Center, invoicing, creating sales receipts, customer reports, and a lot more.

NOTE

If you perform a search using the Find field, the view of the Customers & Jobs list is automatically changed to the Flat View, in which jobs are not indented but listed directly beneath the customer and entitled "<Customer Name>:<Job Name>." To return to the indented view, right-click anywhere in the list and select **Hierarchical View** from the shortcut menu.

Understand the Customer Center

Since the Customer Center is a hub for all customer-related activity, it's a good place to start this chapter. Obviously, the first thing to do is open the Customer Center seen in Figure 4-1. This can be done by clicking the **Customers** button on the Icon Bar or pressing **CTRL+J**.

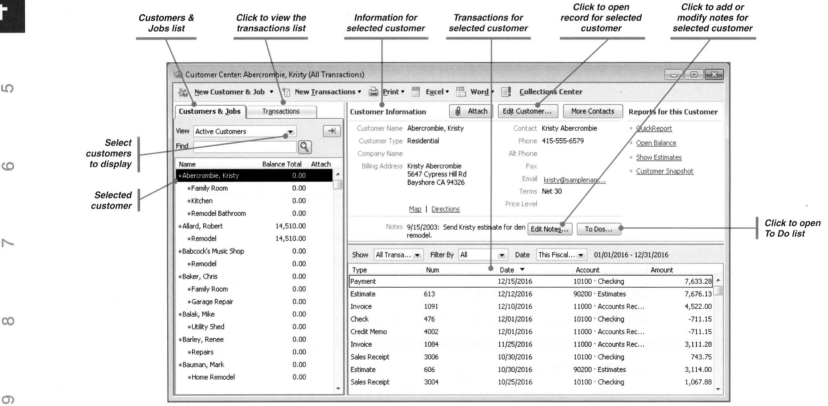

Figure 4-1: Customers, jobs, and their related transactions are at your fingertips.

TIP

Right-clicking in the Customers & Jobs list in the left pane displays a lengthy shortcut menu that contains a large number of customer-related commands, such as adding a new customer, editing an existing customer, creating customer transactions, and so on.

QUICKSTEPS

ADDING CUSTOMERS

If you have a customer base that you want to track, you must first add each customer to the QuickBooks customer database.

1. Press **CTRL+J** to open the Customer Center.

2. Click the Customers & Jobs tab, and then press **CTRL+N** to open a New Customer dialog box. If you're entering a number of new customers, click the **New Customer & Jobs** button, and select **Add Multiple Customers:Jobs** to open the Add/ Edit Multiple List Entries window.

3. You must enter a unique name in the Customer Name field.

4. It's best to leave the Opening Balance field empty and enter the necessary historical data for the customer to arrive at an accurate balance that also provides details.

5. Fill in the **Address Info** tab with as much information as you require. One thing to note on this tab is the Add New button below the Ship To address box. It enables you to add multiple ship-to addresses.

Continued . . .

As you can see, the Customer Center is composed of a left pane containing two tabs and a right pane displaying details of selections from either of those two tabs.

View the Customers & Jobs Tab

The Customers & Jobs tab is a listing of all your customers and their associated jobs (if any). The View field enables you to apply a filter to the list based on active status, customer balance, due or almost due invoices, or a custom filter of your choosing. The Find field is a search tool that lets you locate customers in the list based on the criteria you enter there.

You'll also notice that Customers:Jobs are shown in the list, indented under the customer with whom they are associated.

To view details about a customer or job, simply select the customer or job name in the Customers & Jobs list. Basic customer information from the customer record is displayed in the top portion of the right pane, while the customer's transactions are listed in the bottom-right pane.

Using the buttons at the top of the Customer Center window, you can add customers and jobs, create customer transactions, export data to Microsoft Excel, generate customer letters using Microsoft Word, and open the Collections Center.

Merge Customers

It is not uncommon to end up with multiple customer records for the same customer, especially if you have not instituted and enforced a standard customer naming convention. Fortunately, you can resolve the problem by merging multiple customers, as long as they do not both have jobs attached. If only one has jobs, you can merge the customer without jobs into the customer with jobs.

1. Press **CTRL+J** to open the Customer Center.

QUICKSTEPS

ADDING CUSTOMERS (Continued)

6. Click the **Additional Info** tab, where you can add customer type, terms, sales tax, and price-level information. The only information required on this tab is the sales tax information.

7. Click the **Payment Info** tab, and enter information for the customer's internal account or other method of payment.

8. If you are performing a single job for this customer and don't intend to create any others, you can fill in the **Job Info** tab with data about the status, start and end dates, and other job-related information.

9. Click **Next** to save the new customer and create another, or click **OK** to save the job and return to the Customer Center.

Over time, your customer list will undoubtedly evolve and need to be revised occasionally. To remove a customer, select the customer in the Customers & Jobs tab, right-click, and choose **Delete Customer:Job** from the shortcut menu. If the customer has jobs, you must first delete the jobs. Also, keep in mind that you cannot delete customers for whom you've generated any transactions. You can, however, make a customer inactive by right-clicking the customer name and selecting **Make Customer:Job Inactive** from the shortcut menu that appears.

TIP

To ensure you don't end up with multiple entries for the same customer, it's a good idea to invent a naming convention that everyone follows strictly, such as LastNameFirstName. Try to keep it simple to minimize confusion and mistakes. Eliminating all punctuation (hyphens, commas, and so on) will help to that end.

2. In the Customers & Jobs tab, double-click the customer you want to eliminate (or the one with no jobs) to open the Edit Customer dialog box.

3. Change the **Customer Name** field to match the Customer Name field of the customer you want to retain. The match must be precise. Therefore, if the name of the customer you want to retain is Smith, William, you must rename the original customer Smith, William, not William Smith or Bill Smith.

4. Click **OK** to complete the merge. As soon as you click OK, QuickBooks asks if you want to merge the customers.

5. Click **Yes**, and the two become one. You can also merge jobs belonging to the same customer using this procedure.

NOTE

By default, QuickBooks records and sorts the names as you enter them. This means that if you enter FirstName LastName, that's the way it appears on the Customers & Jobs tab. So, be sure to enter names the way you want them to show up on the customer list.

CAUTION

If you retain customer credit card information, you must comply with the Payment Card Industry Data Security Standard or face stiff penalties in the event there is a security breach in your organization. To protect yourself, you should enable QuickBooks Customer Credit Card Protection by selecting **Company I Customer Credit Card Protection** from the menu bar and completing the Customer Credit Card Protection Setup.

Create Jobs

If you perform multiple jobs for the same customer, you'll probably want to track each job separately. QuickBooks makes this easy by allowing you to create as many jobs as you need for each customer. Creating jobs is easy. Just remember that each job must be attached to a customer.

1. Press **CTRL+J** to open the Customer Center.

2. Click the **Customers & Jobs** tab, and select the customer for whom you want to create a new job.

3. Right-click the customer name, and select **Add Job** from the shortcut menu that appears to open a New Job dialog box (see Figure 4-2).

4. Enter a unique name for the job in the Job Name field.

5. As always, leave the opening balance field blank and enter historical data if needed.

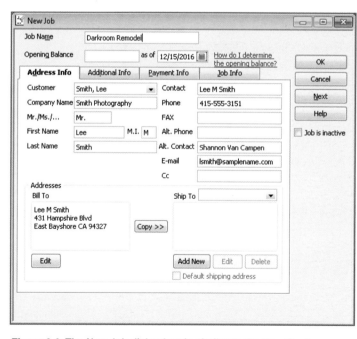

Figure 2-2: The New Job dialog box is similar to the New Customer dialog box.

6. Unless the Address Info, Additional Info, or Payment Info data is different for this job, you can skip to the Job Info tab and fill out the fields as needed:

- **Job Status**   Use the Job Status field to keep track of the state of the job. By default, QuickBooks populates the list with what it considers to be the most common status descriptions—Pending, Awarded, In Progress, Closed, and Not Awarded.
- **Start Date**   This is the actual date on which the job starts.
- **Projected End**   This is the date you hope to finish the job.
- **End Date**   This is the date that you actually finish the job (hopefully, the same as or earlier than the Projected End date).
- **Job Description**   A brief description will help minimize confusion if you're performing multiple jobs for the same client.
- **Job Type**   If you offer different services, you'll probably want to create and use job types.

7. Click **Next** to save the job and create another, or click **OK** to save the job and return to the Customer Center.

One of the great things about using jobs is the variety of reports you can generate. If you check out the Jobs, Time & Mileage submenu on the Reports menu (**Reports | Jobs, Time & Mileage**), you'll see that there are more than a dozen job-related reports that you can run:

- **Job Profitability Summary**   For a quick look at just how much profit you're making on your various jobs, run the Job Profitability Summary report. It provides total costs, total income, and the difference (profit) for each job.
- **Job Profitability Detail**   If you see something on the summary report that piques your interest, run the Job Profitability Detail report to see all the cost and revenue transaction details for a particular job.
- **Job Estimates vs. Actuals Summary**   Want to see how good your estimating skills are? Take a look at the Job Estimates vs. Actuals Summary report. This report compares your cost and revenue estimates for each job with the actual cost and revenue. Of course, this report is only valid for the jobs for which you've created estimates.
- **Job Estimates vs. Actuals Detail**   While reviewing the summary report of the same name, you may want to dig deeper and see exactly how the totals are arrived at.

TIP

You can change the terminology QuickBooks uses in the Job Status drop-down list by accessing the Jobs & Estimates Company Preferences (**Edit | Preferences | Jobs & Estimates | Company Preferences**) and editing the descriptions you find there.

Run the Job Estimates vs. Actuals Detail report to see the cost and revenue numbers broken down. You can even drill down to the individual transactions by double-clicking numbers in the report. As with the summary report, this one is only useful if you've created estimates for the jobs.

- **Job Progress Invoices vs. Estimates** If you do progress invoicing from your estimates, this report will come in handy. You can see just where your estimates and progress invoices stand. It tells you which estimates are active, the total of each estimate, and how much has been invoiced so far.

- **Profit & Loss by Job** This is an actual profit and loss report, but broken down by job. Of course, it only includes those numbers that were assigned to the individual jobs; therefore, it's only accurate if everyone has been diligent about assigning jobs.

- **Estimates by Job** If you're using estimates, this report gives you a quick overview of outstanding estimates. Broken down by job, the report provides basic estimate information, such as date and estimate number, as well as active status and estimate total.

- **Unbilled Costs by Job** If you don't seem to be making as much money on your jobs as you should, you might want to run this report to see how much is outstanding in costs not yet billed. All costs marked billable, but for which the customer has not yet been billed, appear in the Unbilled Costs by Job report.

- **Open Purchase Orders by Job** This is the Open Purchase Orders report broken down by jobs. Check this report to see job items that are still on order and when you expect to receive them.

- **Time by Job Summary** How much time is being expended on each job? That's the question this report answers. The Time by Job Summary report gives you a breakdown of how much time is being spent on each service item (type of work) for each job.

- **Time by Job Detail** Who's doing what for whom and for how long? If you want to know, run this report. You can see how much time each worker is spending on each service item broken down by job.

- **Mileage by Job Summary** If you track mileage for customer jobs, this report will keep you up-to-date on how many miles are being logged for each customer and the dollar amount that is billable.

- **Mileage by Job Detail** The Mileage by Job Detail report is especially helpful if you have multiple vehicles. In this report, you can see the mileage logged for each job, broken down by incident and vehicle. It provides the trip end date, the mileage, the mileage cost, and the billable amount.

Figure 4-3: The Transactions tab provides easy access to all customer transactions.

With all these reports at your fingertips, you'll be able to analyze the performance of your individual jobs and make sure each one is running smoothly, efficiently, and profitably.

Use the Transactions Tab

The Transactions tab, shown in Figure 4-3, provides a listing of all customer transactions broken down by transaction type.

As you can see, the left pane contains the various transaction types, while the right pane displays the existing transactions for the transaction type selected. In addition to viewing the list of transactions, you can apply custom sorts and filters, using the Filter By and Date fields, that enable you to locate specific information quickly.

You can even add and remove columns by right-clicking the transactions list on the right and selecting **Customize Columns** to display the Customize Columns dialog box.

The Available Columns list includes columns presently hidden, while the Chosen Columns list contains columns currently displayed. By moving the columns between the two lists, you can control exactly which columns are displayed.

1. To remove a column from the transactions list, select it in the Chosen Columns pane and click the **Remove** button.

2. To include a column in the transactions list, select it from the Available Columns pane and click the **Add** button. Since the position in the Chosen Columns pane determines the placement of the column in the transactions list, you must move the column up or down to get it exactly where you want it.

NOTE

The position of the column in the Chosen Columns pane determines where it appears in the transactions list. The further up a column is located in the Chosen Columns pane, the further to the left it will appear in the transactions list. Moving a column down in the Chosen Columns pane moves it to the right in the transactions list.

SETTING SALES & CUSTOMERS PREFERENCES

Customizing the way QuickBooks handles customer-related functions is easy.

1. From the menu bar, select **Edit I Preferences** to open the Preferences dialog box.

2. Click the **Sales & Customers** icon in the left pane.

3. Click the **My Preferences** tab to set the **Add Available Time/Costs To Invoices For The Selected Job** option. This option tells QuickBooks how to handle unpaid billable items, such as expenses, time, mileage, and so on, when creating invoices and sales receipts. Your choices are

   - **Prompt For Time/Costs To Add**   If the selected customer has any outstanding billable items, QuickBooks will open the Choose Billable Time And Costs window when this option is enabled.

   - **Don't Add Any**   When you select this option, QuickBooks ignores all unpaid billable items for the selected customer.

   - **Ask What To Do**   If you want QuickBooks to ask each time, select this option.

4. Show or hide the Payment Toolbar by checking or unchecking the **Show Payment Toolbar On Receive Payment And Sales Receipt Forms** option. This toolbar offers quick access to payment options as well as payment preferences and the Payment Snapshot tab.

5. Click the **Company Preferences** tab to set the company-wide options.

6. From the **Usual Shipping Method** drop-down list, choose the shipper you use most frequently. Your choice will automatically appear in the Via field on invoices.

Continued . . .

3. To move a column up, highlight it and click the **Move Up** button until the column is in the correct position.

4. To move a column down, highlight it and click the **Move Down** button until it's where you want it.

5. When you have the columns where you want them, click **OK** to return to the transactions list.

When you right-click a transaction, you can also perform a couple of other handy tasks—view the transaction history, the transaction journal, or the customer or job information. You can even edit the transaction if you need to.

Set Payments Preferences

Receiving payments is what keeps you in business. Therefore, be sure to set the payment preferences to suit your needs. There are no user-specific options; therefore, the Company Preferences tab is the only tab with settings you can change.

1. Open the Preferences dialog box, and click the **Payments** icon in the left pane.

2. Click the **Company Preferences** tab to display the payments options seen in Figure 4-4.

3. Move to the **Receive Payments** section and set the options:

   - **Automatically Apply Payments**   If you want QuickBooks to decide how to apply customer payments to open invoices, select this option. If the amount of the payment matches an open invoice, QuickBooks applies the payment to that invoice, regardless of age. Otherwise, QuickBooks applies the payment to the oldest invoices first.

   - **Automatically Calculate Payments**   With this option enabled, you can check off open invoices in the Receive Payments window, and QuickBooks will calculate the total and place it in the Amount field. If this option is not enabled, you must enter a payment amount before selecting invoices to pay.

SETTING SALES & CUSTOMERS PREFERENCES

(Continued)

7. To automatically enter an FOB (Free On Board) site on sales forms containing the FOB field, enter it in the **Usual FOB** field. FOB is a legal term that has no accounting (QuickBooks) significance. It generally refers to the point at which responsibility for goods shifts from the seller to the buyer, so it may have financial significance.

8. It's a good idea to select the **Warn About Duplicate Invoice Numbers** option to ensure that QuickBooks alerts you when you try to use an invoice number that has already been assigned to another invoice.

9. If you have created price levels (or plan to), select the **Use Price Levels** option to have QuickBooks automatically apply them in customer-related forms.

10. Use the **Choose Template For Invoice Packing Slip** drop-down list to set the default packing-slip template for printing. This is especially useful if you've created a custom packing slip that you want to use all the time.

11. Click **OK** to save your changes and close the Preferences dialog.

TIP

If you're using Premier or Enterprise Editions, you'll also find a Sales Order option. QuickBooks Pro users can utilize sales orders created in Premier or Enterprise, but cannot create their own.

- **Use Undeposited Funds As A Default Deposit To Account**   Select this option to make the Undeposited Funds account the default deposit-to account. When this option is enabled, the Deposit To field is hidden in the Receive Payments window and all customer payments are automatically assigned to the Undeposited Funds account. If you want to choose a deposit-to account each time you receive payments, disable this option.

4. The final set of options on the Company Preferences tab, Invoice Payments, relates to the Intuit PaymentNetwork, a fee-based service that enables customers to make payments electronically. If you sign up for the service you can then elect to show a payment link on both e-mailed and printed invoices. The last option, Intuit PaymentNetwork Email, is important to fill in accurately if you sign up for the service.

5. Click **OK** to save your changes and return to QuickBooks.

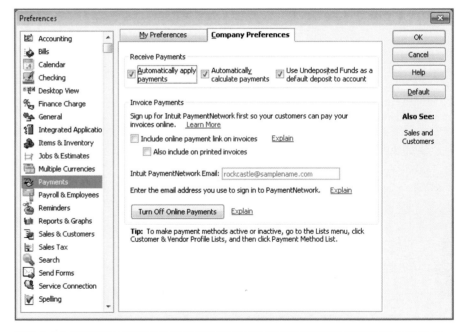

Figure 4-4: Receiving payments is easier when you let QuickBooks know how you work.

Configure Sales Tax

If you collect sales tax, you must enable this feature and then create sales tax items (sales taxes you collect and remit) and vendors (agencies to whom you remit sales tax payments) before you can begin invoicing, or selling to, customers.

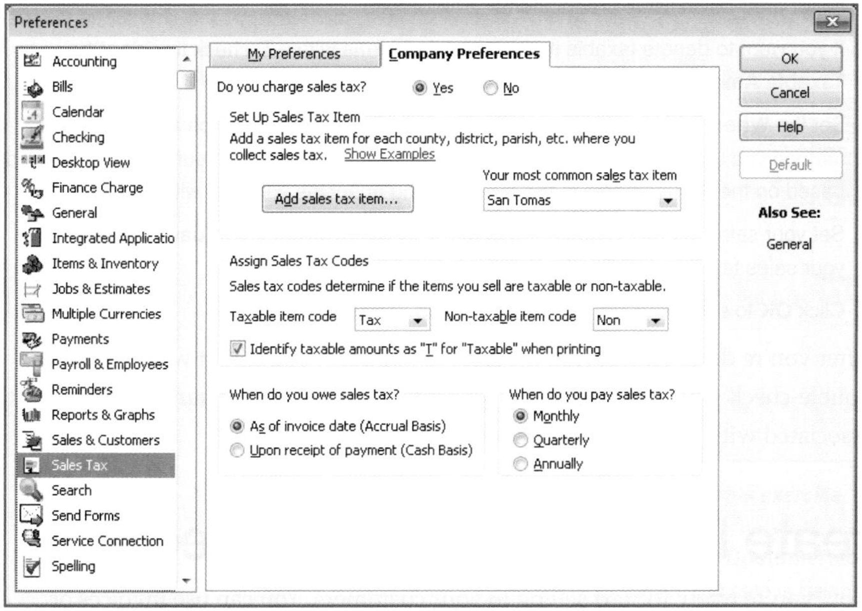

Figure 4-5: QuickBooks offers plenty of options to help you stay on top of your sales tax obligations.

1. Select **Edit I Preferences** from the menu bar to open the Preferences dialog box.

2. Click the **Sales Tax** icon in the left pane, and then click **Company Preferences** to display the sales tax options, shown in Figure 4-5.

3. To enable sales tax tracking, set the Do You Charge Sales Tax? option to **Yes**.

4. Next, you must create sales tax items to use on sales forms. Normally, that means at least a state sales tax item, and possibly additional items for county, city, and/or local sales taxes. Click the **Add Sales Tax Item** button to open the New Item dialog box.

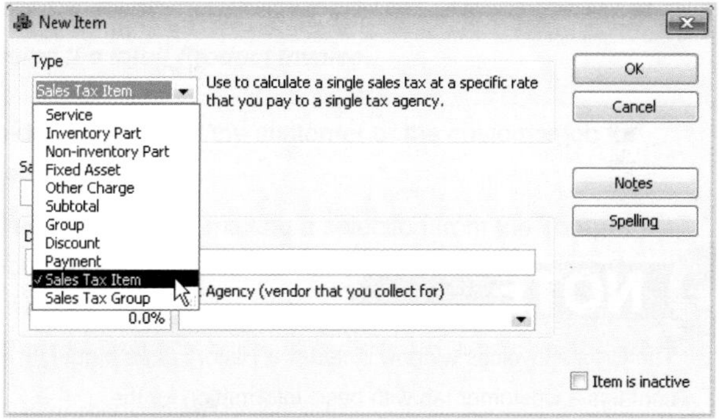

TIP

If you have to collect multiple sales taxes (i.e., state, county, and city), you can create a Sales Tax Group item that automatically inserts all the tax items into sales forms without having to select each individual sales tax item. Create a new item, and select **Sales Tax Group** instead of Sales Tax Item.

5. Give the new item a name (e.g., NYS Sales Tax), a description, the percentage of the tax, and the agency to whom the tax is remitted. If you haven't created any tax agencies, you can do so by selecting **<Add New>** from the drop-down list. Then click **OK** to return to the Sales Tax Preferences.

6. Create as many tax items as you need.

TIP

By default, discounts are applied only to the last line item above the discount item. If you want to apply a discount to multiple line items, insert a subtotal item between the last line item and the discount item. The subtotal item totals all items appearing before it. The discount item then applies the discount to the last item before it, which is the subtotaled amount.

NOTE

If you have changed any customer information in the invoice, QuickBooks will ask if you want to save it to the customer record when you click one of the save buttons. If you want to make the change permanent, click **Yes**. If it was a temporary change for this invoice only, click **No**.

- **Class**   If you have classes turned on (**Edit I Preferences I Accounting I Company Preferences**), a Class field appears on the invoice as well. Select the appropriate class from the drop-down list.
- **Amount**   As soon as you add a quantity and a price, QuickBooks automatically calculates the amount.
- **Tax**   When sales tax tracking is turned on (**Edit I Preferences I Sales Tax I Company Preferences**), a Tax field appears containing the tax code for the selected item.

5. Continue entering line items until you've recorded all items for this sale.

6. To enter a discount, select the appropriate discount item from the **Item Code** drop-down list.

7. Select a message to print on the invoice from the **Customer Message** drop-down list.

8. The Tax field should, by default, contain your most common sales tax item. However, you can change it by making a different selection from the drop-down list.

9. If the selected customer has billable time and costs or credits, you can add them to the invoice by clicking the **Add Time/Costs** button or the **Apply Credits** button, respectively.

10. Indicate the manner in which you want to send the invoice to the customer by checking either the **To Be Printed** or **To Be E-mailed** option.

11. If you have signed up for Intuit's online payment service, be sure to check the **Show Online Payment Link On Invoices** option so your customer can use the service to pay you electronically.

12. In the **Memo** field, add any relevant text that you want to see on-screen and in a statement. Text in the Memo field does not appear on the printed invoice, but it does appear on printed statements.

13. Click **Save & New** to create another invoice, or **Save & Close** to save this one and return to working in QuickBooks.

Memorize Invoices

If you find yourself creating the same invoice over and over for the same customer, or even for different customers (leave the Customer:Job field blank), you can save yourself some time by memorizing the invoice and using it as

QUICK**FACTS**

PREPARING CUSTOMERS FOR BATCH INVOICING

Batch invoicing is a great tool for creating the same (or almost the same) invoice for multiple customers all at once rather than one at a time. For example, if you provide a monthly (quarterly, annual, and so on) service to a number of your customers, you can invoice them all at the same time by using batch invoicing. However, to ensure the process works smoothly, you should make sure some basic customer information is configured correctly. To do this, press CTRL+J to open the Customer Center and check the following customer settings for all customers to be included in the batch invoicing:

- **Terms** Edit the customer record by selecting the customer and pressing CTRL+E. Click the **Additional Info** tab, and then select the correct payment terms for this customer from the Terms drop-down list.

- **Preferred Send Method** The method for sending invoices to the customer is located on the Additional Info tab as well. From the Preferred Send Method drop-down list, choose **E-mail**, **Mail**, or **None**.

- **Sales Tax Information** You'll also find the customer sales tax information on the Additional Info tab of the customer record. From the Tax Code drop-down list, indicate whether the customer is taxable or non-taxable. Move to the **Tax Item** field, and choose the correct sales tax item for this customer.

- **E-mail Address** If any of your customers' preferred send method is e-mail, make sure you have the correct e-mail address in the E-mail field of the Address Info tab.

- **Mailing Address** For those customers receiving invoices by mail, you'll want to confirm the Bill To address found on the Address Info tab.

Once all the customer information is configured correctly, you're ready to begin using the batch invoicing feature.

a template. Before saving the invoice, press **CTRL+M** to open the Memorize Transaction dialog.

Give the memorized invoice a recognizable name, check the **Do Not Remind Me** option (unless you want to be reminded), and click **OK** to save the invoice to the Memorized Transaction List. To use the memorized invoice, press **CTRL+T** to open the Memorized Transaction List, and double-click the invoice to open it. Finish filling it out and save it.

Use Batch Invoicing

For those us who have the need to create invoices for multiple customers all at once, the batch invoicing feature is a godsend. Now, when you have to create the same invoice (regular service charge, retainer, dues, and so on) for 20 customers there's no need to repeat the Create Invoices process 20 times.

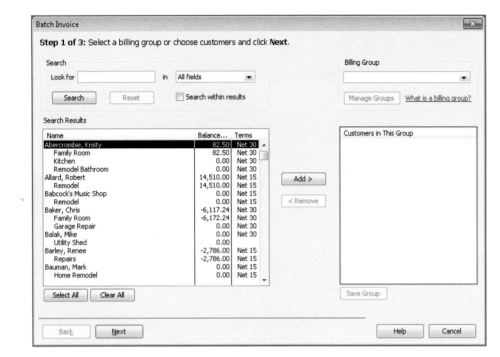

Figure 4-7: *The Batch Invoice wizard is quick and easy to use.*

Simply fire up the Batch Invoice wizard seen in Figure 4-7, and you'll be done in a fraction of the time.

1. Select **Customers | Create Batch Invoices** from the menu bar to launch the Batch Invoice wizard (refer to Figure 4-7).

2. The first time you use this command, QuickBooks displays a dialog box suggesting that you make sure your customers are set up properly. Check the **Do Not Display This Message In The Future** option, and then click **OK** to continue.

3. Select the customers to include in this batch of invoices using one of the following methods:

   ● Search for customers by entering your search criteria in the Look For field, selecting the field(s) to search from the In drop-down list, and clicking the **Search** button.

   ● Select individual customers or jobs from the Search Results list, and click the **Add** button.

   ● Select (or create) a billing group from the Billing Group drop-down list. A billing group is just what it sounds like—a collection of customers that have one or more billing/invoicing conditions in common—for example, all customers who pay a monthly service charge or all members who pay an annual membership fee. To create a billing group, select **<Add New>** from the Billing Group drop-down list and give the group a name. Then add the customers to the group. When you're done, click the **Save Group** button.

4. Click **Next** to fill in the invoice details (see Figure 4-8).

   ● Set the date if the default is not accurate.

   ● Select the invoice template to use from the Template drop-down list.

   ● Enter the line item(s) for the invoice.

   ● Add a message in the Customer Message field.

5. Click **Next** to review the invoices about to be created. As you can see in Figure 4-9, you can deselect (remove the check mark from) any invoice that you do not want created at this time. This is handy when you use billing groups and need to pull one or two invoices from a batch.

TIP

If you have a lot of customers to check, you might want to use the Add/Edit Multiple List Entries feature (**New Customer & Job | Add/Edit Multiple List Entries**).

TIP

To save yourself some time and aggravation, read the "Preparing Customers for Batch Invoicing" Quick Facts in this chapter.

NOTE

To add customers to an existing billing group, select the group from the Billing Group drop-down list and include additional customers from the Search Results list. Then click the **Save Group** button to save the group with the new members. You can also rename and delete groups by clicking the **Manage Groups** button and making the desired changes.

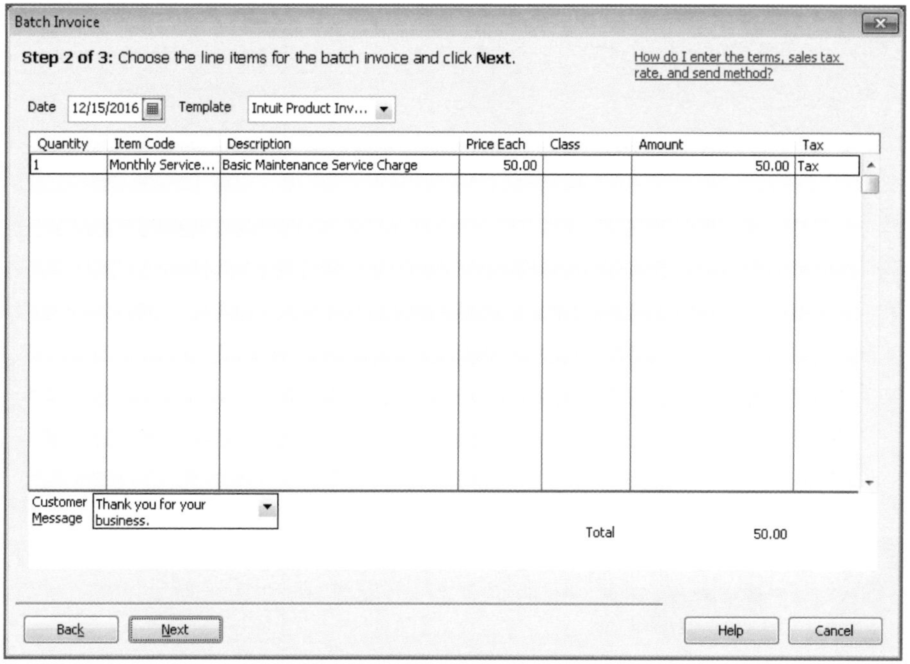

Batch Invoice

Step 2 of 3: Choose the line items for the batch invoice and click **Next**.

How do I enter the terms, sales tax rate, and send method?

Date 12/15/2016   Template Intuit Product Inv... ▼

Quantity	Item Code	Description	Price Each	Class	Amount	Tax
1	Monthly Service...	Basic Maintenance Service Charge	50.00		50.00	Tax

Customer Message: Thank you for your business.

Total   50.00

Back   Next   Help   Cancel

Figure 4-8: Create as many line items as you need.

6. Click the **Create Invoices** button to generate the invoices. QuickBooks creates the invoices and displays a Batch Invoice Summary dialog like the one seen in Figure 4-10.

7. Click the appropriate button(s) to print or e-mail invoices. Clicking the **Print** button opens the Select Invoices To Print dialog. Clicking the **E-mail** button displays the Select Forms To Send dialog box. When you're done, click the **Close** button to finish.

Use Sales Receipts

Sales receipts are used for cash sales. Those are the ones where the customer pays for the product in full at the time of the sale. Remember, it doesn't mean that the customer literally pays in cash—just that the transaction is completed at the time of the sale. Sales receipts, which are accessed by selecting **Customers |**

Batch Invoice

Step 3 of 3: Review the list of invoices to be created for this batch and click **Create Invoices**.

Invoice Date: 12/15/2016

Select	Customer	Terms	Send Method	Amount	Tax Code	Tax Rate	Tax	Total	Status
✓	Abercrombie,...	Net 30	Email	50.00	Tax	7.75%	3.88	53.88	OK
✓	Baker, Chris	Net 30	Email	50.00	Tax	7.75%	3.88	53.88	OK
✓	Bristol, Sonya	Net 30	Email	50.00	Tax	7.75%	3.88	53.88	OK
✓	Burch, Jason	Net 30	Email	50.00	Tax	7.75%	3.88	53.88	OK
	Campbell, He...	Net 15	None	50.00	Tax	7.75%	3.88	53.88	OK

Back   Next   Create Invoices   Help   Cancel

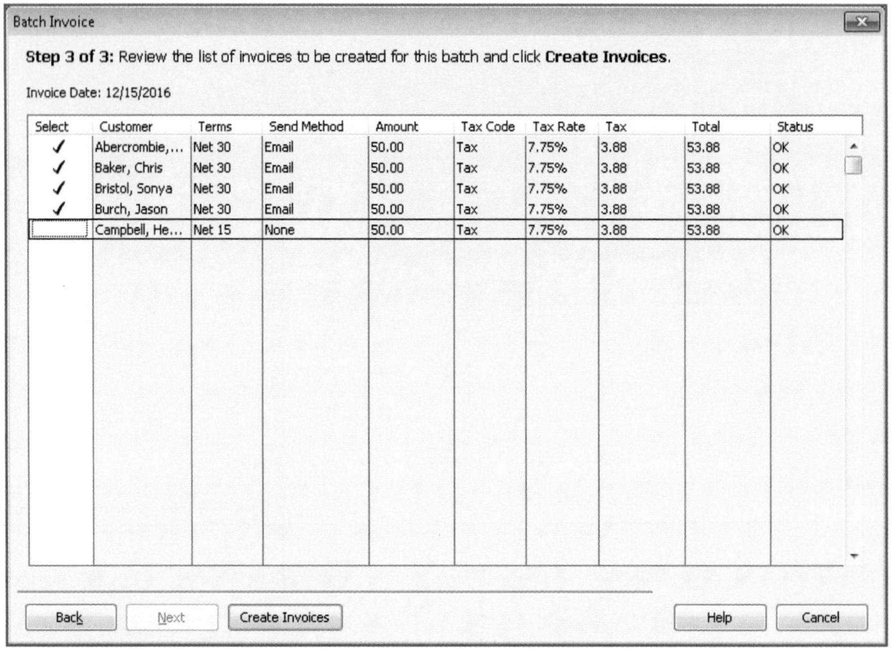

Figure 4-9: You can't modify the invoices, but you can choose which invoices to create.

TIP

If you have a lot of sales that are made to one-time customers, or if you have no need to track individual customers, you might want to create a customer called "Cash," and assign all sales of that type to this one customer.

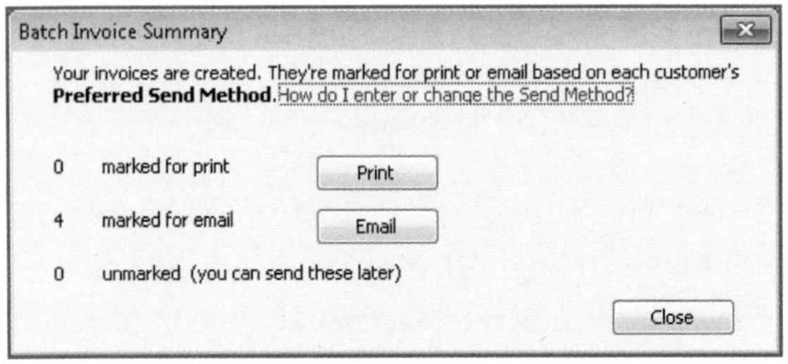

Batch Invoice Summary

Your invoices are created. They're marked for print or email based on each customer's **Preferred Send Method.** How do I enter or change the Send Method?

0	marked for print	Print
4	marked for email	Email
0	unmarked (you can send these later)	

Close

Figure 4-10: If you don't prepare your customers ahead of time, you may end up with a summary like this.

Enter Sales Receipts from the menu bar, are similar to invoices in that the same basic information is required for both (see Figure 4-11).

The header information on the default sales receipt is limited to a check number field and payment type field. The line-item information is the same as the invoice, with two exceptions. One, the order of the fields is different, and two, the Price Each field is called Rate. Other than that, filling out a sales receipt is pretty much the same as filling out an invoice.

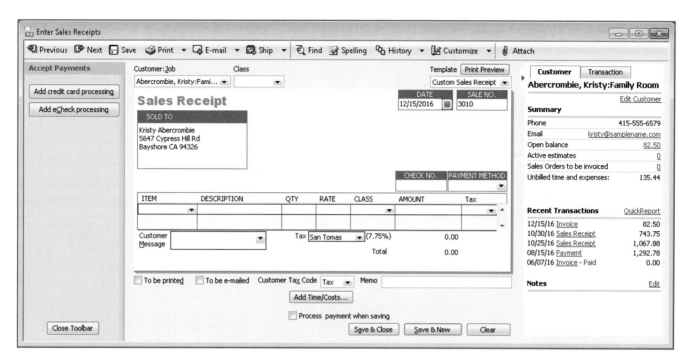

Figure 4-11: Like invoices, sales receipts include a History pane.

Send Statements

If you invoice your customers and occasionally need to remind them of accounts past due, you can use statements as reminders. If you bill your customers for regular monthly charges, you might want to use statements for your billing. Creating statements is a four-part process.

First, make sure all invoices and payments have been accurately recorded. Next, assess any statement charges you want to add. These might include those monthly billings mentioned earlier or other charges that don't require an invoice. To add statement charges, select **Customers | Enter Statement**

TIP

If the credit memo is related to a specific, existing invoice, you can open the invoice, click the **Create** button on the Create Invoices window, and select **Credit Memo For This Invoice** to create a new credit memo that contains all the information from the original invoice. If only some items are to be included, just delete the others and you're all set to go. Select **Customers | Create Credit Memos/ Refunds** from the menu bar to open the Create Credit Memos/Refunds window.

QUICKSTEPS

ISSUING CREDIT MEMOS

When a customer returns an item or is inadvertently overcharged, you can use a credit memo to reimburse the customer.

1. Select **Customers | Create Credit Memos/ Refunds** from the menu bar to open the Create Credit Memos/Refunds window, which now contains a History pane.

2. From the Customer:Job drop-down list choose the customer or customer job to whom the credit should be issued.

3. Enter the line items for which the customer is to receive the credit.

4. Add a customer message if you want one.

5. Click **Save & Close** to save the credit, or click **Save & New** to create another. Regardless of which you click, QuickBooks automatically displays the Available Credit dialog, asking how you want to use the new credit.

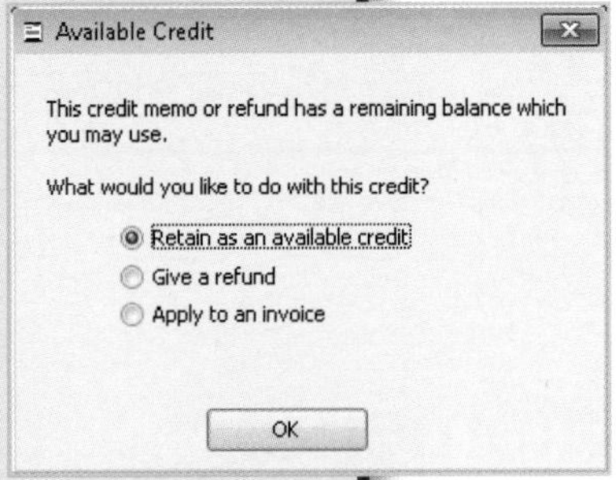

6. Choose the appropriate method of dealing with the credit:

   • **Retain As An Available Credit** Use this option to retain the credit on the customer's account so that it can be applied to future invoices.

   • **Give A Refund** If you select this option, QuickBooks opens the Issue A Refund dialog box, in which you can specify the type of credit to issue (cash, check, credit card refund, and so on).

Continued . . .

Charges from the menu bar to open the accounts receivable register. Select the appropriate customer (or job), and enter the charge.

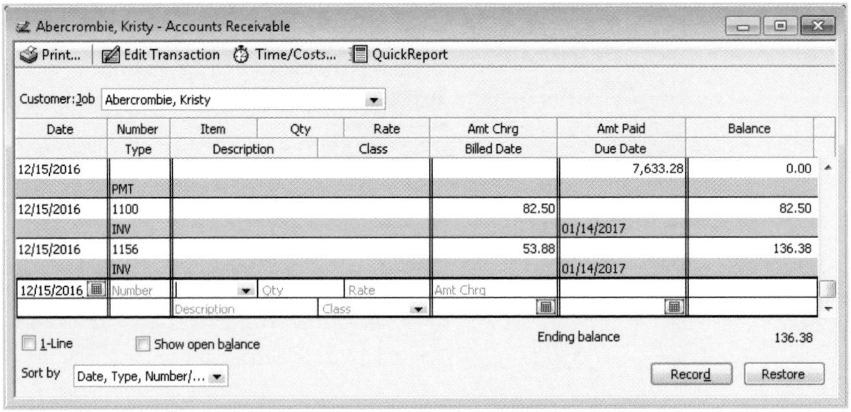

Third, assess finance charges, if any are due, by choosing **Customers | Assess Finance Charges** to open the Assess Finance Charges dialog box shown in Figure 4-12.

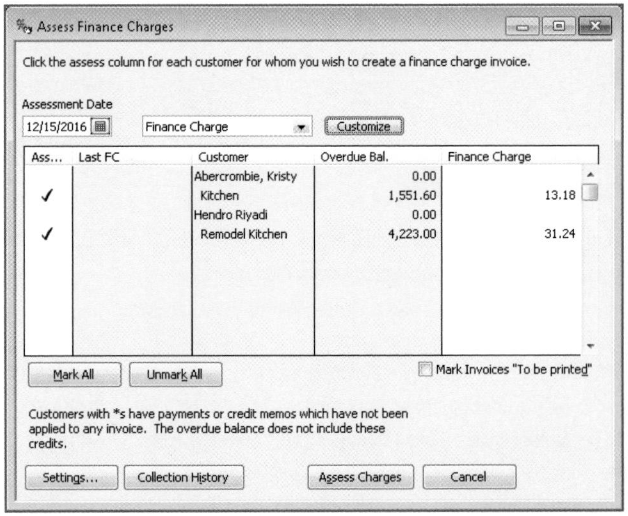

Figure 4-12: QuickBooks automatically calculates finance charges using the settings in the Finance Charges preferences.

UICKSTEPS

ISSUING CREDIT MEMOS (Continued)

- **Apply To An Invoice** Selecting this option opens the Apply Credit To Invoices dialog, which displays all the open invoices for the customer. Select the invoice(s) against which to apply the credit, and click **Done**. If the customer has no open invoices, QuickBooks alerts you to the fact.

Once you finish applying the credit, you are returned either to QuickBooks to work or to a new Create Credit Memos/Refunds window, depending on the save button you clicked.

NOTE

QuickBooks will warn you if any customers have unapplied payments to ensure you don't incorrectly assess finance charges.

To change the Finance Charges preferences, click the **Settings** button in the bottom-left corner. You can pick and choose who receives finance charges by adding or removing the **Assess** column check mark for each customer in the list. You can also modify the **Finance Charge** column if you want to change the amount. When you're satisfied, click the **Assess Charges** button to add finance charges to those customers with a check mark in the Assess column.

Finally, generate the statements.

1. Select **Customers | Create Statements** from the menu bar to open the Create Statements dialog shown in Figure 4-13.

2. QuickBooks uses today's date as the statement date, which appears on the printed statements. You can change it if you need to.

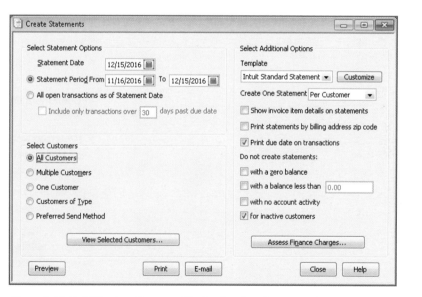

Figure 4-13: QuickBooks offers a multitude of options for generating statements.

3. Determine the transactions to include by clicking **Statement Period From** and entering the start and end dates, or by clicking **All Open Transactions As Of Statement Date**:

- **Statement Period From**   All transactions posted on those dates falling within the range will appear on the statement. This includes the start and end dates. Make sure you set the start date to be the next day following the end date used on the last statement generated for the selected customers.

- **All Open Transactions As Of Statement Date**   If you don't send statements on a regular schedule but only as a reminder for overdue customers, this is probably a good choice—especially when combined with the Include Only Transactions Over *<number of days>* Days Past due date, which becomes available when you select the parent option.

4. Choose those customers for whom you want to create statements:

- **All Customers**   This one's self-explanatory.

- **Multiple Customers**   When you select this option, a Choose button appears that opens the Print Statements dialog when clicked. The dialog box contains a customers and jobs list. Check the customers to whom you want to send statements.

- **One Customer**   Select this option, and a drop-down list of customers and jobs appears, from which you can select one name.

- **Customers Of Type**   Choosing this option displays a drop-down list of customer types.

- **Preferred Send Method**   Another option with a drop-down list, this one is populated with send methods. This is handy if you send some customers electronic statements via e-mail and others printed statements via snail mail.

5. If you've designed your own custom statement template, you can select it from the Template drop-down list. To modify the template, click the **Customize** button.

6. Configure the **Create One Statement** option. If you want all customer jobs included on a single statement, choose **Per Customer**. If you want to print a separate statement for each job, choose **Per Job**.

7. Set the other printing options, which allow you to include invoice details, sort the statements by ZIP code for bulk mailing, and print the due date for each transaction.

8. Set the options telling QuickBooks when not to generate statements. Generally, customers without a balance (or with a very low balance), with no account activity, or those who are inactive don't need a statement.

9. Finally, QuickBooks offers you once last chance to assess or change the assessed finance charges. Click the **Assess Finance Charges** button to open the Assess Finance Charges dialog box.

10. It's always a good idea to review the statements before printing or e-mailing them, so click the **Preview** button to take a look at them on-screen.

11. After reviewing the statements, click **Close** to return to the Create Statements dialog box, where you can either make necessary changes or proceed to print/send the statements.

12. To send the statements to the printer, click the **Print** button, which opens the Print Statement(s) dialog box (different from the one mentioned earlier). Here you can select the printer and printing options.

NOTE

If you attempt to send statements via e-mail without having a company e-mail address entered for your company or for the customers receiving the statements, QuickBooks displays a series of Information Missing Or Invalid dialog boxes, asking for the missing addresses.

TIP

If you receive a payment that is to be applied to a specific invoice, you can open the original invoice, click the **Create** button, and select **Payment For This Invoice** to open a Customer Payment window with all the information from the original invoice already filled in.

Print Statement(s)

Settings | Fonts

Printer name: Artisan 810(Network) on EP01E5F2:AR... ▼   Options...

Printer type: Continuous (Perforated Edge) ▼

Note: To install additional printers or to change port assignments, use the Windows Control Panel.

Print on: ○ Intuit Preprinted forms.   Note: The form Template provides additional print settings such as Logo selection. Templates are accessed by selecting Templates from the List menu.
● Blank paper.
○ Letterhead.

☐ Do not print lines around each field.

Number of copies: 1
☑ Collate

Print
Cancel
Help
Preview
Align

13. To e-mail the statements, click the **E-mail** button, which generates Portable Document Format (PDF) copies of the statement and attaches them to e-mail messages.

14. If you click the **E-mail** button, QuickBooks creates the PDF files. If multiple files are being sent, the Select Forms To Send dialog displays. If only a single e-mail is being sent, the Edit E-mail Information dialog appears. If you use Outlook for your e-mail, the Sending E-mail Using Outlook dialog appears.

15. If the Select Forms To Send dialog appears, select the statements to send. If necessary, edit the accompanying e-mail message, and then click the **Send Now** button. QuickBooks opens the web browser and sends the e-mails with the attached statements.

RECEIVING PAYMENTS

This, of course, is one of the main reasons for being in business—collecting payments from customers.

1. Select **Customers | Receive Payments** to open the Receive Payments window. Keep in mind that the settings in the Payments preferences, covered in the earlier "Set Payments Preferences" section, determine how QuickBooks handles payments.

2. From the **Received From** drop-down list, choose the customer or job to which the payment should be applied.

3. If your Receive Payments preference is set to Automatically Apply Payments, you must enter the amount of the payment in the Amount field. QuickBooks will then apply the payment either to the oldest invoice or to an exact match (regardless of age).

4. If your Receive Payments preference is set to Automatically Calculate Payments, you can either enter the amount and check the invoices against which to apply the payment or you can leave the Amount field blank and check the invoices to which you want the payment applied and QuickBooks will calculate the Amount field for you.

5. If you have neither option selected, you'll have to enter the payment amount and check off the invoices to apply it to, or you can click the **Auto Apply Payment** button to have QuickBooks decide for you. It uses the same criteria as the Automatically Apply Payments preference.

6. Choose the payment type from the Pmt. Method drop-down list. If you select a credit card, QuickBooks displays a Card No. field and an Exp. Date field.

Continued . . .

Use the Collections Center

The Collections Center tracks customers with overdue or nearly overdue balances. You access the Collections Center through the Customer Center. Press **CTRL+J** to open the Customer Center, and then click the **Collections Center** button at the top of the Customer Center window to launch the Collections Center. As you can see in Figure 4-14, the Collections Center contains two tabs: Overdue and Almost Due. The tab names are self-explanatory.

The Collections Center is straightforward. What you see is what you get. Customers with overdue balances (or nearly overdue) are listed with basic information, including amount overdue, days overdue, contact phone number, and notes. To see an invoice, double-click the invoice link under the customer name. In the Notes/Warnings column you'll see a warning icon if the customer does not have an e-mail address on file. Click the icon to open the customer record and add the e-mail address. To read any notes associated with the

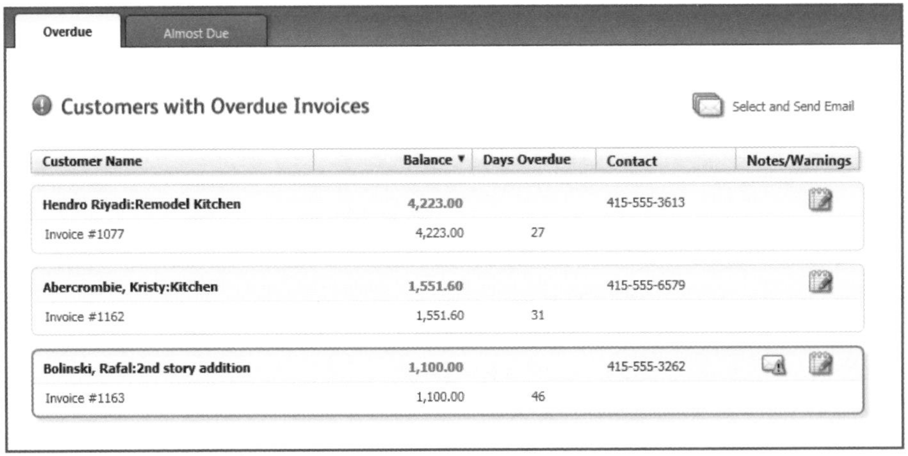

	Overdue	Almost Due			

⊘ Customers with Overdue Invoices   Select and Send Email

Customer Name	Balance ▼	Days Overdue	Contact	Notes/Warnings
Hendro Riyadi:Remodel Kitchen	4,223.00		415-555-3613	
Invoice #1077	4,223.00	27		
Abercrombie, Kristy:Kitchen	1,551.60		415-555-6579	
Invoice #1162	1,551.60	31		
Bolinski, Rafal:2nd story addition	1,100.00		415-555-3262	
Invoice #1163	1,100.00	46		

Figure 4-14: The Collections Center offers an easy way to remind customers with overdue balances.

QUICKSTEPS

RECEIVING PAYMENTS (Continued)

7. If the payment type is a check, enter the check number in the **Check #** field, which appears when you select **Check** from the Pmt. Method drop-down list.

8. If your Use Undeposited Funds As A Default Deposit To Account preference is not checked in the Sales & Customers preferences, the Deposit To field appears. Select the account in which you want the payment deposited.

9. If you want to search for a different customer, job, or invoice, you can click the **Find A Customer/ Invoice** button to open the Search dialog box.

10. To view an invoice, double-click its listing.

11. If the customer has sent an amount that leaves any invoice with a partial balance, QuickBooks considers this an underpayment and offers two options in the bottom-left corner of the Receive Payments dialog—Leave This As An Underpayment or Write Off The Entire Amount. Select the appropriate option.

12. If the customer sends more than the total of all outstanding invoices, QuickBooks considers this an overpayment and offers two different options— Leave The Credit To Be Used Later or Refund The Amount To The Customer. Choose the appropriate option.

13. To apply credits or discounts, click the **Discounts & Credits** button.

14. Click **Save & Close** to record the payments and return to work in QuickBooks, or click **Save & New** to enter another payment.

customer, click the **Notes** icon. The only other thing you can do here is send an e-mail message to all customers with an overdue balance.

1. Click the **Select And Send Email** link at the top of the tab to display the Send Mass Email – <tab name> window (see Figure 4-15).

2. Select or deselect (check or uncheck) those invoices you want to include in this mass mailing.

3. Edit the message on the right as needed.

4. Click **Send** to remit the e-mail message to the selected customers.

Actually, there is one other thing you can do in the Collections Center, and that is sort the list by the various fields (Customer Name, Balance, and Days Overdue). All you have to do is click the column header to change the sort order.

Figure 4-15: Only those customers with e-mail addresses are listed.

Run Sales and Customer Reports

QuickBooks provides a wealth of reporting information about both your sales and your customers. If you check the Reports menu, you see that there's one category for each: Customers & Receivables and Sales.

To open a sales report, choose **Reports | Sales** and select the desired report from the submenu. Once the report is opened, you can customize it by using the filter fields at the top of the report (Dates, From, To, Columns), the Sort By field, or by clicking the **Customize Report** button to open the Modify Report dialog box. The Modify Report dialog offers a variety of options for changing the display, applying filters, and even changing the headers and footers.

After you customize a report, you can save it with the customizations by clicking the **Memorize** button and giving it a unique name. When you want to use it again, choose **Reports | Memorized Reports** and select it from the submenu that appears.

View Customers & Receivables Reports

The Customers & Receivables section is where you'll find accounts receivables reports, customer reports, an open invoice report, a collections report, and more. You can access them through the Reports menu or through the Report Center (see Figure 4-16):

- **A/R Aging Summary** This report should be on the top of your list of reports to run regularly. It lets you know the status of your outstanding accounts receivable (the money owed to you). Performing the work, selling the product, and invoicing the customers are only part of what you need to do to run a profitable business. Making sure the money is collected is the final step in the process. The A/R Aging Summary report will tell you, at a glance, which customers have outstanding invoices and for how long.

- **A/R Aging Detail** Once the A/R Aging Summary report alerts you to potential problems, you can see the specifics by running the A/R Aging Detail report. Here you'll find all outstanding invoices broken down by due date.

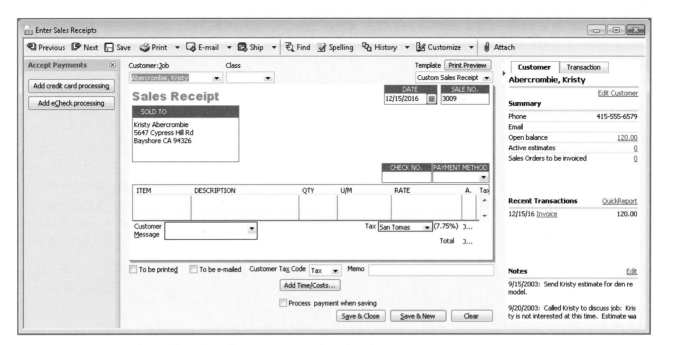

Figure 4-16: The Report Center Grid View offers a sample preview of each report.

- **Customer Balance Summary**   This is another useful report for making sure your outstanding balances don't grow too large. Running the Customer Balance Summary report gives you a quick overview of which customers and jobs have outstanding invoices and their totals.

- **Customer Balance Detail**   Once you spot potential problems on the summary report, you can run the Customer Balance Detail report to drill down to see which particular invoices are outstanding for each customer and job. Since it is sorted by due date, you can immediately ascertain which invoices are current, which are past due, and which, if any, are seriously overdue.

- **Open Invoices** A good report for reviewing outstanding invoices, the Open Invoices report provides a listing of open invoices broken down by customer and job. Included are the invoice and due dates, the customer terms, the invoice number, the number of days past due, and, of course, the amount due.

- **Collections Report** This is the report you never want to have to run but are glad it's available when you need it. It gives you a rundown of only those customers with open invoices that are past due.

- **Average Days To Pay** If you want to see which customers pay in a timely fashion and which ones are somewhat lax, run this report. It gives you the average number of days in which each customer pays invoices. It comes in both a summary and a detail format.

- **Accounts Receivable Graph** While numbers are great, there's nothing like a graphical representation of those numbers to make the financial implications clear. The Accounts Receivable Graph does just that with your outstanding customer balances.

- **Unbilled Costs by Job** If you're faithful about assigning costs to customers and jobs, this report will keep you informed about outstanding costs that have yet to be billed.

- **Transaction List by Customer** To get a complete picture of all your dealings with each customer, run the Transaction List by Customer report. It offers a listing of all transactions (invoices, credits, and payments) for each customer and job.

- **Customer Phone List** You might want to print this one out and tape it to the office wall. It's a simple listing of customer names and jobs with their associated phone numbers.

- **Customer Contact List** While the Customer Contact List provides more detail than the Customer Phone List, it's probably not appropriate for taping on the office wall, since it also contains customer balances. It is, however, a good list to print out when you're making calls about outstanding balances.

- **Item Price List** When you want to review all your service, inventory, and other items, along with their associated prices, this is the report to run. It's also a great place to start when creating a flexible inventory worksheet (see Chapter 6 for more information).

As you can see, QuickBooks offers plenty of powerful reports that will enable you to keep track of your customers and their outstanding balances.

Generate Sales Reports

The Sales submenu of the Reports menu contains a variety of sales-related reports. You'll discover sales reports by customer, item, and rep, as well as a sales graph and a pending sales report. These reports are accessible from the Reports menu as well as from the Reports Center, as seen in Figure 4-17:

- **Sales by Customer Summary**   Any time you want to see a quick overview of sales by customer, run this report. It gives you a breakdown by customer and job of total sales for the selected date range.

Figure 4-17: You can get a preview of each report in the Report Center List View before you open it.

- **Sales by Customer Detail**   When the big sales picture isn't enough, run the Sales by Customer Detail report to see a precise breakdown of your sales to each customer. It offers an itemized listing of customer transactions broken down by line item and includes details such as date, invoice number, item name, quantity, price, total, and balance due.

- **Sales by Item Summary**   How well are your products and/or services doing? Run this report to see a complete listing of each of your sales items, along with some very pertinent information. It provides not only sales totals and percentages of sales, but cost of goods totals and gross margin numbers as well.

- **Sales by Item Detail**   This report is for the terminally curious. It provides the details of every transaction involving each of your sales items.

- **Sales by Rep Summary**   If you're paying your sales reps commission, or just keeping tabs on their performance, this report is extremely useful. It provides total sales for each sales rep.

- **Sales by Rep Detail**   If sales reps' commissions vary by items sold or by volume, you'll want to run the Sales by Rep Detail report to get a more precise picture of each rep's sales numbers.

- **Sales by Ship To Address**   This is a useful report if your customers have multiple locations. You can see which ones are generating the most business.

- **Sales Graph**   Since a picture is sometimes more apt to bring the numbers into focus, the Sales Graph can put all those sales numbers into perspective quickly. It offers both a bar graph and a pie chart.

- **Pending Sales**   If you backorder items for customers or hold orders until paid for, you probably have some outstanding pending sales. Run this report to see just how many, to whom, and for how much.

In addition to the two main categories, you'll find sales- and customer-related reports on some of the other menus. For example, the Company & Financial menu contains a couple of Income by Customer reports. The Accountant & Taxes menu contains a Customer Credit Card Audit Trail report.

How to...

- *Customize the Vendor Center*
- *Add Vendors*
- *Setting Bills Preferences*
- *Enter Bills*
- *Receive Items*
- *Entering Bills for Received Items*
- *Receive Items and Enter Bills*
- *Enter Credits*
- *Entering Recurring Bills*
- *Review and Pay Recorded Bills*
- *Pay Bills as They Arrive*
- *Understand Use Tax*
- *Understanding Vendors & Payables Reports*
- *Track Use Tax*
- *Remit Use Tax*

Chapter 5

Managing Vendors and Paying Bills

Vendors are the other part of the business equation, without whom many of us would not be in business at all. Even if you don't buy products for resale, many facets of your business require essential supplies and services that are provided by vendors. In this chapter we'll go over the vendor-related functions found in QuickBooks, including the Vendor Center, item receipts, bills, vendor reports, and more.

Work in the Vendor Center

The Vendor Center, which you can open by selecting **Vendors | Vendor Center**, is your command center for vendor-related activity. As you can see in Figure 5-1, the layout of the QuickBooks Vendor Center is almost identical to that of the Customer Center.

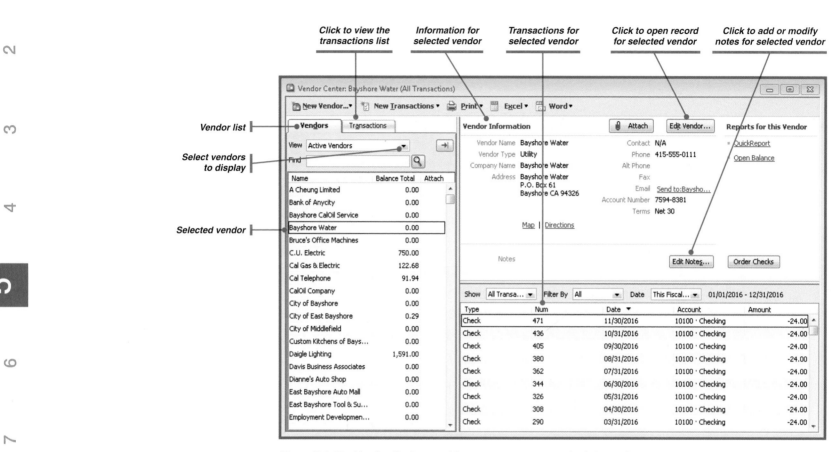

Figure 5-1: *The Vendor Center provides easy access to vendor information.*

The left pane contains two tabs, one for vendors and the other for vendor transactions. Click the **Vendors** tab to view a list of existing vendors and their balance totals. When you select a vendor in the Vendors tab, the upper-right pane displays basic information from the vendor record, while the bottom-right pane lists the selected vendor's transactions.

You can filter the listing of vendors by selecting a filter criterion from the **View** drop-down list at the top of the Vendors tab. If you have a large number of vendors in the list, you can use the **Find** field to search for specific vendors based on the text you enter.

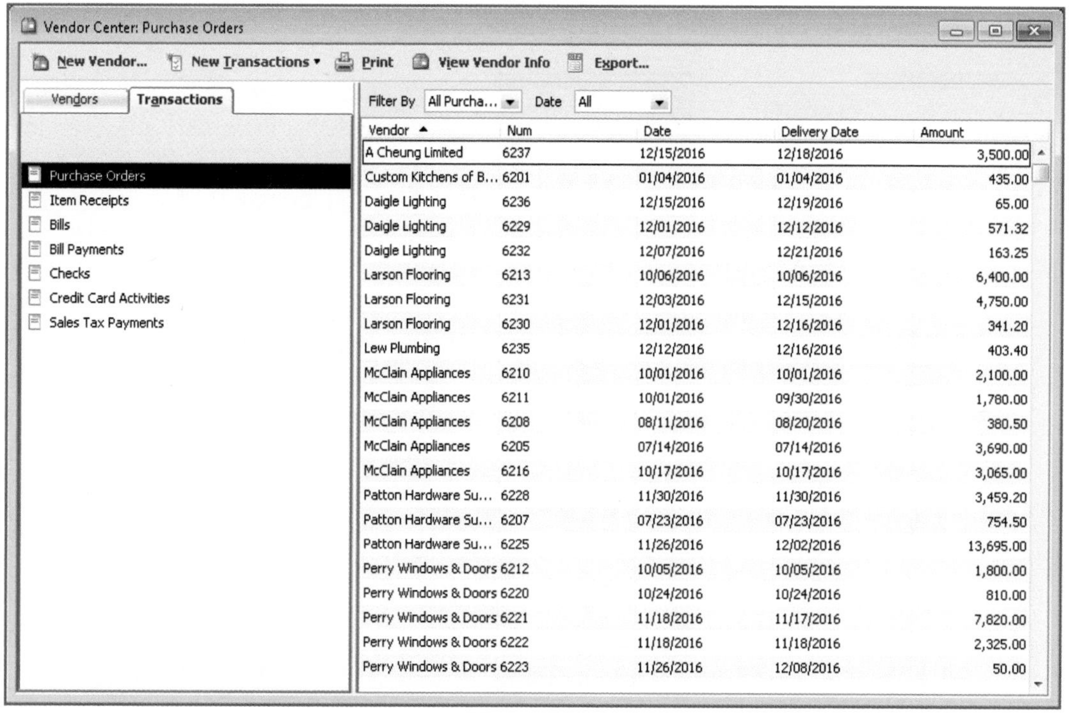

Figure 5-2: *Locating vendor transactions is quick and easy.*

To view all vendor transactions, click the **Transactions** tab (see Figure 5-2). As you can see, the left pane of the Transactions tab contains a listing of the transaction types, while the right pane displays the transactions of the type selected in the left pane.

By default, QuickBooks displays all transactions for the type selected. By using the two filter fields in the right pane (Filter By and Date), you can narrow the listed transactions to only those you're interested in. On the Vendors tab you'll find an additional filter field, Show.

Customize the Vendor Center

In addition to using the filter fields to locate vendors and transactions, you can change the information that is displayed in the Vendor Center. In the

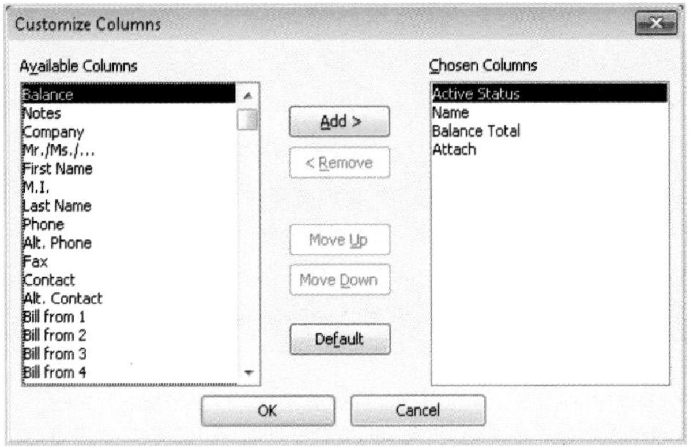

Vendors tab, you can sort the vendor listings by clicking the header in any of the columns. Clicking it once changes the sort order to ascending (A–Z), while clicking it a second time changes the order to descending (Z–A). If you right-click in either of the list panes (vendors or transactions) in the Vendors tab and select **Customize Columns** from the shortcut menu, the Customize Columns dialog box is displayed.

In the Customize Columns dialog, you can add and remove columns, as well as reorder them. By selecting a column in the left pane and clicking the **Add** button, you can add columns to the Vendors tab display. If you select a column in the right pane and click the **Remove** button, the column is deleted from the Vendors tab. To move a column to the left or right in the Vendors tab, select it in the Chosen Columns list, and click **Move Up** to move it to the left or **Move Down** to move it to the right. You can use this same method to customize columns in the transactions list in the right pane of both the Vendors tab and the Transactions tab.

If you decide to add a lot of columns to the Vendors list, you can expand the Vendors tab to see them by dragging the right side of the tab pane further to the right or by clicking the right arrow button next to the View field to completely expand the Vendors tab.

In addition, you can resize columns in any listing with columns by placing your cursor on the separator between column headers, left-clicking (and holding) when the cursor turns into a cross, and dragging the divider left or right.

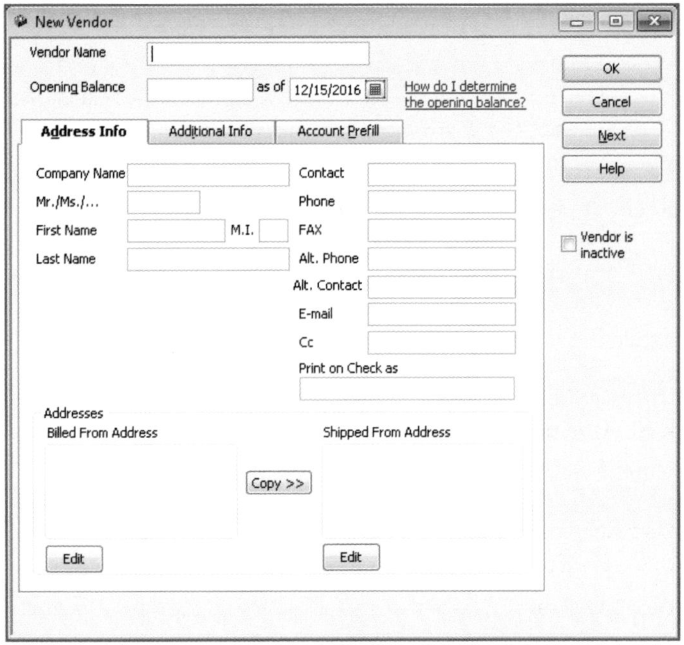

Add Vendors

If you plan to track purchases from vendors, the first step is, obviously, to enter the vendors in QuickBooks.

1. Click the **Vendors** button on the QuickBooks Icon Bar to open the Vendor Center.

2. Click the **Vendors** tab, and press **CTRL+N** to open the New Vendor dialog box shown in Figure 5-3.

Figure 5-3: *The New Vendor form provides billed from and shipped from addresses.*

3. Enter a unique vendor name. As with customers, it's important to use a standardized naming convention to ensure you don't end up with multiple entries for the same vendor.

4. Unless you've discussed it with your accountant, it's preferable to leave the **Opening Balance** field blank and enter historical transactions for the vendor so QuickBooks can calculate an accurate opening balance.

5. Enter the basic contact information on the **Address Info** tab. As you can see in Figure 5-3, you can now add both a billed from and a shipped from address. This is great for those vendors whose accounting offices and warehouses are located at different addresses.

6. If the company name is not the name you want to appear on checks written to the vendor, enter the correct name for checks in the **Print On Check As** field.

7. Click the **Additional Info** tab, and enter the vendor's account number, type, terms, credit limit, and tax ID as necessary.

8. For vendors that provide services as independent contractors and whose payments you are required to report to the IRS, you should check the **Vendor Eligible For 1099** option. If you check this option, remember to enter the vendor's Social Security number (for sole proprietors) or government-issued tax identification number in the **Tax ID** field. If you don't, QuickBooks reminds you when you try to close the vendor record.

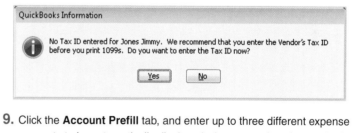

9. Click the **Account Prefill** tab, and enter up to three different expense accounts to be automatically displayed when you select the vendor in the Write Checks window, the Enter Bills window, or the Enter Credit Card Charges window (see Figure 5-4). The accounts appear in the Expenses tab of each of those windows.

10. Click **OK** to save the record and return to the Vendor Center, or click Next to add another vendor.

Figure 5-4: Let QuickBooks do the work by filling in the account field for you.

SETTING BILLS PREFERENCES

Before jumping into the process of entering bills and receiving items, you might want to check the settings for the Bills preferences to ensure things are configured to your satisfaction.

1. Select **Edit | Preferences** from the menu bar to open the Preferences dialog.

2. Click the **Bills** icon in the left pane, and then **Company Preferences** in the right.

3. Set the number of days after receipt that bills are due. If your terms are on receipt, then the number is 0. However, if your terms are 2%10Net30 (due in 30 days, but with a 2% discount if paid within 10 days), it would be 30.

4. I would recommend checking the **Warn About Duplicate Bill Numbers From Same Vendor** option to ensure you don't end up paying the same bill twice.

5. Check the **Automatically Use Credits** option to force QuickBooks to apply existing vendor credits without asking.

6. If your vendor offers terms that include a discount for early payment, you should probably check the **Automatically Use Discounts** option to take the discount automatically.

7. If you check the Automatically Use Discounts option, the Default Discount Account field is enabled. Select the correct discount account, which can be either an expense account or an income account. Check with your accountant to determine which you should use.

8. Click **OK** to save your changes and return to work in QuickBooks.

If, by chance, you have a vendor who is also a customer, you'll have to modify the vendor name (or the customer name) slightly, since QuickBooks will not accept exact matches on the two lists.

Enter Bills and Receive Items

Once your vendors are added to the system, you're ready to start tracking your business activity with them. The primary functions you will perform for vendors are entering bills and receiving items purchased from those vendors. Fortunately, QuickBooks offers several ways to accomplish these tasks.

Enter Bills

Generally, most bills for items are received either with the items or after the items have been delivered. Therefore, most bills that you enter without items will be for expenses such as rent or utilities, in which case, you should use the Enter Bills function.

1. Select **Vendors | Enter Bills** from the menu bar to open the Enter Bills window seen in Figure 5-5. As you can see, the Enter Bills window has a History pane, in which you'll find the company phone number as well as a list of recent transactions and a link to a quick vendor report. This is a great addition that allows you quick access to all the information you might need when entering bills.

2. Select the vendor from the **Vendor** drop-down list. Address and terms information will appear automatically if you previously entered it in the vendor record.

3. If necessary, change the date to match the bill date to ensure discounts and due dates are accurately recorded.

4. Enter the bill number in the **Ref. No.** field.

5. Enter the total amount of the bill in the **Amount Due** field.

6. If the terms did not fill in automatically, enter them now. As soon as terms are entered, a Discount Date field appears. It will be empty unless the terms include a discount, in which case QuickBooks enters it automatically.

7. Use the **Memo** field to enter a note about the bill. The text you enter here will appear in reports as well as on the **Memo** field of the check you write to pay the bill (unless the vendor record contains an account number, which replaces the memo on the check).

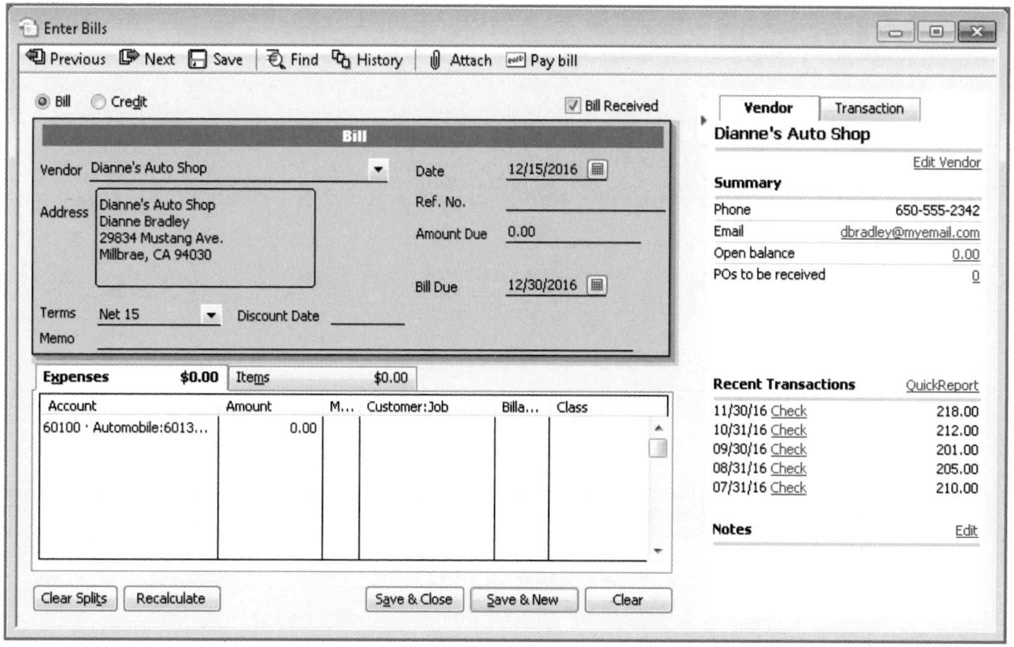

Figure 5-5: *You can track expenses as well as inventory and non-inventory items.*

NOTE

If you have more than one accounts-payable account in your Chart of Accounts, QuickBooks displays an A/P Account field at the top of the window so you can assign the bill to the correct account. Even if all your accounts-payable accounts but one are inactive, the list still appears.

NOTE

The Bill Due (date) field is calculated using data from one of two sources. If the Terms field is populated, QuickBooks uses the terms to determine the Bill Due date. If no terms appear, QuickBooks uses the settings in the Bills preferences. By default, the Bills preferences set the terms to 10 days. If necessary, you can manually change the Bill Due field.

8. Move to the **Expenses** tab, and enter the account to which the first expense should be assigned.

9. Since the amount is automatically transferred from the Amount Due field, you don't have to enter it now unless the bill includes additional expenses or items. If the bill covers other expenses, change the amount to reflect the first expense.

10. Fill in the remaining fields as needed. If the expense is for a specific customer or job, enter the customer or job in the **Customer:Job** field. If you're going to bill the customer for the expense, place a check mark in the **Billable** column.

11. If the bill covers more than one expense, move to the second line and enter a new expense account. If you changed the amount on the first line to reflect the first expense, QuickBooks automatically calculates the second line as the difference between the amount due and the amount of the first line.

12. Continue adding expenses as needed.

13. If the bill is for items, click the **Items** tab and enter the item information.

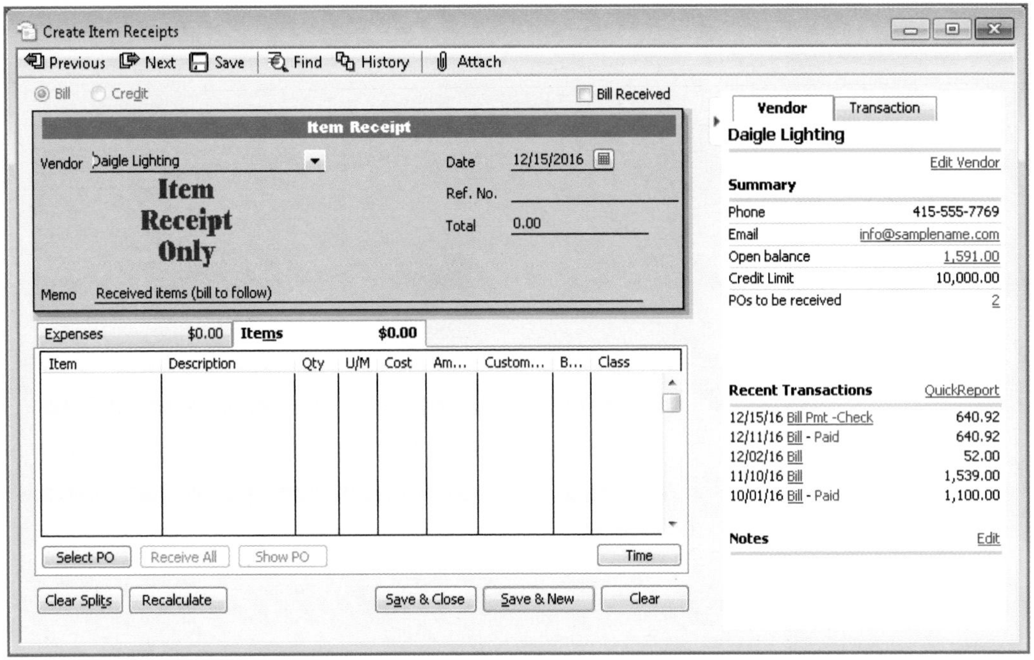

Receive Items

Figure 5-6: *As it says, this form is only for receiving items.*

It is not unusual to receive a shipment of items with only a packing slip, followed by the bill at a later date. When this occurs, you'll want to record the receipt of those items immediately and record the bill when it arrives.

1. From the menu bar, select **Vendors | Receive Items** to open the Create Item Receipts dialog box shown in Figure 5-6. This window also contains a history pane providing you with relevant information concerning the selected vendor.

2. Select the vendor from whom the items were purchased from the **Vendor** drop-down list.

3. If there's an outstanding purchase order from the vendor, QuickBooks displays an alert. Click **Yes** to display the Open Purchase Orders window, and select the corresponding purchase order. If you inadvertently click No, you can always reopen the Open Purchase Orders dialog by clicking the **Select PO** button below the Expenses tab.

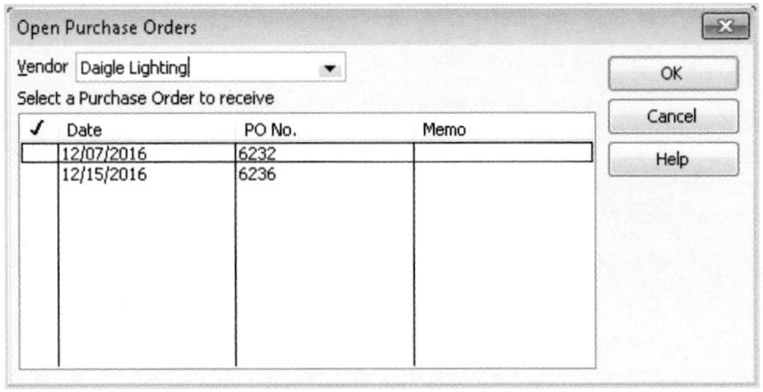

4. If there's no purchase order, enter the packing slip or invoice number into the **Ref. No.** field. This field is optional, so you don't have to enter anything at this point. If you prefer, you can wait and enter the bill number when it arrives.

5. If you know the amount of the purchase, enter it in the **Total** field.

NOTE

If the bill is for items, you can use the Expenses tab to include shipping or other miscellaneous charges.

NOTE

If the packing slip that came only has items and quantities, QuickBooks will fill in the Cost and Amount fields using the information from the item record. When you convert the item receipt into a bill (after the bill arrives), you can adjust the costs to reflect the actual costs paid.

QUICKSTEPS

ENTERING BILLS FOR RECEIVED ITEMS

When the bill finally arrives for items you've already received, you must be careful how you enter the bill. If you use the *wrong* function (Enter Bills), you will add the received items to your inventory for a second time, completely throwing your inventory numbers out of whack. You must use the Enter Bill For Received Items command to ensure QuickBooks handles the bill properly.

1. Select **Vendors | Enter Bill For Received Items** to open the Select Item Receipt dialog box.

2. From the **Vendor** drop-down list, choose the vendor from whom the bill was sent.

3. Select the item receipt that matches the bill you received, and click **OK** to open the Enter Bills window with the selected receipt showing. You'll notice that the Bill Received option at the top of the window is now checked. By adding that check mark, the item receipt has been converted to a bill. Remove the check mark and see for yourself. Of course, don't forget to check it again to continue recording the bill.

4. Double-check all the information and make any necessary changes.

5. Enter any expenses that did not appear on the packing slip but that appear on the bill.

6. Click **Save & Close** to save the bill and close the window, or **Save & New** to enter another bill.

The only thing left to do is pay the bill when it comes due.

6. In the **Items** tab, which is selected by default, enter the items received.

7. If the items are for a specific customer or job, use the **Customer:Job** drop-down list to select the appropriate customer or job.

8. If the customer or job is to be billed for the item, place a check mark in the **Billable** column if it doesn't appear automatically.

9. If there are any charges, such as shipping charges, click the **Expenses** tab and enter them there.

10. Click **Save & Close** to save the item receipt and close the window, or click Save & New to create a new item receipt.

The items are immediately added to inventory and ready for use. When the bill arrives, you can record it using the procedures outlined in the "Entering Bills for Received Items" QuickSteps.

Receive Items and Enter Bills

When the bill arrives with the items, you can enter both at the same time. Select **Vendors | Receive Items And Enter Bill** from the menu bar to open the Enter Bills window. The Enter Bills window opens with the Items tab selected so you can immediately start entering items. Other than that, the process is identical to entering bills of any type. Choose the vendor; enter the correct date, terms, and amount; and then enter the items received. If you have any related expenses, such as shipping charges, click the **Expenses** tab and enter them there.

Enter Credits

When you receive a credit from a vendor for returned or defective merchandise (or whatever reason), you must let QuickBooks know about it so it gets deducted from the amount you owe the vendor.

1. From the menu bar, select **Vendors | Enter Bills** (that's right, Enter Bills).

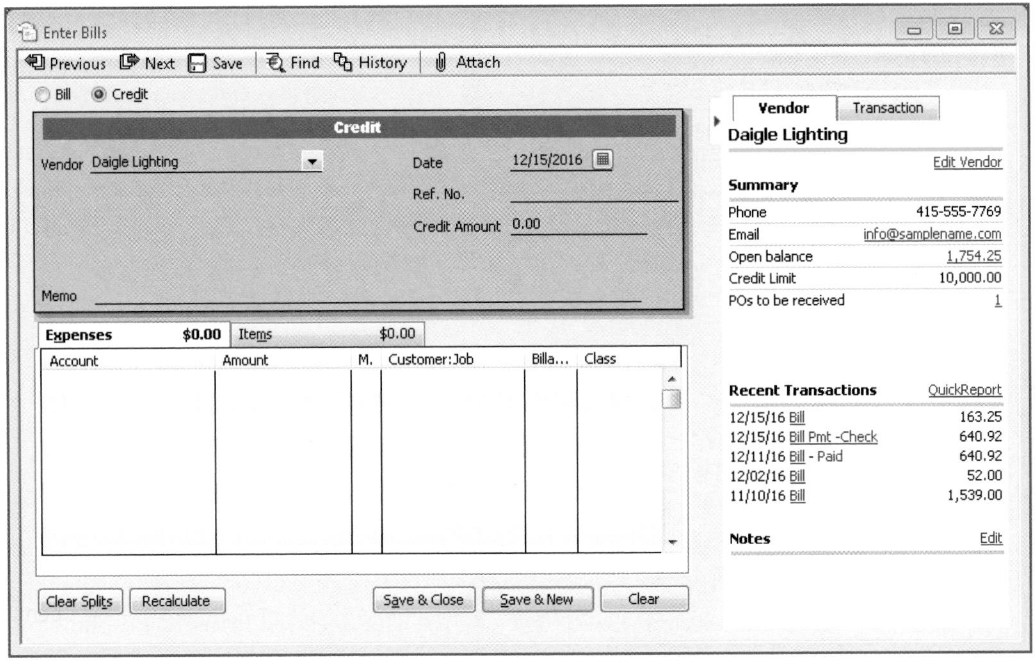

Figure 5-7: *Entering a credit is similar to entering a bill.*

2. The first thing to do is click the **Credit** option at the top of the window to change the bill to a credit, as seen in Figure 5-7.

3. Select the vendor from the **Vendor** drop-down list.

4. Use the optional **Ref. No.** field to enter the credit, invoice, or other relevant number.

5. Enter the credit total in the **Credit Amount** field.

6. If you want to include a brief note about this credit, enter it in the **Memo** field.

7. By default, the Expenses tab is selected. If the credit includes expenses, add them in this tab.

8. If the credit is for returned or defective merchandise, click the **Items** tab and enter the item(s) there.

9. Click **Save & Close** to save the credit and return to work in QuickBooks, or click **Save & New** to create another credit.

When you're paying your vendor bills, you can then apply the credit toward your balance.

QUICKSTEPS

ENTERING RECURRING BILLS

If you have recurring bills such as rent or monthly payments that generally don't vary from month to month, you can simplify the data entry by creating a bill for the vendor and the amount, and memorizing it for future use.

1. Choose **Vendors** | **Enter Bills** to open the Enter Bills window.

2. Follow the steps in the "Enter Bills" section found earlier in this chapter to create the bill. If the amount never varies, enter it in the **Amount Due** field. However, if the amount is always different, leave the **Amount Due** field blank.

3. When you've finished entering the bill, right-click anywhere in the bill (not in the history pane), and select **Memorize Bill** from the shortcut menu to open the Memorize Transaction dialog box. You can also press **CTRL+M** to display the Memorize Transaction dialog.

4. Enter a unique (and recognizable) name for the bill.

5. If you don't want QuickBooks to tap you on the shoulder periodically and remind you about this bill, click **Do Not Remind Me**, which turns off all reminders.

6. If you want to be reminded, leave **Add To My Reminders List** checked and make the appropriate selection from the **How Often** drop-down list.

7. Change the **Next Date** field to reflect the due date for the next payment.

Continued ...

Pay Bills

Eventually, there comes a time when all those bills you've been entering (and some you haven't) have to be paid. Fortunately, QuickBooks makes it relatively easy to decide who and when to pay. Actually, QuickBooks offers two methods of bill paying. The first is for bills that have been entered into QuickBooks previously, and the second is for bills that you don't want, or need, to enter into QuickBooks.

Review and Pay Recorded Bills

If you've been recording bills as they arrive, you can review them by opening the Pay Bills window and then decide which ones to pay.

1. Select **Vendors** | **Pay Bills** to open the Pay Bills window (see Figure 5-8).

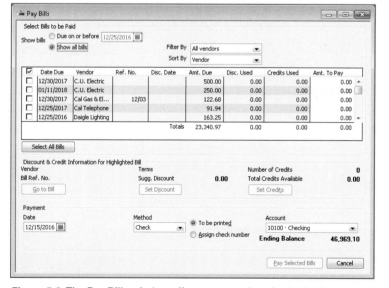

Figure 5-8: **The Pay Bills window offers a comprehensive look at your accounts payable.**

ENTERING RECURRING BILLS (Continued)

8. If you want QuickBooks to enter the bill automatically, check the **Automate Transaction Entry** option and complete the remaining fields. The bill will then appear in the Pay Bills window at the time indicated.

   a. **Number Remaining**   This is the number of payments left to pay. If it is a mortgage or loan payment, enter the number of payments remaining. If, however, it's an ongoing payment such as rent, leave it blank.

   b. **Days In Advance To Enter**   Tell QuickBooks how far in advance of the due date it should create the bill.

9. If you've created transactions groups, which enable you to trigger reminders for a whole series of transactions, the Add To Group option appears. Check the option to include this bill within a transaction group.

10. From the **Group Name** drop-down list, choose the transaction group in which you want this bill to be included. When the reminder or automatic entry for this group is triggered, the bill will be included.

11. Click **OK** to save the memorized transaction and return to the Enter Bills window.

Keep in mind that unless you've configured reminders to display automatically (**Edit | Preferences | Reminders | My Preferences**), you'll have to access the Reminders List manually (**Company | Reminders**) to see which bills are due.

---

2. Decide which bills you want QuickBooks to display by either setting a **Due On Or Before** date or selecting **Show All Bills**.

3. If you have multiple accounts-payable accounts, select the appropriate one from the **A/P Account** drop-down list, which only appears if you have more than one accounts-payable account.

4. If you have a large number of bills, you can sort the list by making a sort selection from the **Sort By** drop-down list. You can also use the **Filter By** drop-down list to display bills from a single vendor.

5. Now, place a check mark next to each bill in the list that you want to pay this time around.

6. As you select a bill, you'll see that the discount and credit information for that particular bill appears below the list of bills. To see the original bill, click the **Go To Bill** button.

7. If you are past the discount date and still want to take the discount, click the **Set Discount** button to open the Discount And Credits window with the Discount tab selected. Enter the discount amount and the account to which it should be assigned.

8. To apply an existing credit to the bill, click the **Set Credits** button, which opens the Discount And Credits window with the Credits tab selected. Check the credit(s) to apply, and click the Done button to return to the Pay Bills window.

9. Move to the **Payment** section, and enter the payment date.

10. Select the method of payment from the **Method** drop-down list. If the method selected is Check, indicate whether it is to be printed by QuickBooks or if a check number should be assigned so you can handwrite the check.

11. Select the appropriate bank account or credit card account (depending on the method selected) from the **Account** drop-down list.

12. Click the **Pay Selected Bills** button to proceed:

    a. If you chose Check as the method and To Be Printed as the option, QuickBooks processes the payment and displays the Payment Summary window.

    b. If you chose Check as the method and Assign Check Number as the option, QuickBooks opens the Assign Check Numbers dialog box in which you can assign a check number or choose to let QuickBooks assign the number. After you make your choice, the payment is processed and the Payment Summary dialog opens.

    c. If you chose Credit Card or Online Bank Pmt as the method, the payment is processed and the Payment Summary dialog appears.

Each Payment Summary dialog offers a Pay More Bills button that returns you to the Pay Bills window so you can continue paying additional bills. Continue until you've finished paying bills for this session.

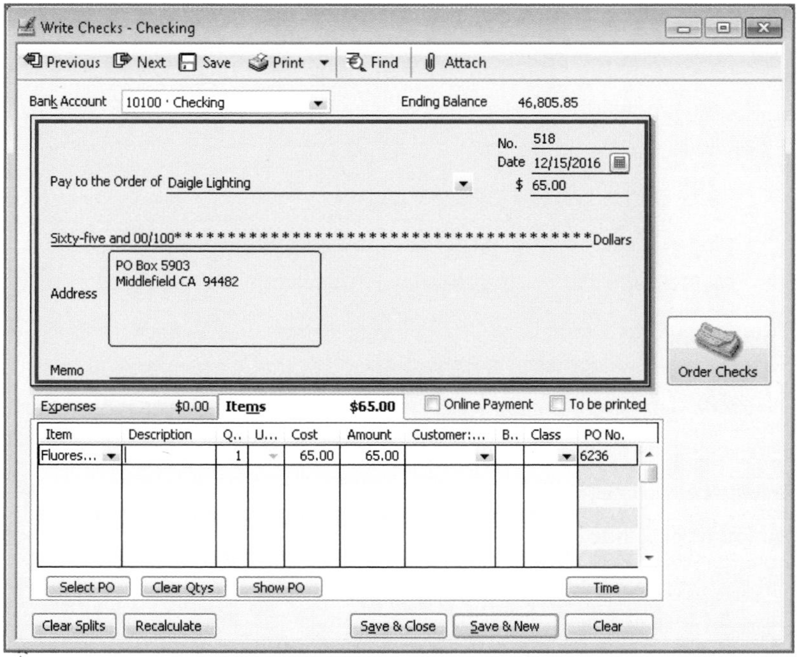

Pay Bills as They Arrive

If you have cash on delivery (COD) deliveries or bills that don't need to be tracked, you can pay them directly using the Write Checks window or the Enter Credit Card Charges window. This eliminates the need to record the bill before paying it.

USE THE WRITE CHECKS WINDOW

The Write Checks window is similar to a bill, except the bill is replaced by the facsimile of a paper check. Using the Write Checks window follows closely the steps needed to fill out a paper check.

1. Press **CTRL+W** to open the Write Checks window shown in Figure 5-9.

2. If you have multiple checking accounts, choose the account to use from the **Bank Account** drop-down list.

3. From the **Pay To The Order Of** drop-down list, select the vendor to pay.

4. QuickBooks automatically assigns the next available check number. You can change it if you need to.

Figure 5-9: *The Write Checks window presents a familiar interface.*

5. Enter the total amount to pay the vendor in the amount ($) field. QuickBooks then fills in the text for the Dollars field. If you select a vendor with an open (previously recorded) bill, QuickBooks alerts you to this fact to ensure you don't pay this bill using the Write Checks window.

6. Enter the **Address** and **Memo** fields if QuickBooks doesn't enter them automatically.

7. If you want to print the check in QuickBooks, check the **To Be Printed** option, and QuickBooks will store the check for printing at a later time.

8. If you've signed up for online bill paying, check the **Online Payment** option.

9. Move to the **Expenses** tab, and enter any expenses you're paying with this check.

10. If you've items to pay for, click the **Items** tab and enter those items.

11. Click **Save & Close** to save the check and close the window, or click **Save & New** to write another check.

If you selected the To Be Printed option, the check is stored for printing and can be accessed by selecting **File | Print Forms | Checks** to open the Select Checks To Print dialog.

If you checked the Online Payment option, QuickBooks saves the payment to the Online Banking Center in the Items Ready To Send section.

PAY BILLS WITH A CREDIT CARD

If you don't want to pay for an unrecorded bill by check, QuickBooks offers the alternative of paying by credit card.

1. Select **Banking | Enter Credit Card Charges** from the menu bar to open the Enter Credit Card Charges window seen in Figure 5-10.

2. From the **Credit Card** drop-down list, select the credit card you want to use to pay the bill.

3. Select the vendor to pay in the **Purchased From** drop-down list.

4. Enter a reference number, if you have one.

5. In the **Amount** field, enter the total amount of the bill.

6. Enter expenses in the **Expenses** tab and/or items in the **Items** tab.

7. Click **Save & Close** or **Save & New** to save the charge and either close the window or create a new charge.

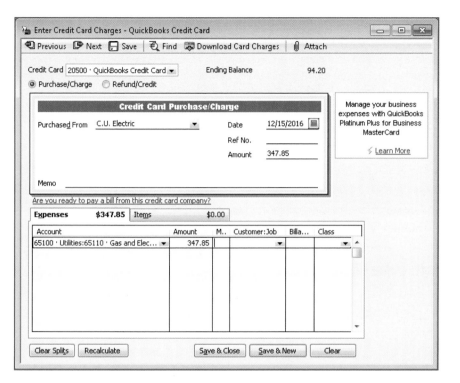

Figure 5-10: *Entering credit card charges is not much different from entering regular bills.*

NOTE

The use tax you owe is based on the sales tax you would have paid in your own location. If your state has "surtax" sales tax based on your county, city, ZIP code, and so on, you owe use tax on the total sales tax rate.

If you want to take a look at the current charges on this account, you can click the **Download Card Charges** button at the top of the Enter Credit Card Charges window to open the Online Banking Center, where you can complete the download.

Manage Use Tax

Unfortunately, there's one more vendor bill that's becoming more prevalent these days: the use tax bill. Most states that impose a sales tax also impose a use tax. Recently, states have begun aggressive measures to collect use tax due. If you collect sales tax, you'll probably be contacted by your state tax agency to report and remit use tax in addition to remitting sales tax you collect from customers.

Technically, all businesses and individuals are responsible for tracking and paying use tax, but businesses that pay state taxes of any kind are easy for the state to find (and pursue).

Understand Use Tax

Use tax is the amount that your state would have collected in sales tax if a taxable product or service were purchased in your state. Generally, the rules for use tax are similar across all states, and the following scenarios represent the common rules:

- If you purchase a product or service that's taxable in your state from a vendor in another state (including a purchase made on the Internet) and the vendor didn't add sales tax, you owe the state use tax on the purchase (to make up for the revenue the state would have received if you'd purchased the product/service in your own state). The reason the vendor did not add sales tax to your purchase could be because the vendor is in a state that doesn't impose a sales tax, or because the vendor is in a state that doesn't require imposing sales tax on out-of-state sales.

QUICKFACTS

UNDERSTANDING VENDORS & PAYABLES REPORTS

While much of the work in QuickBooks is tedious, one of the things that makes it all worthwhile is the ability to create and customize comprehensive reports. The Vendors & Payables reports are invaluable for analyzing that side of your business. To access the Vendors & Payables reports, select **Reports | Vendors & Payables** to display the submenu of related reports:

- **A/P Aging Reports** Want to know how your accounts stand with vendors? Then these are the reports for you. QuickBooks offers two A/P Aging Reports: a Summary version and a Detail version. Both let you know how much (and for how long) you owe your vendors. The Detail report breaks down your accounts payables by status (current, 1–30 days, and so on), while the Summary report gives you totals due (with status) for each vendor.

- **Vendor Balance Reports** If you just want to know how much you owe a vendor, the Vendor Balance Summary report gives you a quick breakdown by vendor with no additional information. To see all the transactions for each vendor, choose the Vendor Balance Detail report.

- **Unpaid Bills Detail** The A/P Aging reports are great for an overview of what you owe, but to see all outstanding (unpaid) bills for each vendor, choose the Unpaid Bills Detail report.

- **Accounts Payable Graph** For a visual representation of the accounts payable numbers, try the Accounts Payable Graph, which includes both a bar chart and a pie chart of your accounts payables.

Continued . . .

- If you purchase a product or service that's taxable in your state from a vendor in another state, and the vendor added sales tax for its own state, and that sales tax rate is lower than your state's rate, you owe the state use tax on the difference. (Some states will not let you report sales tax you paid at a rate that's higher than your state's rate and get a credit for the difference.)

- If you sell taxable products and you remove a product from your warehouse to use it in your business (or remove it for personal use), you owe the state use tax (to make up for the sales tax the state would have received if you'd sold the product).

Use tax is an expense to your business, unlike sales tax. (If you have a sales tax license and collect sales tax from your customers for taxable goods and services, that sales tax is neither income nor an expense. It's a liability, because you're only holding the money temporarily until you send it to the state.)

Track Use Tax

You need to keep records on purchases you make that are liable for use tax. The way you keep those records depends on the forms your state uses to calculate and collect use tax.

- Some states ask for a report on the total purchases for which use tax is due, as well as the total taxable products removed from your inventory for your own use.

- Some states want a complete report that displays the total of all purchases, a subtotal of purchases liable for use tax (similar to the sales tax report that many states require), and a list of inventory removed for business use.

You can design any method that seems efficient to track use tax owed to your state. Your method can be implemented within QuickBooks or outside of QuickBooks. Here are the common methods that businesses are using:

- Create a Vendor Type for out-of-state vendors from whom your purchases are for products or services that are taxable in your state. Then create transaction reports for vendors of that type to determine the total purchases liable for use tax.

- Keep a list of purchases liable for use tax outside of QuickBooks (a spreadsheet works better than sticky notes attached to your monitor).

Depending on the type of reporting your state requires, you may have to work with your accountant to set up a more complex method of tracking these purchases.

QUICK**FACTS**

UNDERSTANDING VENDORS & PAYABLES REPORTS *(Continued)*

- **Transaction List By Vendor** This report is similar to the Vendor Balance Detail report, but includes a few more columns and is automatically filtered to include only transactions for this month to date.

- **1099 Reports** If you have 1099 vendors (independent contractors), these reports come in handy. The summary report lists all your 1099 vendors along with their total (non-employee) compensation for the last calendar year. The detail report, of course, includes all of the transactions for each 1099 vendor for the last calendar year.

- **Sales Tax Liability** If you collect sales tax, you'll want to keep current on how much you owe the sales tax collection agencies in your state. This report gives you a breakdown for each agency (tax vendor), including both taxable and non-taxable sales, the tax rate, and the total tax collected.

- **Sales Tax Revenue Summary** If you just want to see your taxable and non-taxable sales for each tax vendor, use this report.

- **Vendor Lists** Need a phone list of vendors to tape on the wall next to the phone? Or maybe a more comprehensive list of vendors to take with you on your next business trip? No problem: Just print out a Vendor Phone List with vendor names and phone numbers, or a Vendor Contact List with name, address, phone number, fax number, contact, and balance.

Remit Use Tax

To remit use tax, you must create an Expense account for use tax in your Chart of Accounts.

- If your state accepts printed reports, create a check posted to the Use Tax Expense account, and attach the check to the report.

- If your state insists on online filing (many states have moved to online filing for sales tax, and those states also provide use-tax reporting online), your use-tax payment is probably deducted automatically from your bank account. Enter the transaction in your bank register (use ACH for the check number, or leave the Number field blank), and post it to the Use Tax Expense account.

Run Purchase Reports

In addition to Vendor & Payables reports, QuickBooks offers a number of purchases-related reports. You can access them by selecting **Reports | Purchases** from the menu bar. Here you'll find reports that break down purchases by vendor and by item, either in a summary version or a detail version. In addition, there are three open purchase-order reports.

For more information on running and customizing QuickBooks reports, see Chapter 8.

How to...

- Configuring Inventory Preferences
- Add Inventory Items
- Understanding Inventory Tracking Basics
- Create Subitems
- Use the EasySaver Feature
- Create Custom Fields
- Use Add/Edit Multiple List Entries
- Generating Purchase Orders
- Change the Display Options
- Preparing for an Inventory Count
- Use Filters on the Inventory Worksheet
- Change the Worksheet Appearance
- Memorize the Worksheet
- Adjust Inventory Quantity
- Adjust Inventory Value
- Track Inventory Giveaways
- Understanding Inventory Reports
- Manage Damaged Inventory

Chapter 6
Tracking Inventory

If you run an inventory-based business, you know what a major investment (and headache) inventory can be. Keeping track of it without the proper tools is an impossible job. Fortunately, QuickBooks provides everything you need to manage your inventory and keep your business running smoothly. Some of the things we'll cover in this chapter include setting inventory preferences, creating inventory items, making inventory adjustments, and more.

Configuring Inventory Control

If your business involves the buying and selling of products, even if you're primarily a service business that also sells parts, you'll want to enable inventory tracking. The ability to keep tabs on hundreds or even thousands of individual inventory items is an absolute must.

CONFIGURING INVENTORY PREFERENCES

The QuickBooks inventory preferences are not at all complicated. They pretty much amount to turning on inventory tracking and setting a couple of warnings.

1. Select **Edit | Preferences** from the menu bar to open the Preferences dialog box.

2. Click the **Items & Inventory** icon in the left pane, and click **Company Preferences** in the right pane to display the available inventory options.

3. To enable inventory tracking in QuickBooks, check the **Inventory And Purchase Orders Are Active** option. As soon as you enable the option, two more options become available.

4. If you want QuickBooks to warn you when you attempt to use a purchase order number that is already in use, leave the check mark next to the **Warn About Duplicate Purchase Order Numbers** option. The only real reason to deselect this option is if your QuickBooks file is extremely large, resulting in a significant performance deterioration due to the time it takes to search for duplicate numbers.

5. It's a good idea to leave the next option, **Warn If Not Enough Inventory Quantity On Hand (QOH) To Sell**, enabled. It's much easier to let a customer know immediately that a product is out of stock than to wait until it's discovered in the warehouse.

Continued . . .

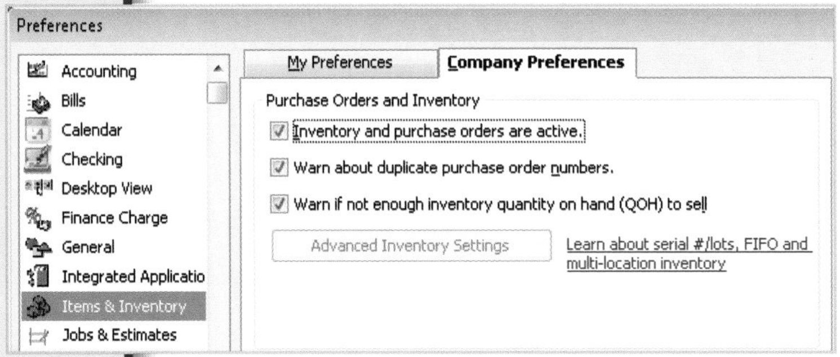

If you used the EasyStep Interview to set up your company file, you may already have inventory tracking turned on. If not, you can still do it now using the Items & Inventory preferences.

Working with Inventory Items

Once inventory is enabled in QuickBooks, you can begin adding inventory items in the Item List. Without a list of all the items that you stock for resale, it will be a little difficult to track your inventory accurately.

Add Inventory Items

In order to track inventory in QuickBooks, you first have to let QuickBooks know exactly what inventory items you have.

1. Select **Lists | Item List** from the menu bar to open the Item List window (see Figure 6-1).

2. Press **CTRL+N** to open a New Item dialog box.

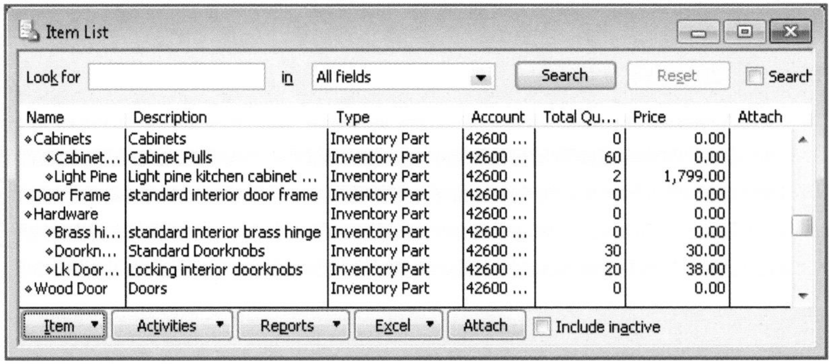

Figure 6-1: **The Item List is your repository for all items, including inventory items.**

6. If you're running QuickBooks Premier Accountant, Contractor, or Manufacturing & Wholesale, or any of the Enterprise editions, you will have a functioning Unit Of Measure option available. It's a handy feature that enables you to sell products in different units. For example, if you sell cans of soda, you can sell individual cans, six packs, or cases.

7. Click **OK** to save your settings and close the Preferences dialog box.

Although Advanced Inventory is only available in the Enterprise Edition, you'll see a grayed-out button for Advanced Inventory Settings in this section. Click the link next to it to learn more about the feature.

NOTE

If you're running QuickBooks Enterprise Edition you'll see a new menu dedicated entirely to Inventory. It appears on the menu bar as soon as you turn inventory tracking on. This new menu includes a number of inventory-related commands that were formerly scattered around on different menus.

---

3. From the Type drop-down list, choose **Inventory Part** to open a blank New Item form for an inventory part. If you have the EasySaver feature turned on, you'll see an additional pane to the right of the New Item form. See the section later in this chapter, entitled "Use the EasySaver Feature," for more information.

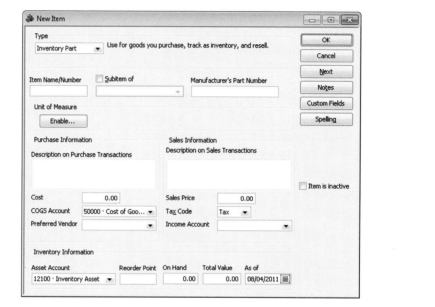

4. Enter a unique name or number to identify the item. The text you enter here appears on item drop-down lists in sales and purchase transaction forms.

5. Include a manufacturer's part number if you have one.

6. In the **Description On Purchase Transactions** field, enter the description you want to appear on purchase orders, bills, item receipts, and other purchase forms.

7. In the **Cost** field, you can enter the most recent cost of the item. If you're going to use a default markup to automatically calculate the sales price, you must enter a number in the Cost field. However, keep in mind that QuickBooks uses the Avg. Cost (a calculated field), not the Cost field, when posting to the Cost of Goods Sold account.

8. If you have more than one Cost of Goods Sold account, select the appropriate one for this item from the **COGS Account** drop-down list.

9. If you have multiple vendors for this item, select your vendor of first choice from the **Preferred Vendor** drop-down list.

QUICK**FACTS**

UNDERSTANDING INVENTORY TRACKING BASICS

Before jumping into the QuickBooks inventory tracking feature, it will help if you have a few of the basics under your belt:

- **Inventory part vs. non-inventory part** QuickBooks offers both inventory and non-inventory parts. Most people understand what an inventory part is—an item that you buy, stock, and resell. It's pretty straightforward. It's usually the non-inventory part that causes the confusion. It is not, as many people think, for tracking office supplies, paper towels, and other items that you buy and use in your business. Those items are considered expenses. It's for items that you resell to your customers (or charge them for) but do not stock. If an item is going to be used in sales transactions but not have its on-hand quantity tracked, it should be a non-inventory item.

- **Inventory accounts** When you create your first inventory item, QuickBooks automatically creates two new inventory-related accounts—an Other Current Asset account called Inventory Asset and a Cost of Goods Sold account named, appropriately enough, Cost of Goods Sold. These become the default accounts used as you create new inventory items.

- **Inventory adjustments** If you need to make inventory adjustments, either to the count or the value, use the **Adjust Quantity/Value On Hand** command (**Vendors | Inventory Activities | Adjust Quantity/Value On Hand** or **Inventory | Adjust Quantity/Value On Hand** for Premier and Enterprise users). The first time you use it, you will

Continued . . .

10. In the **Description On Sales Transactions** field, enter the text you want to appear on sales receipts, invoices, and other sales transaction forms.

11. If the Sales Price is not automatically calculated, you can enter it now, or if you prefer, leave this field blank and enter it on sales transactions as you create them.

12. If you've enabled the sales tax feature, assign the appropriate tax code to the item in the **Tax Code** field.

13. QuickBooks will not let you save the new item unless you have assigned it to an income account, so select the appropriate account from the **Income Account** drop-down list.

14. QuickBooks assigns the item to the Inventory Asset account it automatically created the first time you added an inventory item. If you have multiple Inventory Asset accounts, you can select a different one from the **Asset Account** drop-down list.

15. If you would like QuickBooks to alert you when you start running low on this item, enter a number in the **Reorder Point** field. When the on-hand quantity reaches the number you enter here, it automatically triggers a reminder.

16. If you have stock on hand, you can enter it in the **On Hand** field. However, it is better to use the Adjust Quantity/Value On Hand window to ensure the adjustment is assigned to the correct account. If you decide to use the On Hand field and the item has a cost, QuickBooks automatically calculates the Total Value field.

17. Click **OK** to save the item and return to the Item List, or click **Next** to open another New Item form.

Enter as many inventory items as needed. If you're entering quite a few, you might want to take advantage of the Add/Edit Multiple List Entries feature by right-clicking in the Item List and selecting **Add/Edit Multiple Items** from the shortcut menu (see "Use Add/Edit Multiple List Entries" later in this chapter).

Create Subitems

If your inventory items come in different sizes, shapes, colors, and so on, you'll be glad to hear that you can accommodate them all by using subitems. If your inventory includes men's golf shirts in four sizes and four colors, that means you've got 16 possible variations. While you could add 16 different items for the shirts, a more effective method would be to create a single item for Men's Golf Shirt and 16 subitems for each color/size combination. While both methods

QUICKFACTS

UNDERSTANDING INVENTORY
TRACKING BASICS *(Continued)*

have to create an inventory adjustment account. While your first impulse may be to use an income or expense account, you should really check with your accountant first, as accountants are frequently more inclined to opt for a cost of goods sold account.

- **Purchase orders** Purchase orders should be used for inventory items only. The reason is simple. Purchase orders are meant to be turned into item receipts or bills once the products arrive. Since non-inventory items will never be brought into inventory, you'll have a collection of unneeded purchase orders building up in QuickBooks. One other thing to note about purchase orders is that the first time you create a purchase order (or even just open the Create Purchase Orders window), QuickBooks creates a Non-Posting account called Purchase Orders.

TIP

If you want QuickBooks to automatically calculate the sales price for an item based on its cost, turn on the Markup function. Select **Edit | Preferences | Time & Expenses | Company Preferences**, and enter a percentage in the **Default Markup Percentage** field. Next, select (or create) an account in the **Default Markup Account** drop-down list, and click **OK** to save your changes. From then on, QuickBooks will calculate the sales price of a new item by increasing the item's cost by the percentage you entered here.

achieve the same end result, using subitems gives you more control when it comes to creating effective reports and graphs.

Creating subitems is not much different from creating items. Use the steps outlined in the previous section, "Add Inventory Items," with one small change. Check the **Subitem Of** option and select the parent item from the drop-down list below the option. Fill out the rest of the item form as explained earlier, and save the item when you're done. When you review the Item List, you'll see that the subitems appear below the parent item and are indented (as long as you are using the Hierarchical View—click the **Item** button and select **Hierarchical View**).

Use the EasySaver Feature

New in QuickBooks 2012 is the EasySaver feature. Intuit has contracted with a number of vendors to (theoretically) obtain the best price on a wide range of products that you might use in your business. When you add either an Inventory Part or a Non-Inventory Part to your Item List, QuickBooks automatically checks the Intuit database for matches on the Item Name and presents a listing of related items and their prices in the EasySaver pane that appears to the right of the New Item form (see Figure 6-2).

As long as you have an active Internet connection, QuickBooks will search the Intuit database as soon as you enter something in the Item Name/Number field and move to the next field. Only the first ten matches are listed in the EasySaver pane. Hovering your mouse over an item listing displays a description and picture (if available). To see additional items, click the **See More** link at the bottom of the pane. This will open a QuickBooks browser window with a listing of all the matches. You can purchase items by clicking the check box next to the item(s) and clicking the **Add Selected Items To Cart** button.

To turn the EasySaver feature on, open the Preferences dialog box (**Edit | Preferences**), click the **General** icon in the left pane, the **Company Preferences** tab in the right, and check the **Show Me EasySaver Recommendations By Analyzing My Item Descriptions** option.

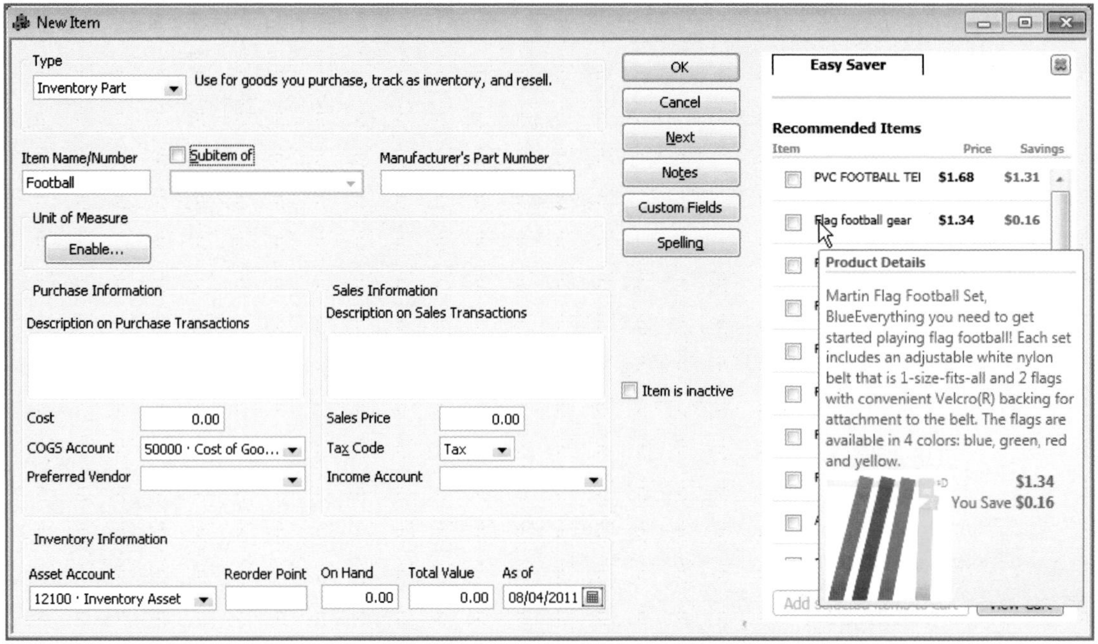

Figure 6-2: *Now you can do comparison shopping from within QuickBooks.*

NOTE

When you enter a quantity into the On Hand field, QuickBooks assigns it to the Opening Balance Equity account, which is an account found only in QuickBooks. Most accountants prefer not to use this account, so check with your accountant before entering on-hand quantities.

TIP

If you plan to take periodical physical inventories, you can create a custom field called Dept or Bin to indicate where the item is located. For detailed instructions, see the section entitled "Create Custom Fields."

Create Custom Fields

While QuickBooks provides a large number of fields for recording information about inventory items, there may be some information you would like to keep track of for which there are no fields. For example, certain inventory items may come in different sizes or colors, or perhaps your warehouse uses departments or bins to organize stock. These are ideal candidates for custom fields, which you create for your own personal use.

1. Select **Lists** | **Item List** to display the Item List.

2. Double-click the item for which you want to add the custom field to open the Edit Item dialog box.

3. Click the **Custom Fields** button to open the Custom Fields dialog box (if no custom fields exist, QuickBooks displays an information dialog to that effect).

4. Click the **Define Fields** button to open the Set Up Custom Fields For Items dialog.

5. Enter a name (e.g., Dept or Bin) in the **Label** field, and check the **Use** column.

6. Click **OK** to return to the Custom Fields dialog that now contains your new field, fill in the necessary information, and then click **OK** to save it.

Now, most of the items in your Item List contain the custom field(s) you created. The Subtotal, Sales Tax, and Sales Tax Group items do not contain custom fields.

Use Add/Edit Multiple List Entries

If you have a lot of items to either add or edit, it can be time-consuming to perform each task individually. Fortunately, QuickBooks offers a speedy alternative for Service, Inventory, and Non-Inventory items. It's called the Add/Edit Multiple List Entries feature.

1. Select **Lists | Add/Edit Multiple List Entries** from the menu bar. Or, if you're in the Item List, right-click in the list and choose **Add/Edit Multiple Items** from the shortcut menu that appears. Either way, the Add/Edit Multiple List Entries window appears (see Figure 6-3).

2. From the **List** drop-down list, select the item type you want to add or edit. Your choices (of items) are limited to Service Items, Inventory Parts, and Non-Inventory Parts.

TIP

Unless you plan to enter data in every field of the item record, you should rearrange the columns of the Add/ Edit Multiple List Entries window so all the fields you want to use appear at the beginning of the list. Click the **Customize Columns** button to open the Customize Columns dialog box. Here you can add, remove, and reposition all the available columns (fields) for the item record.

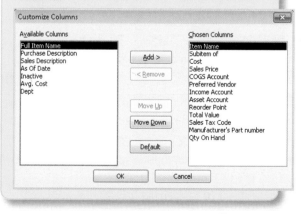

Add/Edit Multiple List Entries

① Select a list.   ② Customize columns to display.   ③ Paste from Excel or type to add to or modify your list.   🖳 See how to quickly update your lists

List [Inventory Parts ▾]   View [Active Inventory Items ▾]   Find [🔍]   [Customize Columns]

Currently Editing: [   ]

Item Name	Subitem of	Cost	Sales Price	COGS Account	Preferred Vendor	Income Account	Asset Account
Cabinets		0.00	0.00	50000 · Cost of Goods Sold	Thomas Kitchen & Bath	42600 · Construction Income:Materia...	12100 · Inventory Ass
Cabinet Pulls	Cabinets	3.00	0.00	50000 · Cost of Goods Sold	Patton Hardware Supplies	42600 · Construction Income:Materia...	12100 · Inventory Ass
Light Pine	Cabinets	1,500.00	1,799.00	50000 · Cost of Goods Sold	Patton Hardware Supplies	42600 · Construction Income:Materia...	12100 · Inventory Ass
Door Frame		12.00	0.00	50000 · Cost of Goods Sold	Patton Hardware Supplies	42600 · Construction Income:Materia...	12100 · Inventory Ass
Hardware		0.00	0.00	50000 · Cost of Goods Sold	Patton Hardware Supplies	42600 · Construction Income:Materia...	12100 · Inventory Ass
Brass hinges	Hardware	3.00	0.00	50000 · Cost of Goods Scroll	Perry Windows & Doors	42600 · Construction Income:Materia...	12100 · Inventory Ass
Doorknobs Std	Hardware	15.00	30.00	50000 · Cost of Goods Sold	Perry Windows & Doors	42600 · Construction Income:Materia...	12100 · Inventory Ass
Lk Doorknobs	Hardware	34.95	38.00	50000 · Cost of Goods Sold	Perry Windows & Doors	42600 · Construction Income:Materia...	12100 · Inventory Ass
Wood Door		0.00	0.00	50000 · Cost of Goods Sold	Patton Hardware Supplies	42600 · Construction Income:Materia...	12100 · Inventory Ass
Exterior	Wood Door	590.39	120.00	50000 · Cost of Goods Sold	Perry Windows & Doors	42600 · Construction Income:Materia...	12100 · Inventory Ass
Interior	Wood Door	35.00	72.00	50000 · Cost of Goods Sold	Perry Windows & Doors	42600 · Construction Income:Materia...	12100 · Inventory Ass

[Save Changes]   [Close]   [Help]

Figure 6-3: **The Add/Edit Multiple List Entries window speeds up data entry considerably.**

TIP

If you only want to edit certain records, you can use the Find field to create a custom filter. Don't enter anything in the Find text box (clear it if it contains anything). Instead, click the magnifying glass icon to the right of the field to open the Custom Filter dialog box. From the **Search** drop-down list, choose the item group you want to search. In the **For** field, enter the search word or phrase. Finally, select the field(s) to search within from the **In** drop-down list. Click **Go** to locate the records that match your search criteria.

Custom Filter

Search [All Inventory Items ▾]   For [door]

in [All fields ▾]

[Go]   [Cancel]   [Help]

3. To add new items, scroll to the bottom of the list, and start entering data in the first blank line. Or you can start from the top by selecting **Unsaved <item name> Items** from the View drop-down list. Unless you started creating new items earlier and failed to save them, the list should be blank.

4. Fill in the fields as needed, and repeat for all items you want to enter. When you're done, click **Save Changes** to add the new items to the Item List.

5. To edit an item, locate the item, move to the column (field) that you want to modify, click in the field, and make the desired change.

6. Repeat for all edits, and click **Save Changes** to record the changes.

This is especially handy for entering information into custom fields you create. When you open the Customize Columns dialog box, you'll find the custom fields in the Available Columns pane. Add them to the Chosen Columns pane, and use the **Move Up** and **Move Down** buttons to shift them into position so they're easily accessible, and then click **OK** to save the new list layout.

QUICKSTEPS

GENERATING PURCHASE ORDERS

As mentioned earlier, purchase orders are better suited for inventory items than for service or non-inventory items. There is nothing to prevent your using purchase orders for everything; you just end up bloating your QuickBooks file with unnecessary transactions.

1. From the menu bar, select **Vendors | Create Purchase Orders** to open the Create Purchase Orders window.
2. Select the appropriate vendor from the **Vendor** drop-down list. Once you select a vendor, the History pane displays some basic vendor information as well as recent transactions.
3. If you're tracking classes, a Class field appears so you can assign this transaction to the proper class.
4. By default, QuickBooks uses your company address as the Ship To address. However, if you want to have the order sent directly to a customer (or other vendor, employee, or other name), use the **Drop Ship To** drop-down list to select the correct address.
5. If you've customized a purchase order template, select it from the **Template** drop-down list.
6. QuickBooks automatically uses today's date and assigns the next available purchase order number. You can change either as needed.
7. Now fill in the line items that you are ordering. Depending on the information entered in the individual item records, some of the line-item information appears automatically (Description and Rate appear if included in the item record).
8. If an item is being purchased for a specific customer, select the name from the **Customer** drop-down list.

Continued . . .

Print the Worksheet

A good worksheet is invaluable for taking an accurate count during a physical inventory. The good news is that QuickBooks provides a worksheet that you can print and use. Even better news is that Intuit finally improved it to the point that it is a useful inventory worksheet. The Physical Inventory Worksheet (see Figure 6-4), which can be accessed by selecting **Reports | Inventory | Physical Inventory Worksheet**, is much more flexible than in older versions. Before printing the worksheet you might want to make a few modifications.

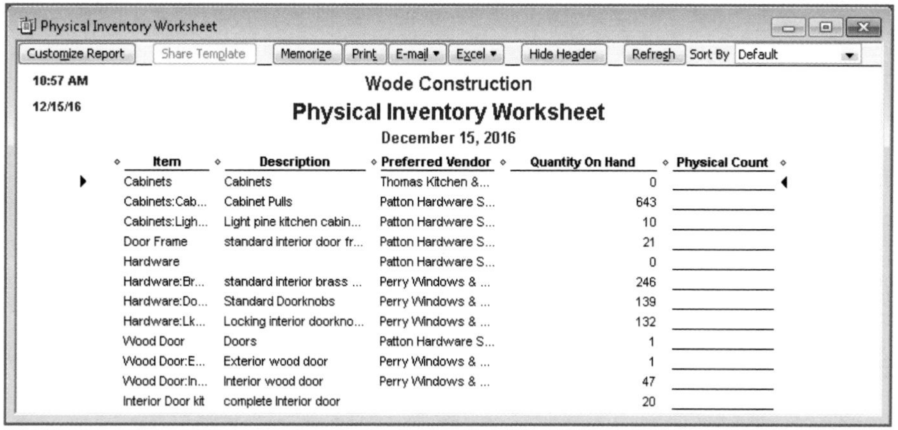

Wode Construction
Physical Inventory Worksheet
December 15, 2016

Item	Description	Preferred Vendor	Quantity On Hand	Physical Count
Cabinets	Cabinets	Thomas Kitchen &...	0	
Cabinets:Cab...	Cabinet Pulls	Patton Hardware S...	643	
Cabinets:Ligh...	Light pine kitchen cabin...	Patton Hardware S...	10	
Door Frame	standard interior door fr...	Patton Hardware S...	21	
Hardware		Patton Hardware S...	0	
Hardware:Br...	standard interior brass ...	Perry Windows & ...	246	
Hardware:Do...	Standard Doorknobs	Perry Windows & ...	139	
Hardware:Lk...	Locking interior doorkno...	Perry Windows & ...	132	
Wood Door	Doors	Patton Hardware S...	1	
Wood Door:E...	Exterior wood door	Perry Windows & ...	1	
Wood Door:In...	Interior wood door	Perry Windows & ...	47	
Interior Door kit	complete Interior door		20	

Figure 6-4: ***The QuickBooks inventory worksheet can be customized to suit the needs of your physical inventory.***

Change the Display Options

The Physical Inventory Worksheet is fully customizable like the other QuickBooks reports. This means that you can control which fields appear on the report and in which order. This is especially helpful if you have created custom fields for such things as department or bin location, or for inventory item attributes such as color and size. You can now include them on the inventory worksheet you print out.

GENERATING PURCHASE ORDERS

(Continued)

9. Fill in the **Vendor Message** field, if needed (i.e., special shipping instructions). Since vendor messages are less frequently used than customer messages, there is no list in which to save your vendor messages.

10. If you are going to send the purchase order via snail mail, check the **To Be Printed** option. If you're going to e-mail it, check the **To Be E-mailed** option. If you're just going to phone the order in, leave both unchecked.

11. The Memo field can be used to enter a note to yourself or your staff. It does not appear on the printed purchase order.

12. Click **Save & Close** to save the purchase order and close the window, or click **Save & New** to create another purchase order.

The purchase order is nothing more than a placeholder in QuickBooks, and has no accounting ramifications (nothing is posted to any QuickBooks accounts). It is only when the merchandise or bill arrives and you convert the purchase order into an item receipt or a bill that the amounts are recorded in QuickBooks.

To change the fields displayed and the order in which they're sorted:

1. Click the **Customize Report** button in the top-left corner of the report. This opens the Modify Report dialog box seen in Figure 6-5.

2. Scroll through the **Columns** list on the Display tab, and select those fields you want to appear on the report and deselect those you want to eliminate.

3. Move to the **Sort By** drop-down list and choose the field by which you want the report sorted. If you added a location field such as Dept or Bin, this is a good candidate for the Sort By field.

4. Next, select the sort order you wish to impose. Click **Ascending Order** to sort the worksheet from A to Z. If you wish to do a reverse sort (Z to A), choose **Descending Order**.

If you change your mind about the modifications you made, simply click the **Revert** button.

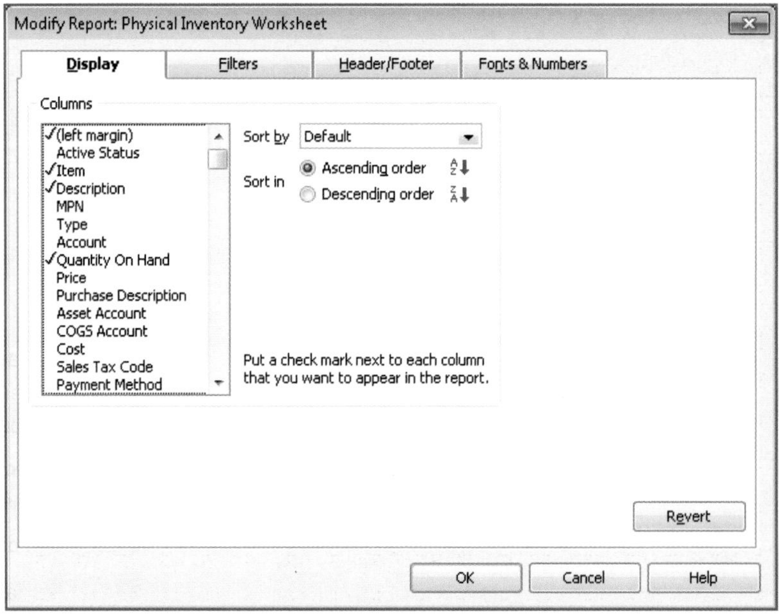

*Figure 6-5: **The Display tab lets you add and remove fields from the inventory sheet.***

PREPARING FOR AN INVENTORY COUNT

Everyone knows that taking an inventory means you grab your clipboard and run around counting each of the items you have sitting in the store or warehouse. Unfortunately, for all too many businesses, that is the sum of the preparation and execution of a physical inventory. To get an accurate count, you need to prepare properly for taking inventory by doing the following:

- **Get organized** Plan ahead so you can close the store or warehouse while you perform the count. If you must take a count during business hours, formulate a plan for manually recording sales, returns, and incoming merchandise to ensure they don't get entered into QuickBooks.

- **Clean up QuickBooks** Make sure your inventory items are current and have good descriptions, part numbers where available, and location (department or bin) information.

- **Clean up the location** Trying to take an inventory while items are strewn all over the place is practically impossible. Organize your store or warehouse so things are where they belong before starting to take the count.

- **Location map** Create a map of your location indicating where each department or bin (or other location designation you use) is situated.

- **Train the staff** Make sure everyone knows how the count is to be conducted, what to do in the case of items appearing that are not listed on the count sheets, how to resolve confusion about individual items, and last but not least, who is in charge.

Use Filters on the Inventory Worksheet

Another nice feature of the Physical Inventory Worksheet is the ability to apply filters. This enables you to do a couple of things. First of all, you can use filters to create and print separate worksheets for the different areas of your warehouse, or for different categories of inventory items. You can also employ filters to eliminate certain items that you don't want to include in the physical count.

Applying filters is easy.

1. Click the **Customize Report** button on the Physical Inventory Worksheet report to open the Modify Report dialog box.

2. Click the **Filters** tab to display the filter options. By default, two filters are already applied: one to include only active items and the other to include all inventory and assembly items (assembly items can only be created in Premier or Enterprise Editions).

3. If you want to change the default filters, highlight each one and make changes to the options that appear to the left of the Current Filter Choices box, or click the **Remove Selected Filter** button to eliminate the filter entirely.

4. Move to the **Choose Filter** list, and select the field on which to base the filter. As soon as you do, options for that filter type appear to the right.

5. Set the filter options as needed.

As with the Display tab, if you change your mind, all you have to do is click the **Revert** button to put everything back to its original state.

Change the Worksheet Appearance

The final two tabs of the Modify Report dialog box give you the opportunity to change the way the report looks. In the Header/Footer tab you can change the titles and other informative data that appear on the report. You can add or remove page numbers and footers.

The Fonts & Numbers tab lets you customize the fonts used for the individual elements of the report. In addition, you can change the way numbers are presented. Don't be afraid to experiment. If you make changes that you don't like, you can always use the Revert button to restore the report to its earlier condition.

Memorize the Worksheet

Once you expend the effort to customize the worksheet so it fits your needs, you'll want to memorize it so you don't have to duplicate your work the next time you do a physical inventory.

1. Make all the necessary modifications to the report.

2. Click the **Memorize** button to display the Memorize Report dialog box.

3. Give the report a unique name that will enable you to easily recognize it the next time you need to use it.

4. If you've created a report group for inventory reports, check the **Save In Memorized Report Group** option, and select the appropriate group from the drop-down list.

5. If you think others may find your customized worksheet valuable, you can share it by checking the **Share This Report Template With Others** option.

6. Finally, click **OK** to save the memorized report.

To access the report the next time you perform a physical inventory, select **Reports | Memorized Reports | Memorized Report List**, and double-click the report name.

Take the Physical Count

Open the Physical Inventory Worksheet and make the necessary modifications. Then click the **Print** button and print the sheet(s) you need. Once you have your count sheets distributed among all the counters and one person designated as the person in charge, you can grab your clipboard and start running around counting all the items on the shelves. If you have a lot of inventory to count and a lot of people counting, it's a good idea to have someone make random audits of the counting to ensure everyone's doing a good (accurate) job.

Make Inventory Adjustments

When the inventory count is over and all the data is tallied up, there are going to be some, if not a lot of, discrepancies between what QuickBooks says you have in stock and the actual numbers revealed by your physical count. The reasons for this are simple and straightforward. Breakage, human errors, and theft are the main culprits. Whatever the reason, you have to let QuickBooks know about those discrepancies.

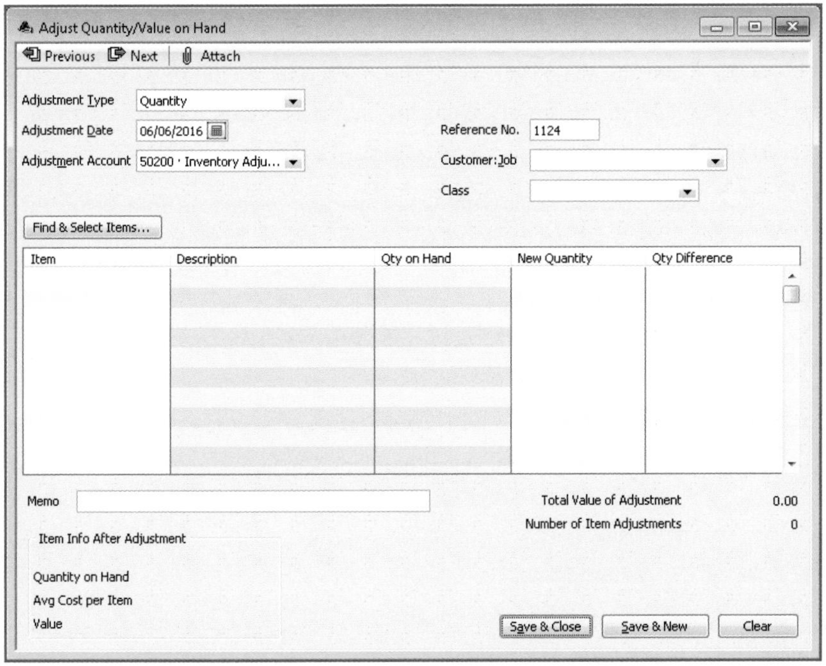

Adjust Inventory Quantity

Whenever you are aware of a change in your inventory quantities, whether it's after a physical count or after someone breaks an inventory item, you should let QuickBooks know about it as soon as possible. Fortunately, QuickBooks has a simple process for adjusting inventory quantities.

1. Select **Vendors I Inventory Activities I Adjust Quantity/Value On Hand** (**Inventory I Adjust Quantity/Value On Hand** for Enterprise users) to open the Adjust Quantity/Value On Hand dialog box (see Figure 6-6).

2. Select the appropriate account from the **Adjustment Account** drop-down list. If this is your first time making an adjustment, you'll have to create an inventory adjustment account. Check with your accountant for the correct account type to use. While QuickBooks suggests expense or income accounts, many accountants prefer to use cost of goods sold accounts.

3. If the adjustment is related to a customer or job, you can choose a name from the **Customer:Job** drop-down list.

4. If you're tracking classes, you can assign a class to this adjustment by making a selection from the **Class** drop-down list that appears.

Figure 6-6: **Adjusting inventory quantities in QuickBooks is a breeze.**

NOTE

Nearly half of retail shrinkage (inventory loss) is due to employee theft. Therefore, if your physical counts reveal substantial losses, you might be forced to take a closer look at implementing security measures that reduce employee theft.

NOTE

You can elect to make adjustments to both quantity and value at the same time by selecting **Quantity And Total Value**.

5. Click the **Find & Select Items** button to display the Find & Select Items window.

6. Locate and select the item(s) to be adjusted, and then click the **Add Selected Items** button.

7. Highlight each item and enter the new (accurate) quantity in the **New Quantity** field. QuickBooks automatically calculates the difference between the current quantity and the new quantity, and enters the result in the Qty Difference field.

8. Repeat for all the items that need to be adjusted.

9. Click **Save & Close** to save the changes and close the window, or click **Save & New** to enter another adjustment.

As you make adjustment entries, QuickBooks calculates the total value of those entries and enters them in the bottom-right corner of the window, with the label Total Value Of Adjustment. This figure is calculated using the Avg. Cost figure.

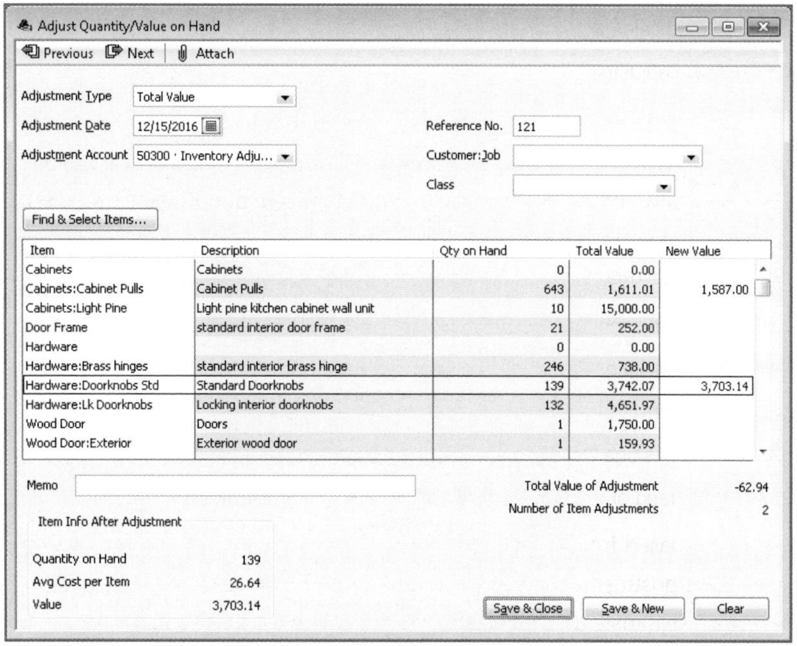

Adjust Inventory Value

If you need to change the value of inventory items, you can use the same basic procedure described in the previous section, "Adjust Inventory Quantity," with a couple of minor changes.

1. Open the **Adjust Quantity/Value On Hand** dialog box.

2. From the Adjustment Type drop-down list choose **Total Value**. As you can see in Figure 6-7, the New Quantity and Qty Difference columns are removed and two new columns, Total Value and New Value, are added.

3. Select (or add) an account from the **Adjustment Account** drop-down list.

4. Enter optional fields (Customer:Job and Class) as needed.

5. Click the **Find & Select Items** button, select the item(s) to change, and click the **Add Selected Items** button.

6. Highlight each item and enter the new value of the item in the New Value column.

7. Change all items as needed.

8. Click **Save & Close** to save the adjustment(s) and close the window, or click **Save & New** to enter another adjustment.

Figure 6-7: **You can easily modify the quantity, the value, or both.**

QuickBooks calculates the value of the adjustment using your new numbers rather than the average cost used for quantity adjustments.

Make Special Inventory Adjustments

Now that you've got inventory adjustment basics down, let's see how they work in the real world. The following sections cover some specific situations in which you might find you need to make adjustments to your inventory.

Track Inventory Giveaways

Sometimes you give away an inventory item instead of selling it. You may make a donation of the inventory item to a charitable organization, or you may send sample products to customers and potential customers.

You have two ways to create a transaction for a giveaway of an inventory item:

- Use a zero-based sales receipt (the sales price is entered as 0.00).
- Use an inventory adjustment.

USE A SALES TRANSACTION TO RECORD A GIVEAWAY

The zero-based sales receipt transaction appears to be the quickest and easiest way to give away an inventory product, but it doesn't track the details properly. For example, when you create a zero-based sales receipt for an inventory item that's linked to your Income account, the following postings take place:

- The inventory asset account is reduced by the current average cost of the item.
- The COGS account is increased by the current average cost of the item.
- The Income account is unaffected (because the amount of income is zero).
- The bank account is unaffected (because no income was received).
- The quantity on hand of the item is reduced.

If you use a zero-based invoice instead of a sales receipt transaction, the postings change a bit: The posting to the bank account listed for the postings of a sales receipt doesn't exist; instead, that posting is to accounts receivable. The bank account is affected when you receive invoice payments. (Of course, you'll never receive a payment for this invoice because it has no balance.)

CAUTION

You can only post an expense for a charitable contribution for a product, not for services rendered or for time volunteered. The deductible amount is the cost of the product, not the retail price.

NOTE

If the inventory item is returnable to the manufacturer (your vendor), have the customer return the item to you so you can return it to the manufacturer and get a credit. If the inventory item isn't returnable to the manufacturer, tell the customer not to return it so you don't have to include the cost of shipping it back to you in the credit.

If the giveaway is for a charitable organization, your Charitable Gifts expense account isn't involved. If the giveaway is a sample, your Marketing or Advertising expense account isn't involved. This means you can't accurately analyze what your business is doing. Another good reason for not using a zero-based invoice.

If you use a zero-based transaction (either a sales receipt or an invoice), after you save the transaction, you should move the amounts to their proper expenses by creating a General Journal Entry (GJE). To know what the amounts are for the GJE, open the original transaction window and press **CTRL+Y** to see the transaction journal for the transaction, which should look similar to Figure 6-8. Make a note of the amount posted to the Costs of Goods Sold account.

Open a journal entry window (**Company | Make General Journal Entries**), and make the following entries:

- Credit the COGS account for the amount posted by the transaction.
- Debit the appropriate expense account (charitable contributions or marketing expense) for the same amount. You've moved the expense from COGS to the right category.

USE AN INVENTORY ADJUSTMENT TO TRACK GIVEAWAYS

Okay, now that you learned how to do it the hard way, you'll be pleased to know there's an easier way. The previous exercise was for those folks who already used

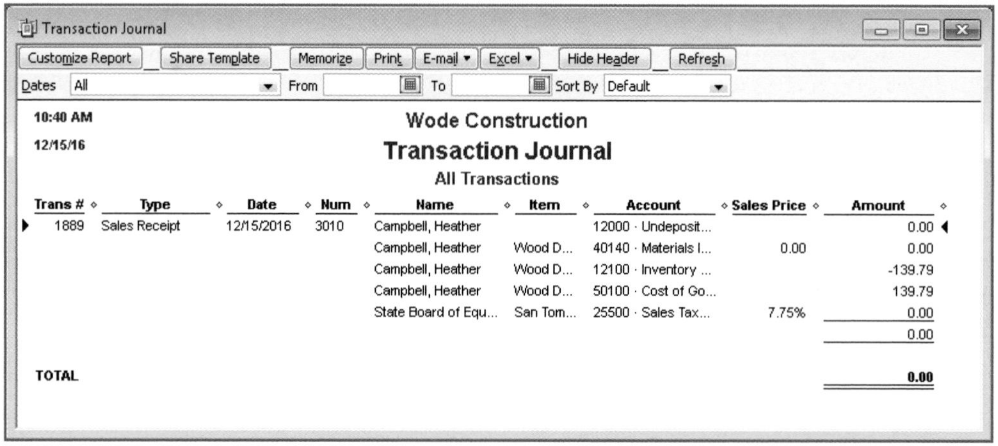

10:40 AM
12/15/16

Wode Construction
Transaction Journal
All Transactions

Trans #	Type	Date	Num	Name	Item	Account	Sales Price	Amount
1889	Sales Receipt	12/15/2016	3010	Campbell, Heather		12000 · Undeposit...		0.00
				Campbell, Heather	Wood D...	40140 · Materials I...	0.00	0.00
				Campbell, Heather	Wood D...	12100 · Inventory ...		-139.79
				Campbell, Heather	Wood D...	50100 · Cost of Go...		139.79
				State Board of Equ...	San Tom...	25500 · Sales Tax...	7.75%	0.00
								0.00
TOTAL								**0.00**

Figure 6-8: ***You need to know the amount posted to Costs of Goods Sold so you can move that amount to the correct expense account.***

a zero-based transaction. If you're starting from scratch, forget the zero-based transaction and journal entry; just use an inventory adjustment to track giveaways. To accomplish this, choose **Vendors | Inventory Activities | Adjust Quantity/ Value On Hand** (**Inventory | Adjust Quantity/Value On Hand** for Enterprise users). In the Adjust Quantity/Value On Hand transaction window, take the following actions:

1. In the **Adjustment Account** field, select the appropriate expense account (charitable contributions or marketing).

2. Optionally, enter the Customer:Job (only if this is a marketing expense and there is a real customer—don't enter a new customer if this is a potential customer).

3. Select a class if you're tracking classes.

4. Use the Find & Select Items window to select the item(s) you're giving away.

5. When you return to the Adjust Quantity/Value On Hand window, enter -1 (minus one) in the Qty Difference column for each item. If you're giving away more than one, enter the appropriate quantity as a negative number.

6. Optionally, enter a note in the **Memo** field to explain the transaction (e.g., enter the charity's name or the potential customer's name).

7. Click **Save & Close** to record the adjustment.

Manage Damaged Inventory

If a customer receives an inventory item that's damaged, you have to issue a credit to the customer. You can't really put the item back into the warehouse because you can't risk shipping it to another customer.

However, issuing the credit for the inventory item automatically returns the item into inventory. Here's what takes place in QuickBooks:

- The quantity on hand is increased.
- The amount of the current average cost is added to the inventory asset account.
- The amount of the current average cost is removed from the COGS expense account.

These postings are neither accurate nor desirable. The workaround is to create an inventory adjustment after you create the credit memo so you can correct the postings.

Continued . . .

QUICKFACTS

UNDERSTANDING INVENTORY REPORTS

QuickBooks offers a variety of inventory reports that enable you to analyze your inventory, whether you want to see your on-hand quantities, the value of your inventory, or what items you have on order. To view the reports, select **Reports | Inventory** to display the submenu of available inventory reports.

- **Inventory Valuation Summary** This report is chock-full of information. It includes the item, the on-hand quantity, the average cost, and the asset value, as well as the retail value and more.

- **Inventory Valuation Detail** If you want to see the value of your inventory and all the transactions involved in determining that number, run this report. It includes sales, purchase, and receipt transactions.

- **Inventory Stock Status by Item** Want to know how many of a particular item you have on order (listed on a purchase order)? Well, run this report and you'll find out.

- **Inventory Stock Status by Vendor** This is the same report as the Inventory Stock Status by Item, with one exception—it is sorted by preferred vendor rather than by item.

- **Physical Inventory Worksheet** A handy worksheet used for taking a physical count of your inventory. It's great for creating a customized count sheet for taking physical inventories.

QUICKFACTS

UNDERSTANDING INVENTORY REPORTS *(Continued)*

- **Pending Builds** Although you can only have pending builds in QuickBooks Premier or Enterprise Edition, this report appears in QuickBooks Pro as well. In the higher versions of QuickBooks, you can create assemblies, which are inventory products that are built using other inventory products. When there are not enough parts to complete an assembly, it is considered a "pending build." This report provides details on all current builds that are pending.

NOTE

If the item and customer are both taxable, QuickBooks automatically calculates the tax and will remove the amount from your Sales Tax liability account.

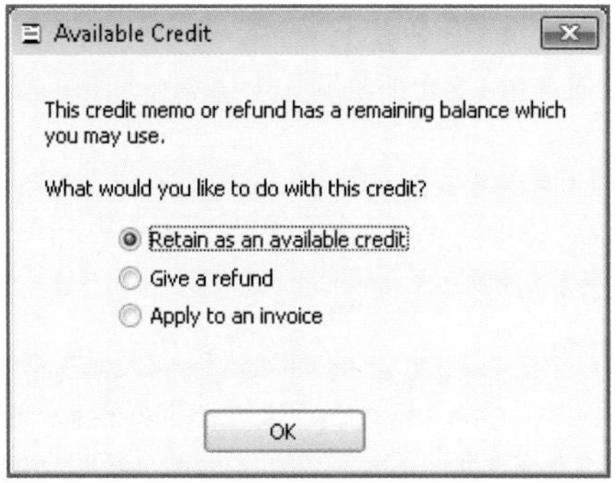

*Figure 6-9: **Select the appropriate option for applying this credit.***

Start by creating a credit. Choose **Customers | Create Credit Memos/Refunds**. In the transaction window, take the following steps:

1. From the **Customer:Job** drop-down list, select the customer.
2. In the line-item section, select the item being returned from the **Item** drop-down list.
3. Enter the quantity being returned in the Qty field (don't use a minus sign).
4. Enter the amount in the Amount field, if it doesn't automatically appear (don't use a minus sign).
5. Optionally, enter a note in the Memo field.
6. Click **Save & Close** to save the credit and display the Available Credit dialog box shown in Figure 6-9.

Depending on the selection you make in the Available Credit dialog box, you may have additional tasks to perform. See Chapter 4 to learn about managing credit memos.

Now that the credit exists, you have to remove the item from inventory. Choose **Vendors | Inventory Activities | Adjust Quantity/Value On Hand** (**Inventory | Adjust Quantity/Value On Hand** for Enterprise users). In the Adjust Quantity/Value On Hand transaction window, take the following actions:

1. In the **Adjustment Account** field at the top of the window, select the appropriate expense account. You can use an Inventory Adjustment expense account, an Inventory Adjustment Cost of Goods account, or a Damaged Inventory account (either an expense or a COGS account), depending on the way your accountant advised you to adjust inventory.
2. Click the **Find & Select Items** button, select the item that's damaged, and click the **Add Selected Items** button to return to the Adjust Quantity/Value On Hand window.
3. Enter -1 (assuming one item was damaged) in the Qty Difference column.
4. Optionally, enter a note in the **Memo** field to explain the transaction (for example, "damaged product returned by BizCom").
5. Click **Save & Close** to record the adjustment.

QuickBooks posts all the appropriate amounts to the correct accounts in addition to reducing the quantity on hand.

How to...

- ⌀ *Getting Organized Before You Start*
- ◔ *Activating Manual Payroll*
- ◔ *Creating Payroll Items as You Need Them*
- • *Enter Wage and Salary Information*
- • *Add Employee Benefits*
- ⌀ *Understanding Employee Types*
- • *Set Up New Employees*
- ⌀ *Understanding Payroll Setup Wizard Limitations*
- • *Configure Payroll Preferences*
- ⌀ *Understanding Payroll Preferences*
- • *Add, Edit, and Delete Employees*
- ⌀ *Setting Employee Preferences*
- • *View Employee Transactions*
- ◔ *Setting Default Employee Information*
- • *Record a Single Activity*
- ◔ *Using the Weekly Timesheet*
- ◔ *Assigning Employees to Payroll Schedules*
- ⌀ *Understanding Payroll Liabilities Payment Options*
- ◔ *Configuring 1099 Vendors*
- • *Configure 1099 Tracking*
- • *Prepare and File 1099 Forms*

Chapter 7

Running Payroll

If you have a small or medium number of employees who get paid on a regular schedule, you may find that running your own payroll in QuickBooks is the right solution for you. For those who decide to do their payroll in-house, QuickBooks offers a set of tools to make the job easier. This chapter will cover those tools and get you up to speed on running payroll in QuickBooks.

Understand Payroll Service Choices

If you've decided to use QuickBooks for payroll, you must first decide which payroll service, if any, you're going to subscribe to. Intuit offers five options (with a couple of suboptions) for doing payroll:

- **No Payroll Service**   If you don't sign up for a payroll service, QuickBooks payroll can be activated and used, but you'll have to do the calculations on your own. Without a subscription to a payroll service, there is no way you can enter the tax table information required for QuickBooks to perform the necessary calculations. You can get those tables from the IRS and your state tax agency and do your own calculations. You can then manually input them and print checks, but it's a lot of work if you have more than a couple of employees.

NOTE

The options you see are somewhat confusing, so be advised that the first option offers to sign you up for Enhanced Payroll, the second for Full Service Payroll, and the third for Basic Payroll. If you're interested in Assisted Payroll you'll have to visit the QuickBooks Payroll website (http://payroll.intuit.com/).

NOTE

When you first sign up for a payroll service, QuickBooks downloads the current tax information. However, both state and federal tax rates may change over the course of time. Therefore, you should periodically update your tax table information. All you have to do is make sure your Internet connection is live, and then select **Employees | Get Payroll Updates**, or press **CTRL+SHIFT+U** to open the Get Payroll Updates dialog.

QUICKFACTS

GETTING ORGANIZED BEFORE YOU START

Before you start configuring QuickBooks payroll, you should gather all the documents and information you're going to need to complete the process. It will go a lot faster if you prepare ahead of time:

- **Company data** What types of compensation do you offer? Perhaps you have some employees on hourly wages, others on salary, and some working for commissions. Do you offer bonuses? Do some employees earn tips? QuickBooks wants to know about it all. Next come the benefits. Do you offer health insurance, retirement plans, and vacations?

Continued . . .

- **Basic Payroll** With the basic service, QuickBooks calculates earnings, payroll taxes, and deductions; prints the paychecks; runs reports; calculates federal and state payroll taxes; and automatically updates federal and state tax rates. For an extra fee you can also use direct deposit. However, you must fill out all your tax forms manually using the data from QuickBooks.

- **Enhanced Payroll** Here you get everything the basic service offers plus the ability to electronically file and pay payroll taxes. In addition, it automatically fills out payroll tax forms that you can print and sign, and it tracks workers' compensation.

- **Assisted Payroll** This is the service for those who don't want the hassle of worrying about payroll taxes. You enter the payroll information in QuickBooks, print the paychecks (or use direct deposit), and let Intuit take care of the rest, including year-end W-2s. Intuit files your payroll tax forms and makes the payments, while guaranteeing that all will be done in a timely and accurate manner.

- **Full Service Payroll** The only thing you have to do with this service is enter employee hours online and let Intuit do the rest. A payroll specialist sets up your account online and assists with your first payroll. Intuit takes care of tax payments and form filing, including year-end W-2s.

Now, if you're wondering what happened to those suboptions I mentioned, here they are. The basic and enhanced services come in two flavors (actually two prices). The first, and least expensive, is for no more than three employees. The second is for an unlimited number of employees. For more information, select **Employees | Payroll | Learn About Payroll Options** to access the Intuit website for payroll services.

Enable the QuickBooks Payroll Feature

The first step in running payroll of any type is turning on the payroll feature in the QuickBooks Preferences.

1. Select **Edit | Preferences** to display the Preferences dialog box.

2. In the left pane, click the **Payroll & Employees** icon.

QUICKFACTS

GETTING ORGANIZED
BEFORE YOU START *(Continued)*

Are there any other special payments or deductions you offer? Finally, if you're using direct deposit or e-filing, you'll also need bank account information, like routing and account numbers for your payroll account.

- **Employee data**   You'll need to supply employee pay rates and deductions, information from the employees' W-4 forms, hire dates, vacation and sick pay data, and direct deposit information, if applicable.

- **Tax data**   Whom do you have to file with and pay? What are your filing schedules? What's your state unemployment insurance rate? QuickBooks wants to know.

- **Payroll history data**   Unless you're opening your business and starting QuickBooks payroll at the same time, you should have some historical data on prior payrolls. QuickBooks will ask for prior payroll information going back to the beginning of the calendar year.

- **Create vendors**   The payroll wizard drop-down lists for vendors, unlike most other QuickBooks drop-down lists, do not offer an <Add New> choice. That means you can only select vendors for health insurance, life insurance, taxes due, and so on that already exist in QuickBooks. Therefore, create any vendors you'll need for payroll setup before you start.

For a handy checklist of items that you'll need, and some tips on preparing, start the payroll wizard by selecting **Employees I Payroll Setup**. Then click the **Payroll Setup Checklist** link on the introduction screen of the wizard to download the list in PDF format.

3. Next, click the **Company Preferences** tab to display the available options for payroll and employees.

4. In the QuickBooks Payroll Features section, choose **Full Payroll**.

5. Click **OK** to save your changes.

Regardless of which payroll service you use, even manual payroll, you must first let QuickBooks know you're running payroll by enabling this option.

Configure QuickBooks Payroll

After you subscribe to the payroll service of your choice or turn on manual payroll, as indicated in the "Activating Manual Payroll" QuickSteps, it's time to configure QuickBooks for running payroll. To make the task a little easier, QuickBooks provides a couple of ways to accomplish this, including a wizard that walks you through the process.

- **Manage Payroll Items**   You can use the **Manage Payroll Items I New Payroll Item** command on the Employees menu to create payroll items any time you want. It offers two ways of creating those items. The first is called EZ Setup, which actually launches the Payroll Setup wizard to complete the task. The difference is that it opens the wizard to the exact location needed to create the selected item type instead of slogging through the whole wizard. The second option is called the Custom Setup method, which is quicker, but offers no handholding. See the QuickSteps entitled "Creating Payroll Items as You Need Them" for instructions on both methods.

- **Run the Payroll Setup Wizard**   The nice thing about the Payroll Setup wizard, which is officially called QuickBooks Payroll Setup, is that it walks you through payroll setup from the beginning to the end. In addition, you can exit the wizard at any time and pick up where you left off when you return. The bad thing about it is that you have to go through every step, even if you don't need certain items.

For those who want to ensure that they don't miss a single item necessary for payroll, the wizard is the way to go.

1. Select **Employees I Payroll Setup** to launch the QuickBooks Payroll Setup wizard seen in Figure 7-1.

2. If this is your first visit to the Payroll Setup wizard, it opens at the Introduction screen. Click **Continue** to begin the Company Setup portion of the wizard.

3. Follow the on-screen instructions to complete the wizard.

CREATING PAYROLL ITEMS AS YOU NEED THEM (Continued)

- **Custom Setup** With this method you're entirely on your own. You decide which payroll item to create and enter all the necessary data in a series of no-frills screens.

3. In the Payroll Item Type dialog that appears, select the payroll item to create, and then click **Next**. This screen is basically the same no matter which method you select. The only difference is that you cannot create state and local tax items using the EZ Setup method.

4. If you selected the EZ Setup method in step 2, the Payroll Setup wizard launches and takes you to the exact form needed to create the selected item. Complete the wizard steps, and click **Finish**.

5. If you chose Custom Setup in step 2, follow the on-screen instructions to create the new item. The screens you see and the information needed will, of course, vary depending on the payroll item you're creating.

Remember, if you need some assistance with your choices, choose the EZ Setup option. If you're a payroll whiz, choose the Custom Setup option.

---

you are paying piecework. You will only find the Piecework item in the wizard and in the EZ Setup option. The reason is that QuickBooks considers the Piecework item to be a fixed-amount Commission item. If you want to add the item using the Custom option, you have to create a Commission item and name it Piecework (or some other appropriate name). Piecework items must be edited to enter the default rate for each item.

As mentioned earlier, the QuickBooks Payroll Setup wizard (**Employees | Payroll Setup**) offers more handholding than either the EZ Setup option or the Custom Setup option found in the Add New Payroll Item dialog (**Employees | Manage Payroll Items | New Payroll Item**).

Add Employee Benefits

There are a lot of possible benefits that you might offer your employees, and QuickBooks needs information about each one. They are broken down into four different categories:

- **Insurance** Many companies offer some form of health, dental, vision, or even life insurance. If you offer any of these, QuickBooks wants to know who pays—you (the employer), the employee, or do you share the cost? In addition, QuickBooks needs to have the vendor and payment information.

- **Retirement** If your company offers retirement plans, such as 401(k), 408(k) (for 25 or fewer employees), a simple IRA, or a 403(b) (for government, university, or nonprofit employees), you'll have to tell QuickBooks about them. If you add them through the Payroll Setup wizard or the EZ Setup option, QuickBooks adds a payroll item for both your contribution and the employee's contribution. If you use the Custom Setup option, you must remember to create both.

- **Paid Time Off** Do you offer sick days or paid vacation to your employees? Whether you offer one or both, you must tell QuickBooks about it. If you use the wizard or the EZ Setup option, QuickBooks sets up an item for hourly employees and/or salaried employees, depending on the wage types you've configured. If you use the Custom Setup option, remember that QuickBooks considers paid time off as just another wage type. Also, when using the Custom Setup option, you must set up a Paid Time Off item for both salaried employees and hourly employees if you have both on staff.

- **Miscellaneous Additions** If you use the wizard or the EZ Setup option, you'll find that this category includes not only miscellaneous additions, but deductions as well. Here you'll find things like cash advances, taxable fringe benefits (i.e., company car),

QUICK**FACTS**

UNDERSTANDING EMPLOYEE TYPES

It is important to understand (and use) employee types as defined by the IRS to ensure your deductions and payroll reports are accurate and in keeping with current IRS rules:

- **Regular**   No mystery here. This is someone who works for you and for whom you issue a regular compensation check as well as a W-2 form at the end of the year.

- **Officer**   If your business is incorporated, you will have officers, whose payroll should be reported separately on tax returns, since, in some states, corporate officer pay is exempt from state unemployment tax. Other than that, they are considered regular employees.

- **Statutory**   In some cases, independent contractors may, in reality, be considered statutory employees, which means they are subject to some withholding taxes. For details on what constitutes a statutory employee and to which taxes they are subject, check IRS Publications 15 and 15-a.

- **Owner**   Since an owner (or a partner) cannot be an employee, this employee type should not even exist. Owners do not get paychecks, but rather take draws from the business. Owners and partners should be added to the Other Names list, not the Employee list.

For detailed explanations of who the IRS considers an employee, you should download and carefully read Publications 15 and 15-a (Circular E, Employer's Tax Guide, and its supplement), which can be found in the forms and publications section of the IRS website (www.irs.gov). There are many nuances that throw light on the differences between employees, common-law employees, statutory employees, independent contractors, and nonstatutory employees—each of which has different taxing requirements. As always, ask your accountant when in doubt.

mileage reimbursements (employees using their own cars for business), and miscellaneous additions. On the deductions side, there are wage garnishments, union dues, charitable donations, and miscellaneous deductions. If you use the Custom Setup option, these items do not appear as Miscellaneous Additions but rather as Additions and Deductions.

Set Up New Employees

You can add new employees either with the QuickBooks Payroll Setup wizard or in the Employee Center. While the wizard offers a little more handholding, the Employee Center method offers a little more flexibility. Therefore, we're going to cover that method here.

1. Select **Employees | Employee Center** from the menu bar to launch the Employee Center shown in Figure 7-2.

2. Click the **New Employee** button in the upper-left corner of the window to open the New Employee dialog box seen in Figure 7-3.

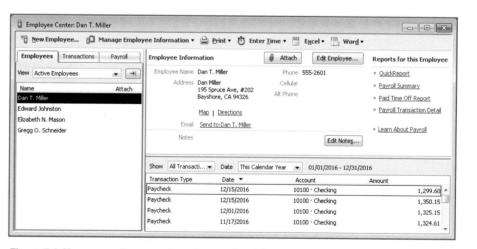

Figure 7-2: **You can perform most employee-related functions in the Employee Center.**

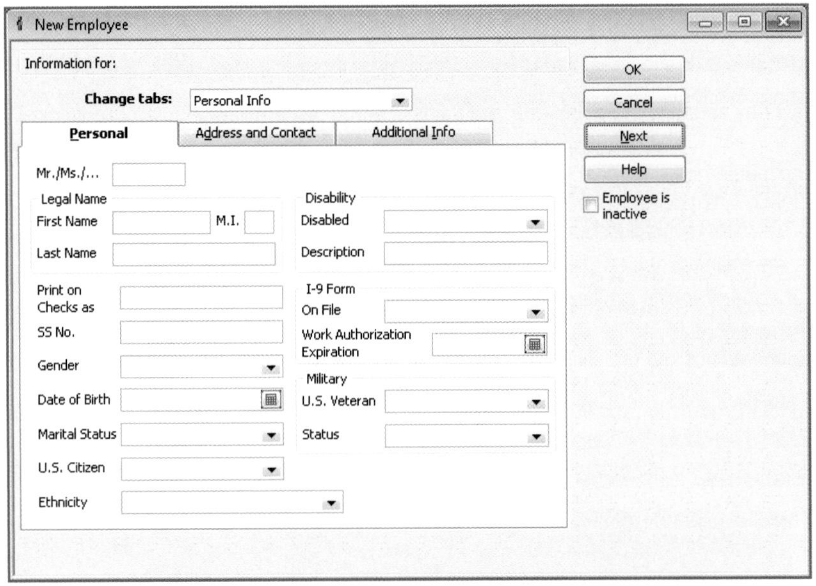

Figure 7-3: *The Enhanced Payroll subscription adds quite a few fields to the Personal tab.*

NOTE

If you have entered data for employee defaults (**Edit I Preferences I Payroll & Employees I Company Preferences I Employee Defaults**), the information appears automatically in the Payroll Info tab of the New Employee dialog.

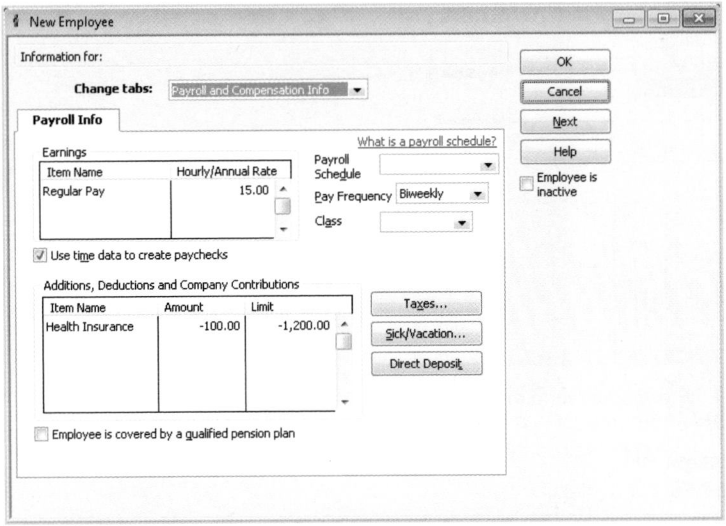

3. Enter the necessary information on the Personal Info tabs:

- **Personal**   The info on the Personal tab is pretty self-explanatory. The only thing you might watch for is the Print On Checks As field. To make your internal records clearer, you may want to enter the name the employee normally goes by (i.e., Eddy Rojeski) in the name fields. However, to ensure paychecks and IRS records are accurate, you might want to enter his complete name (William E. Rojeski) in the Print On Checks As field.

- **Address And Contact**   This tab is straightforward. Address, phone numbers, e-mail address, and so on are all you need to enter here.

- **Additional Info**   If you assign your employees ID numbers, this is the place to enter them. You can also create custom fields for data that you want to track but for which there are no QuickBooks fields.

4. From the Change Tabs drop-down list, select **Payroll And Compensation Info** to display the Payroll Info tab.

TIP

If you need to enter a new wage, addition, or deduction item, select **<Add New>** from the Item Name drop-down list in the appropriate section to launch the Add New Payroll Item wizard.

5. Enter or modify (if the employee defaults are configured) the earnings and the additions, deductions, and company contributions information by clicking a line in the **Item Name** column and selecting the item from the drop-down list. Then move to the rate or amount column and enter the associated amount.

6. To remove a line item, highlight the item name and delete it, and then highlight the amount and delete it as well.

7. If you use payroll schedules, select the schedule for this employee from the **Payroll Schedule** drop-down list. For more on creating payroll schedules, see the "Assigning Employees to Payroll Schedules" QuickSteps later in this chapter.

8. From the **Pay Frequency** drop-down list, select how often this employee receives a paycheck. If you use payroll schedules, this field is filled in automatically.

9. Click the **Taxes** button to display the Taxes dialog box.

10. From the employee's W-4 form, enter the filing status, number of allowances, and any additional withholdings the employee requested. Then check all the federal taxes to which the employee is subject.

11. Move to the **State** and **Other** tabs, and enter the appropriate state and local (city, town, county, and so on) tax information.

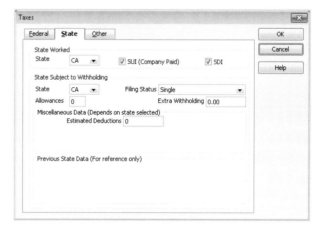

12. When you're finished, click **OK** to return to the Payroll Info tab.

13. Click the **Sick/Vacation** button to display the Sick And Vacation dialog box.

UNDERSTANDING PAYROLL SETUP WIZARD LIMITATIONS

If you decide to use the payroll wizard (**Payroll | Setup**) to set up employees, there are a few things you should be aware of:

- **Payroll items**   The other payroll items, including wages, benefits, and deductions, must already be set up before you can add employees through the wizard.

- **Employee defaults**   The wizard does not automatically insert wage, benefit, and deduction information from the employee defaults that can be set up in the QuickBooks Preferences.

- **New payroll items**   You cannot create new payroll items (wages, benefits, and so on) during the employee setup. None of the drop-down lists includes an *<Add New>* command.

14. Enter the parameters for accumulating sick and vacation time, and then click **OK** to return to the Payroll Info tab.

15. If you've enabled direct deposit and have written permission from the employee to directly deposit his or her paycheck, click the **Direct Deposit** button to configure it for this employee.

16. From the Change Tabs drop-down list, select **Employment Info** to display the Employment tab.

17. Enter the date you hired the employee, and select the employee type from the **Type** drop-down list. If the employee is no longer with you, enter the **Release Date** as well.

18. If you have an Enhanced Payroll subscription, you'll find some additional fields for Job Details and Employment Details. Fill them in as needed.

19. Click **Next** to add another new employee, or click **OK** to save this one and close the New Employee dialog.

Configure Payroll Preferences

Like most other features in QuickBooks, Payroll can be customized using the options found in the Preferences dialog box.

1. Select **Edit | Preferences** to display the Preferences dialog box.

2. Click the **Payroll & Employees** icon in the left pane to activate the payroll options.

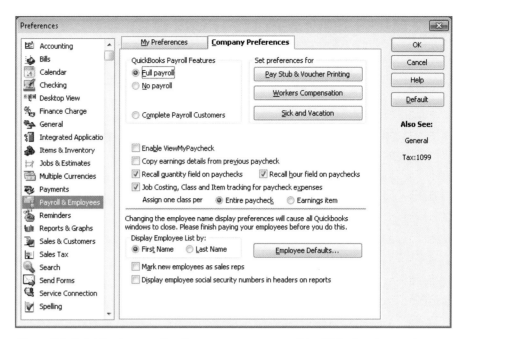

QUICKFACTS

UNDERSTANDING PAYROLL PREFERENCES

QuickBooks provides a variety of options for customizing both payroll and employee information. You'll find the following options on the Company Preferences tab of the Payroll & Employees preferences section:

- **QuickBooks Payroll Features** If you're using Basic, Enhanced, or manual payroll in QuickBooks, set this option to **Full Payroll**. For an outside payroll service, set this to **No Payroll**. Finally, if you're using Intuit Complete Payroll, select the third option, **Complete Payroll Customers**.

- **Pay Stub & Voucher Printing** Click this button to open the Payroll Printing Preferences dialog with options for what to include on paycheck vouchers and stubs.

- **Workers' Compensation** Enhanced Payroll users who are liable for workers' compensation can turn on tracking for the feature, set an alert to assign codes, and exclude overtime from calculations using the options found here.

- **Sick And Vacation** If most of your employees receive the same sick and vacation benefits, click this button to set the default parameters for new employees. That way, you won't have to reenter the same data each time you add a new employee.

- **Enable ViewMyPaycheck** Only available with an Enhanced Payroll subscription, this option enables employees to view their paycheck stub information online.

Continued ...

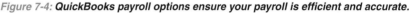

*Figure 7-4: **QuickBooks payroll options ensure your payroll is efficient and accurate.***

3. Click the **Company Preferences** tab to display the options for payroll and for employees (see Figure 7-4).

4. Select or deselect options as needed. See the "Understanding Payroll Preferences" and "Setting Employee Preferences" QuickFacts for a detailed description of each option.

5. Click **OK** to save your changes.

Navigate the Employee Center

As you might imagine, the Employee Center, which you can open by clicking the **Employees** button on the Icon Bar, provides access to all QuickBooks employee-related features (see Figure 7-5). Like the Customer and Vendor Centers, it contains a left pane consisting of two tabs and a right pane in which details of the item selected in the left pane are displayed.

UNDERSTANDING PAYROLL PREFERENCES *(Continued)*

- **Copy Earnings Details From Previous Paycheck** This is a handy option to enable if your employees work regular schedules and their paychecks rarely vary from week to week. Each week, QuickBooks will fill in the paychecks using the previous week's data.

- **Recall Quantity Field On Paychecks** Any payroll items based on quantities are carried forward to the new paycheck each week as long as the payroll items are included in the employee record.

- **Recall Hour Field On Paychecks** If your employees' hours are pretty consistent, check this option to bring them forward from paycheck to paycheck.

- **Job Costing, Class And Item Tracking For Paycheck Expenses** The option only appears (with this wording) if you have both class tracking and time tracking enabled. With one or the other enabled, it changes to reflect which is enabled. With neither enabled, it is simply listed as **Job Costing For Paycheck Expenses**. Enable this option to assign portions of company-paid payroll taxes by job, class, or service item.

- **Assign One Class Per** Use this option, which only appears when class tracking is turned on, to assign a single class to all payroll expenses or to assign multiple classes to individual expenses.

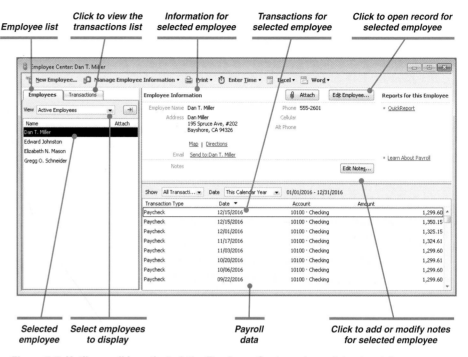

Employee list — **Click to view the transactions list** — **Information for selected employee** — **Transactions for selected employee** — **Click to open record for selected employee**

Selected employee — **Select employees to display** — **Payroll data** — **Click to add or modify notes for selected employee**

*Figure 7-5: **Until payroll is activated, the Employee Center only contains two tabs.***

As you can see in Figure 7-5, the two tabs are Employees and Transactions. The first contains the list of employees, and the second provides access to all employee-related transactions. The right pane simultaneously displays information and transaction details for the employee selected in the Employees tab. When the Transactions tab is selected, the right pane displays the transactions for the category selected in the left pane.

Add, Edit, and Delete Employees

Adding new employees in the Employee Center is easy. Click the **New Employee** button or right-click anywhere in the Employee list, and select **New Employee** from the shortcut menu. Either way, the New Employee dialog appears. See the section entitled "Set Up New Employees," found earlier in this chapter, for details on creating new employees.

SETTING EMPLOYEE PREFERENCES

To set employee preferences, select **Edit | Preferences**, click the **Payroll & Employees** icon, and then click the **Company Preferences** tab. You'll find the following employee options in the lower portion of the tab:

- **Display Employee List By**   How would you like the Employee list sorted? By last name or by first name? Make your choice here.

- **Mark New Employees As Sales Reps**   If you want QuickBooks to automatically add new employees to the Sales Rep List, check this option.

- **Display Employee Social Security Numbers In Headers On Reports**   The name of this option says it all. Reports such as the Employee Withholding report and the Payroll Transactions by Payee report display the employee's Social Security number when this option is checked.

- **Employee Defaults**   To configure default payroll settings for new employees, click this button and fill in the Employee Defaults dialog that appears. See the "Setting Default Employee Information" QuickSteps to learn more.

To edit an existing employee, double-click the employee name in the Employees tab to open the Edit Employee dialog. Make any necessary modifications to the employee information, and click **OK** to save the changes.

Deleting an employee is just as easy, as long as the employee has not been used in any transactions. To delete an employee, select the employee name in the Employees tab and press **CTRL+D**. If the employee has not been used in any transactions, QuickBooks requests a confirmation of the deletion. If the employee has already been used in a transaction, QuickBooks lets you know and offers to make the employee inactive.

View Employee Transactions

The Transactions tab of the Employee Center includes all the transactions created for all your employees. As you can see in Figure 7-6, the Transactions tab contains five different transaction categories. When you select a category in the left pane, all the transactions of that type appear in the right pane.

You can sort the transactions that appear in the right pane by clicking a column header. The first time you click the header, the column is sorted in ascending order (A–Z). If you click the header a second time, the column is resorted in descending order (Z–A). If you want to see only transactions for a certain time period, use the **Date** drop-down list to apply a date filter.

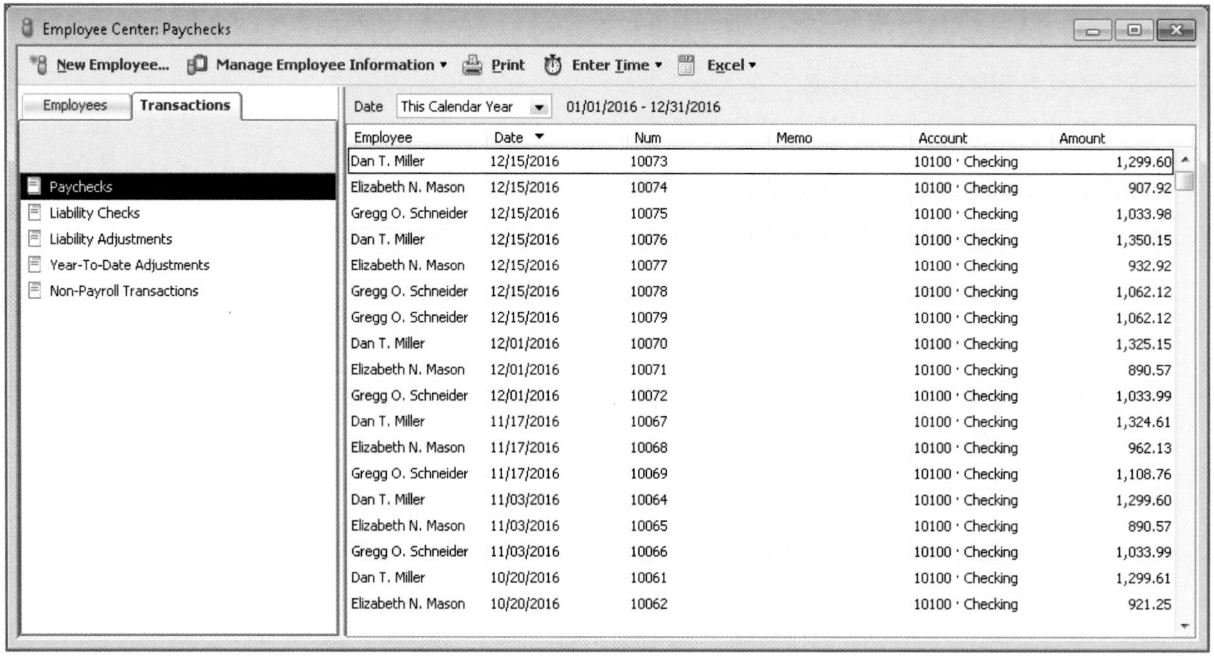

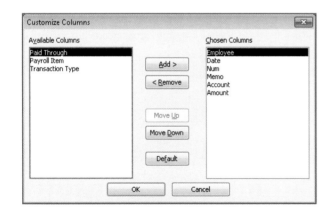

Figure 7-6: *Employee transactions are neatly filed away in the Employee Center.*

You can even customize the right pane to display the columns you want to see, in the order you want to see them.

1. Right-click in the right pane, and select **Customize Columns** from the shortcut menu to open the Customize Columns dialog box shown in Figure 7-7.

2. To add a column to the transaction pane, select the column name from the left pane (Available Columns), and click the **Add** button. This moves the column to the Chosen Columns list. Any item in this list appears in the transactions pane.

3. To remove a column from the transactions pane, select it in the Chosen Columns list and click the **Remove** button.

4. To reposition a column, select it in the Chosen Columns list and use the **Move Up** and **Move Down** buttons. Moving an item up in the list moves it to the left in the transactions list. Moving it down in the Chosen Columns list moves it to the right in the transactions list.

Figure 7-7: *Understanding transaction information is easier when you organize the information to suit your needs.*

SETTING DEFAULT EMPLOYEE INFORMATION

If most of your new employees share the same payroll information, you'll be delighted to learn that you can create default settings that are automatically applied to each new employee you add to the system.

1. Select **Employees | Employee Center** to open the Employee Center.

2. Click the **Manage Employee Information** button, and select **Change New Employee Default Settings** from the menu to open the Employee Defaults dialog box. If you don't see this command, it's because you haven't turned on payroll yet. See the "Configure Payroll Preferences" section earlier in this chapter for more on setting Payroll & Employees preferences.

3. If you use a payroll schedule for most employees, select it now from the **Payroll Schedule** drop-down list.

4. Choose the most common pay period for your employees from the **Pay Frequency** drop-down list. If you selected a payroll schedule in the previous step, this field is filled in automatically.

5. If most of your employees are hourly, click in the **Item Name** column of the Earnings box and select the hourly pay item you use most.

6. If most employees earn the same hourly wage, enter it in the **Hourly/Annual Rate** column. If they get different hourly rates, leave it blank so you can fill it in when you run payroll.

7. If you normally use the QuickBooks timesheets feature to track employee hours, check the **Use Time Data To Create Paychecks** option.

Continued . . .

Use Timesheets

If your workers (employees, contractors, or even partners) are required to track their time either for payroll or for job-costing purposes, you'll probably want to enable and use time tracking. QuickBooks offers two versions of time tracking—single activity or weekly activity tracking. The first allows a worker to enter the time for a single activity, which could be an entire day's work or several different single-activity timesheets if multiple activities were completed. Of course, using weekly timesheets, the worker could also record one or multiple activities for a single day. The only real difference being that it's easier to remember the details of each activity as it's completed rather than wait until the end of the week to compile the data.

Enabling time tracking in QuickBooks is easy. Of course, like most other configuration options, it's located in the Preferences dialog box.

1. Select **Edit | Preferences** from the menu bar to open the Preferences dialog.

2. Click the **Time & Expenses** icon in the left pane to activate the time tracking options. It's the very last one in the left pane, so if you don't see it, you may have to scroll down.

3. Click the **Company Preferences** tab to view the options for time tracking.

4. Set the Do You Track Time? option to **Yes**, and select the first day of your work week.

5. Click **OK** to save your settings.

QUICKSTEPS

SETTING DEFAULT EMPLOYEE INFORMATION *(Continued)*

8. In the **Additions, Deductions, And Company Contributions** section, add those items common to the majority of your new employees.

9. You can use the **Taxes** button to enter default tax information, such as filing status, tax liability, and so on, for new employees as well.

10. If you have a company policy for sick and vacation time that applies to most of your new employees, use the **Sick/Vacation** button to enter that information.

11. If you offer a retirement plan such as a 401(k), most employees are considered covered, even if they do not participate in the plan. Therefore, if you offer such a plan you'll probably want to check the **Employee Is Covered By A Qualified Pension Plan** option. Be sure to check with your accountant to determine which nonparticipating employees are considered covered.

12. Click **OK** to save the default employee information.

Every time you create a new employee (unless you use the Payroll Setup wizard), QuickBooks automatically uses the data from the Employee Defaults dialog to fill in the Payroll Info tab of the New Employee record.

TIP

As noted earlier, workers can encompass employees, outside contractors, or even owners and partners. Be sure to record them properly. Employees are easy—you add them as employees. Outside contractors should be added as vendors, and owners or partners should be added to the Other Names list.

There is actually a third option, online time tracking, which Intuit offers for a fee. For more information about this service, choose **Employees | Enter Time | Let Your Employees Enter Time**.

Regardless of which timesheet you use, the first order of business is to ensure that employees/workers, activities (service items), and customers or jobs that will be used for tracking time are entered in QuickBooks.

Record a Single Activity

For those workers who need or want to record time worked as single activities, the process is fairly simple.

1. Select **Employees | Enter Time | Time/Enter Single Activity** to open the Time/Enter Single Activity dialog.

2. QuickBooks automatically enters today's date. If you're recording an activity for a different date, change the date accordingly.

3. Select the worker's name from the **Name** drop-down list.

4. If the activity is being recorded for job-costing reasons or to bill to a customer, make the appropriate selection from the **Customer:Job** drop-down list.

5. If you plan to bill the customer, be sure to check the **Billable** option.

6. If the recorded time is going to be used to generate a paycheck for an employee, select the appropriate payroll item from the **Payroll Item** drop-down list. This field does not appear unless you've enabled the Use Time Data To Create Paychecks option in the employee record.

7. A Class field appears if you have enabled class tracking. Make the appropriate selection from the **Class** drop-down list.

8. Use the **Notes** field to enter any details or reminders about the task being recorded.

9. Enter the time spent on the activity in the **Duration** field. By default, the field tracks time in minutes and seconds. Therefore, if you enter <u>2.5</u>, the time is automatically converted to 2:30 (2 hours, 30 minutes).

10. To track time with precision, you can use the stopwatch feature. Click **Start** to begin the timer, **Pause** to temporarily halt it, and **Stop** to, you guessed it, stop it.

11. Click **Save & Close** to save the new activity and close the dialog box, or click **Save & New** to record another activity.

When you save a single-activity timesheet, it is automatically recorded on the weekly timesheet for the worker who recorded it. Therefore, by filling out single-activity timesheets, the worker is actually filling out the weekly timesheet one activity at a time.

QUICKSTEPS

USING THE WEEKLY TIMESHEET

The weekly timesheet is useful for those workers whose activities and hours are fairly consistent. For example, an employee working on a long-term project performing the same task day in and day out will have no need to enter single activities each day.

1. To open the Weekly Timesheet dialog box seen in Figure 7-8, select **Employees | Enter Time | Use Weekly Timesheet**.

2. From the **Name** drop-down list, choose the worker for whom you're filling out the weekly timesheet. You can enter each activity as a line item in the timesheet.

3. If the activity is linked to a customer or job, click in the **Customer:Job** column and select the appropriate customer or job.

4. The same applies to the remaining columns. Click in each column either to activate the related drop-down list or to enter data manually.

5. In the day/date fields, enter the number of hours worked. As with the single-activity timesheet, the default time format is Hours:Minutes. Therefore, if you enter <u>2.3</u> in a date field, QuickBooks automatically converts it to 2:18 (2 hours, 18 minutes).

After entering all activities for the week, click **Save & Close** to record the new timesheet, or click **Save & New** to create a new weekly timesheet.

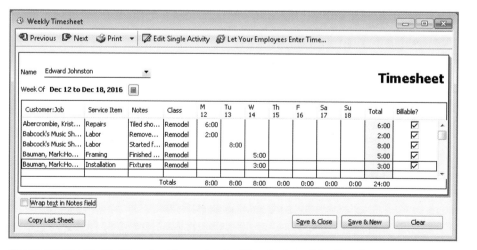

Figure 7-8: **The Weekly Timesheet keeps track of the single-activity timesheets.**

NOTE

If you have not set the option for the selected employee to use time data to create paychecks, QuickBooks will display a dialog here asking if you want to turn the feature on for this employee.

NOTE

If you don't see a Class field (and you have class tracking turned on), check the Company Preferences tab of the Payroll & Employees preferences. Make sure the **Earnings Item** option is checked in the Assign One Class Per section.

NOTE

New in QuickBooks 2012 is the ability to create batch timesheets for multiple employees who are all performing the same weekly tasks. Simply select Multiple Names (Payroll) or Multiple Names (Non-Payroll) from the Names drop-down list, and then select the names to be included. Only employees with the Use Time Data To Create Paychecks option enabled in their employee records will appear when you choose Multiple Names (Payroll).

TIP

If this week's schedule is identical to the last week's schedule, or nearly so, click the **Copy Last Sheet** button to bring forward the data from the last weekly timesheet. Even if there are small differences, it's easier to edit the sheet than to start from scratch.

Create Payroll Schedules

Payroll schedules are handy if you use multiple pay frequencies. For example, if you pay your administrative people weekly and your salespeople monthly, you can set up a different payroll schedule for each group. Even if you pay everyone at the same time, you can set up schedules to separate employees into logical groups. If some employees get paychecks and others use direct deposit, you could create a payroll schedule for each group. Creating payroll schedules is easy.

1. Select **Employees | Add Or Edit Payroll Schedules** to open the Payroll Schedule List.

2. Press **CTRL+N** to open the New Payroll Schedule dialog box shown in Figure 7-9.

*Figure 7-9: **Create as many payroll schedules as you need.***

NOTE

The check date is the date that is used for reporting and tax liability purposes. For example, if the period end date falls in the first quarter (end of March) but the check date falls in the second quarter (beginning of April), the payroll will appear in second quarter reports, and tax liabilities will be due in the second quarter, not the first.

QUICKSTEPS

ASSIGNING EMPLOYEES TO PAYROLL SCHEDULES

Before you can run a payroll using a payroll schedule, you must assign employees to the appropriate schedule(s). If you took QuickBooks up on its offer to make the assignment, your job is done. However, if you elected to do it on your own, or if there are additional employees on a different schedule, you must do it now.

1. Open the Employee Center, and edit the first employee you want assigned to the new schedule.

2. From the Change Tabs drop-down list, choose **Payroll And Compensation Info** to display the Payroll Info tab.

3. From the **Payroll Schedule** drop-down list, select the appropriate schedule.

4. Click **OK** to save the change and return to the Employee Center.

5. Repeat for all employees who need to be assigned payroll schedules.

If the majority of new employees will be assigned to one particular payroll schedule, you can open the Employee Defaults dialog box (click the **Manage Employee Information** button in the Employee Center, and select **Change New Employee Default Settings**), and choose a default payroll schedule to assign to new employees.

3. Give the schedule an easily identifiable name. If the reason for the schedule is a different pay frequency, use the pay frequency as the name. If it's for salaried as opposed to hourly employees, call it Salaried.

4. Next choose the pay frequency for this schedule.

5. Then, use the pop-up calendar to select the period end date for your next pay period.

6. Finally, enter the date that should appear as the check date.

7. Click **OK** to save the new schedule.

When you finish setting up the payroll schedule and click **OK** to save it, QuickBooks asks if you want to assign the schedule to all employees with the same pay frequency as the new schedule. If you do, click **Yes**; otherwise, click **No**. If you choose No, QuickBooks reminds you that if you pass up this opportunity, you'll have to assign each employee individually. It then gives you a second chance to assign all employees with the same pay frequency.

Run Payroll

With or without payroll schedules, you can run payroll as soon as you set up employees and payroll items. If you don't have any payroll schedules set up, selecting **Employees | Pay Employees** launches the Enter Payroll Information dialog seen in Figure 7-10.

If you have created at least one payroll schedule, QuickBooks offers three options for running payroll when you select **Employees | Pay Employees**:

- **Scheduled Payroll**   Selecting this command opens the Payroll Center, which is actually a third tab added to the Employee Center window when you activate a payroll service. In the Pay Employees section, choose the payroll schedule to use, and click the **Start Scheduled Payroll** button to launch the Enter Payroll Information dialog with only those employees assigned to the selected schedule.

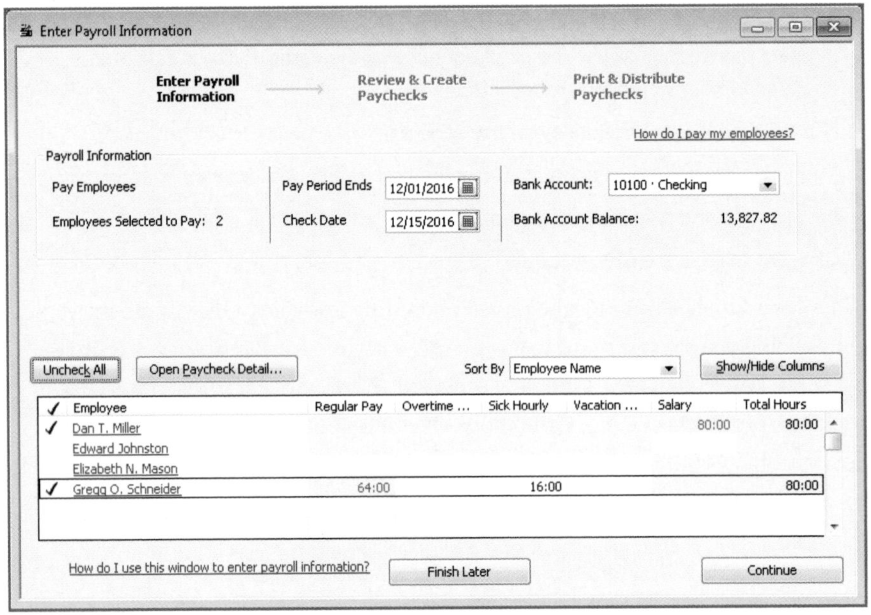

Figure 7-10: *All employees are listed when you don't use payroll schedules.*

NOTE

As you can see in Figure 7-10, all regular pay items (both hourly and salaried) appear as columns in the Enter Payroll Information dialog. If an employee has been assigned a wage or salary payroll item, you can enter the hours worked in that column. If no wage or salary item has been assigned, you must click the employee name and assign a wage or salary item before entering hours worked.

- **Unscheduled Payroll** This command opens the Enter Payroll Information dialog with all employees listed, regardless of any payroll schedule assignments. You can select the individual employees (or click **Check All** to choose all) and run the payroll for the selected employees.

- **Termination Check** If you need to write a check for an employee who is leaving, you can select this command, which opens the Enter Payroll Information dialog with all employees listed. The difference between this command and the Unscheduled Payroll command is that you cannot process a paycheck for any employee here unless a release date has been entered in the Release Date column or in the Employment tab of the employee record.

Regardless of which payroll type you run, the basics are the same.

1. Use one of the commands described earlier to open the Enter Payroll Information dialog.

2. Make sure the information in the Payroll Information section is correct. This includes Pay Period Ends and Check Date fields, as well as the correct payroll bank account.

3. Select the employee(s) to be paid. Even if you're using a payroll schedule, you may want to deselect an employee who has taken an unpaid leave.

4. If the hours are not automatically entered, fill them in under the appropriate hourly or salary wage column.

5. Click **Continue** to display the Review And Create Paychecks dialog box, which displays each employee about to be issued a check, along with the check details.

6. Select the **Print Paychecks From QuickBooks** option to let QuickBooks automatically assign check numbers, or select **Assign Check Numbers To Handwritten Checks** to assign your own.

7. To preview an individual check, select the employee and click the **Open Paycheck Detail** button to display the Preview Paycheck dialog box seen in Figure 7-11. If you click the employee name, which is a link, the Preview Paycheck dialog opens without having to click the Open Paycheck Detail button.

QUICKFACTS

UNDERSTANDING PAYROLL LIABILITIES PAYMENT OPTIONS

If you're using the Intuit Basic Payroll, you'll have to run the appropriate Employees & Payroll reports to calculate your liabilities and then fill out the forms by hand. If, on the other hand, you're using Enhanced Payroll, QuickBooks will do most of the work for you. Select **Employees | Payroll Taxes And Liabilities** to view a submenu of available commands:

- **Pay Scheduled Liabilities**   This opens the Payroll Center where you can view and pay liabilities that are due in the Pay Scheduled Liabilities section of the right pane. Check the liabilities that you want to view or pay, and click the **View/Pay** button to display the check with details.

- **View E-payment History**   If you file tax forms electronically, use this command to open the E-payment History dialog, which contains a listing of all payroll tax payments that have been filed online.

- **Edit Payment Due Dates/Methods**   If you find that you have to modify one of your scheduled liabilities, use this command to launch the QuickBooks Payroll Setup wizard with the Tax Payments section displayed. You can then change the payee or the payment frequency, or make any other necessary edits.

- **Adjust Payroll Liabilities**   This command opens the Liability Adjustment dialog in which you can modify any specific tax liability, either for the company or for an individual employee. If you subscribe to the Assisted Payroll service, you cannot make adjustments to tax liabilities.

Continued . . .

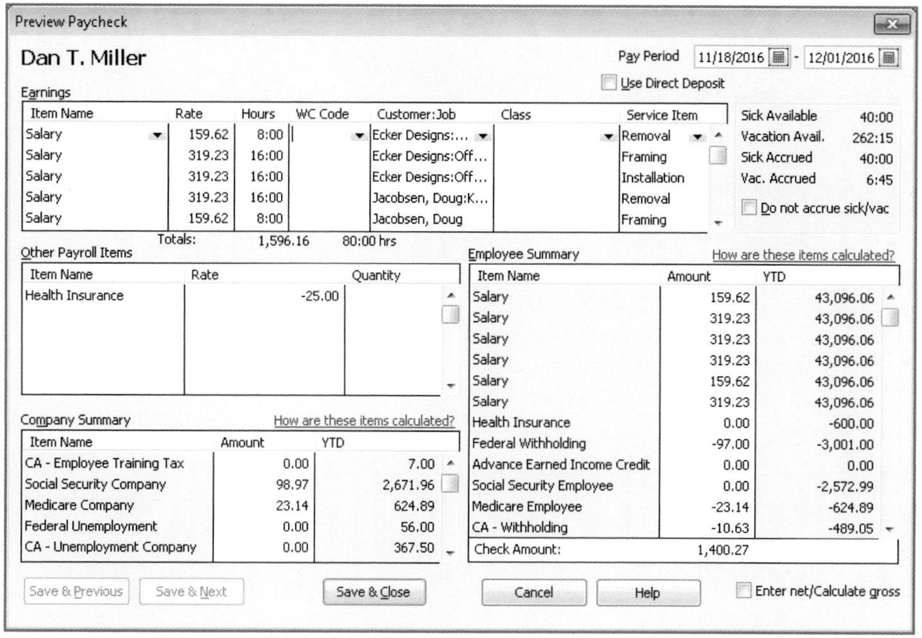

*Figure 7-11: **The Preview Paycheck window provides a detailed look at the selected check.***

8. When you're satisfied with all the entries, click the **Create Paychecks** button to display the Confirmation And Next Steps dialog.

9. Click the **Print Paychecks** button or the **Print Pay Stubs** button, depending on which you want to do.

10. If you prefer to print the check(s) later, click **Close**. You can then use the **File | Print Forms | Paychecks** command when you're ready.

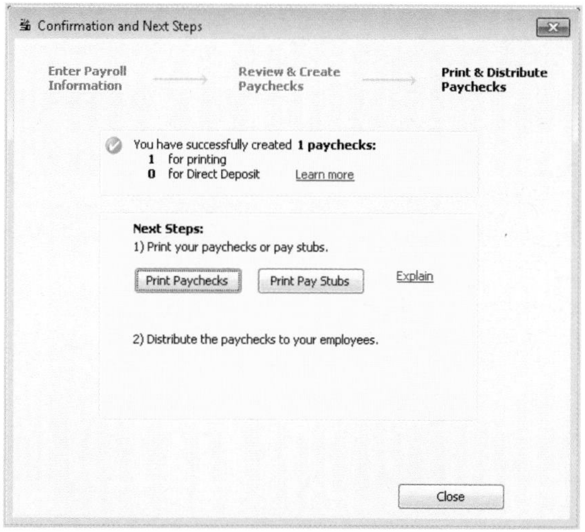

QUICK**FACTS**

UNDERSTANDING PAYROLL LIABILITIES PAYMENT OPTIONS

(Continued)

- **Deposit Refund Of Liabilities**   If you receive a refund check from one of your taxing agencies, use this command to deposit the check to the proper account.

- **Create Custom Liability Payments**   To create an unscheduled liability payment, use this command to open the Pay Liabilities dialog box. There you can select the dates, the payroll item, and the amount to pay.

Run Payroll Reports

Whether you use them for tracking liabilities, keeping an eye on your labor costs, or just reviewing your overall financial situation, QuickBooks offers a variety of payroll reports to suit your needs:

- **Summary reports**   When you only need an overview of certain numbers, you can run the summary reports. These include the Payroll Summary report and the Employee Earnings Summary report. The Payroll Summary report provides a breakdown for each employee of employee and employer numbers (wages, taxes, deductions, and contributions). For a breakdown of employee wages, taxes, and deductions by employee, use the Employee Earning Summary report. You'll also see two Workers Comp summary reports if your subscription supports this and you've turned it on.

- **Detail reports**   When you need to see how those summary numbers were arrived at, use a detail report to view the particulars. You'll find three payroll/employee-related detail reports. First is the Payroll Item Detail report, which gives you a detailed (by paycheck) breakdown of each item on your Payroll Item List. The second is the Payroll Detail Review report, which provides a breakdown of employee and employer wages, taxes, deductions, and contributions, by employee and by pay period. The third detail report is the Payroll Transaction Detail report, which lists the details of each paycheck for each employee. If your subscription supports Workers Comp and you've enabled it, you'll see a Workers Comp Detail report as well.

- **List reports**   When you need to print a simple listing of payroll- or employee-related information, choose one of the four list reports that are available. The Employee Contact List report produces a listing of employee contact information. For a printout of employees and their withholding information (Social Security number, filing status, and so on), use the Employee Withholding report. To see a listing of all payroll items with their account assignments and other details, run the Payroll Item Listing report. For a complete rundown of vacation/sick time available and used, run the Paid Time Off List report.

Track Vendors Who Need a 1099

If you employ subcontractors, you probably have to issue Form 1099 at the end of the calendar year to each subcontractor. Check with your accountant to determine which subcontractors must receive Form 1099.

QUICKSTEPS

CONFIGURING 1099 VENDORS

Each vendor eligible for Form 1099 has to be configured for 1099 tracking. If you only have a handful of vendors to configure, use the Vendor Center.

1. Select **Vendors | Vendor Center** to open the Vendor Center.

2. In the Vendors tab, double-click the listing for the first vendor who fits this category to open the Edit Vendor dialog box.

3. Select the **Additional Info** tab to view the 1099 options.

4. In the Tax ID field, enter the vendor's Social Security number or business employee identification number (EIN) number.

5. Check the **Vendor Eligible For 1099** option.

6. Repeat for each 1099 vendor.

7. Click **OK** to save the changes.

As long as bills entered or checks written for this vendor have the expense posted to an account you selected in the 1099 setup, the amount of the check is tracked for this vendor's 1099. This means you must be careful to use the right account when you create the bill or the direct check.

TIP

If you have a lot of vendors to configure, use the Add/ Edit Multiple List Entries feature, and click the **Customize Columns** button to add the 1099-related fields to the form.

Configure 1099 Tracking

Once you determine that you have vendors who should receive 1099s, you have to enable the feature in QuickBooks.

1. Choose **Edit | Preferences** to open the Preferences dialog box.

2. Click the **Tax: 1099** category in the left pane to activate the 1099 preferences.

3. Click the **Company Preferences** tab to display the available options shown in Figure 7-12.

4. At the top of the dialog box, set the Do You File 1099-MISC Forms? option to **Yes**.

5. Click **OK** to save your changes and close the Preferences dialog.

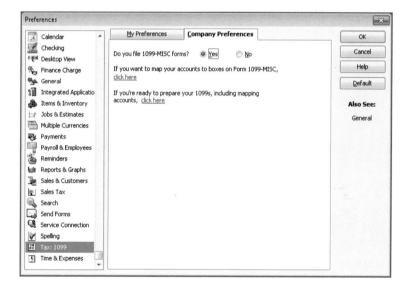

Figure 7-12: **Turning on 1099 tracking is a snap.**

Prepare and File 1099 Forms

One of the nice additions to QuickBooks 2012 is the new QuickBooks 1099 Wizard. It enables you to prepare and file your forms with ease.

1. Select Vendors | Print/E-file 1099s from the menu bar to launch the new wizard.

2. The first screen is informational only. It explains each of the wizard steps. Click the **Get Started** button to proceed to the Verify Your 1099 Vendors screen (see Figure 7-13).

QuickBooks 1099 Wizard

Verify your 1099 vendors

Be sure each vendor that needs a Form 1099-MISC is selected. You can edit vendors' information here, and changes are saved in QuickBooks.

1 — **2** — **3** — **4**
Verify Vendors | Report Payment | Review Form | Choose Filing

Required — Be sure you haven't left any information blank and that you've provided valid tax ID numbers.
* Enter City, State, ZIP with commas separating each part and valid state postal abbreviations, as follows: City, ST, 99999
* Tax IDs must have 9 digits with hyphens seperating them in one of these formats: 99-999-9999 or 99-9999999

Vendor Name*	1099?	Tax ID*	Address*	City, State, ZIP*	Phone
C.U. Electric	Yes ▼	987-65-4321	C. U. Electric, P.O. Box 2816,	Bayshore, CA, 94326	415-555-0797
Hamlin Metal	Yes ▼	13-2456789	Hamlin Metal, 270 Old Baysho	Bayshore, CA, 94326	415-555-8965
Holly Heating and Electric	Yes ▼	94-0102000	Holly Heating and Electric, Att	E. Batshore, CA, 94326	415-555-4300
Kershaw Computer Services	Yes ▼	99-9999999	Kershaw Computer Services, 1	Bayshore, CA, 94326	415-555-1515
Keswick Insulation	Yes ▼	12-3456789	Keswick Insulation, P.O. Box 6	Middlefield, CA, 94482	415-555-0305
Larson Flooring	Yes ▼	98-7654321	Larson Flooring, 2780 County	Bayshore, CA, 94326	415-555-2046
Lew Plumbing	Yes ▼	12-3456789	Lew Plumbing, 221 Old Bayshi	Bayshore, CA, 94326	415-555-5483
Middlefield Drywall	Yes ▼	333-33-3334	Middlefield Drywall, P.O. Box 7	Middlefield, CA, 94482	415-555-0046
Sloan Roofing	Yes ▼	23-4567891	Sloan Roofing, P.O. Box 2431,	Bayshore, CA, 94326	415-555-1284
Vu Contracting	Yes ▼	01-4920394	Vu Contracting, Don Vu, 8930	San Mateo, CA,	829-555-9019
Washuta & Son Painting	Yes ▼	98-7654321	Washuta & Son Painting, P.O.	Bayshore, CA, 94326	415-555-1813
Wheeler's Tile Etc.	Yes ▼	99-8877665	Wheeler's Tile Etc., 650 Old B;	Bayshore, CA, 94326	415-555-9977

Need more information?

Back | Save & Close

*Figure 7-13: **The QuickBooks 1099 Wizard warns you if you're missing necessary vendor information.***

NOTE

If the Continue button is grayed out, it means that not all the required vendor information has been entered. In addition, you'll see a warning message in red above the vendor list. Enter the missing information and the Continue button will become available.

3. Check each vendor that appears in the table to ensure it has the correct 1099 status, Tax ID, and mailing address. You can edit the information in any of the fields.

4. When you're satisfied that all the vendor information is correct click **Continue** to the Report 1099 Vendor Payments screen shown in Figure 7-14.

5. If all the accounts listed are correct, check the Apply All Payments To Box 7 option.

6. If the accounts are not correct, change the settings by making the correct selection from the Apply Payments To This 1099 Box drop down list.

7. To see the filing thresholds set by the IRS, click the Show The Filing Thresholds link.

What payments do I need to report to the IRS?
QuickBooks only prepares Form 1099-MISC if the total you've paid each vendor is above the thresholds set by the IRS. — Hide the Filing Thresholds

Box 1: Rents	600
Box 2: Royalties	10
Box 3: Other Income	0
Box 4: Federal Tax Withheld	0
Box 5: Fishing Boat Proceeds	0
Box 6: Medical Payments	0
Box 7: Nonemployee Compensation	600
Box 8: Substitute Payments	10
Box 9: Direct Sales	5000
Box 10: Crop Insurance Proceeds	0
Box 13: Excess Golden Parachute	0
Box 14: Gross Proceeds to Attorney	0

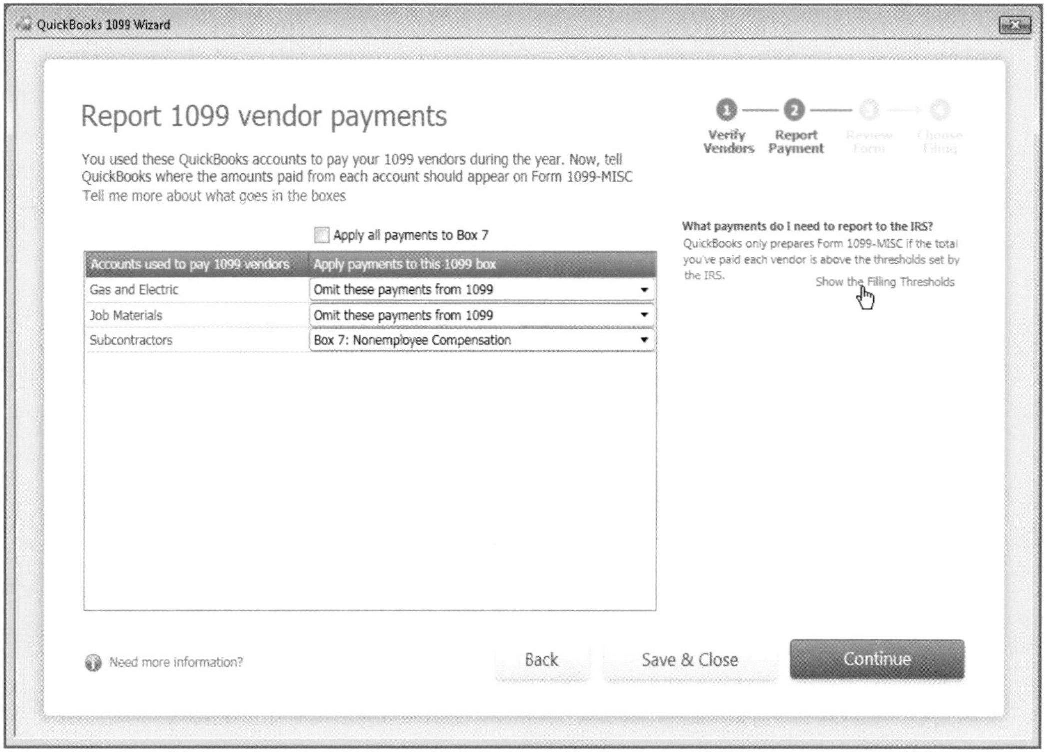

Report 1099 vendor payments

You used these QuickBooks accounts to pay your 1099 vendors during the year. Now, tell QuickBooks where the amounts paid from each account should appear on Form 1099-MISC
Tell me more about what goes in the boxes

Verify Vendors — Report Payment — Review Form — Choose Filing

☐ Apply all payments to Box 7

Accounts used to pay 1099 vendors	Apply payments to this 1099 box
Gas and Electric	Omit these payments from 1099 ▾
Job Materials	Omit these payments from 1099 ▾
Subcontractors	Box 7: Nonemployee Compensation ▾

What payments do I need to report to the IRS?
QuickBooks only prepares Form 1099-MISC if the total you've paid each vendor is above the thresholds set by the IRS.   Show the Filling Thresholds

⊙ Need more information?   Back   Save & Close   Continue

Figure 7-14: The wizard lists all the accounts used to pay 1099 vendors during the course of the year.

8. When all the accounts are correctly assigned to the1099 form, click Continue to view the Review 1099 Summary screen (see Figure 7-15)

9. This is where you can see which vendors require 1099s and the amounts recorded. If everything is ok click **Continue** to proceed, otherwise click **Back** to make the necessary changes.

10. The final screen, seen in Figure 7-16, is the Choose A Filing Method screen. It offers two options which are explained in the following sections.

USE INTUIT 1099 E-FILE SERVICE

If you'd like to e-file your 1099 forms, click this button to access the signup page for the fee-based service. One of the advantages to using this service (aside from the obvious savings in postage and work) is the fact that no 1096 form is required when you e-file. Follow the onscreen prompts.

NOTE

You can leave the wizard anytime you want by clicking the Save & Close button. Any changes you have made thus far will be saved. You can then open the wizard and finish at a later time.

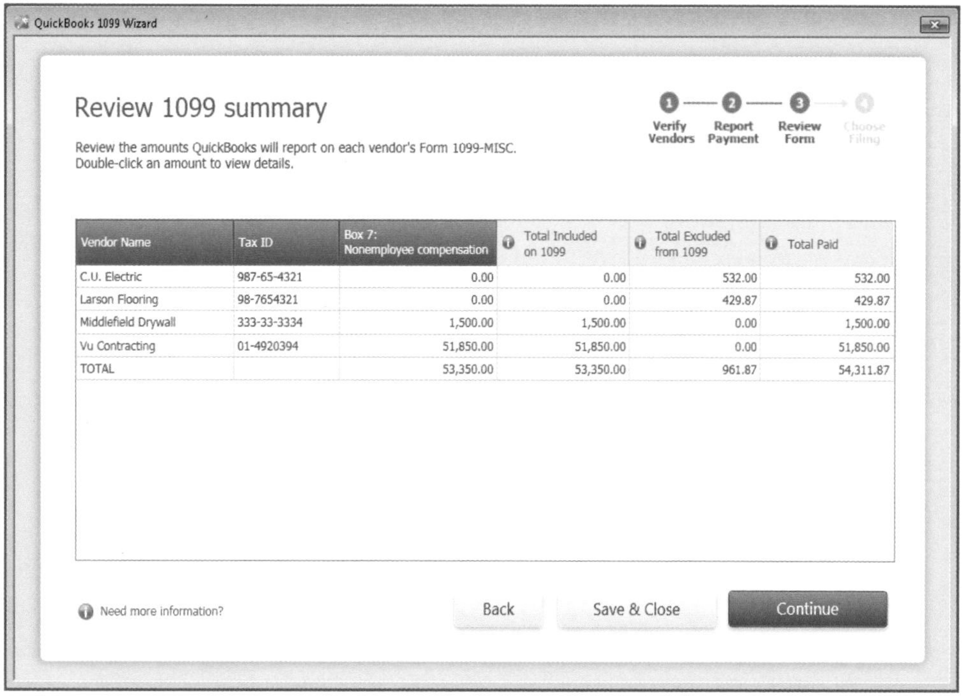

Figure 7-15: *Make sure all the numbers and box assignments are correct before going any further.*

PRINT 1099s

If you've purchased preprinted forms (the IRS will not accept 1099 forms printed on standard printer paper) use the Print 1099s method.

1. Click the **Print 1099s** button in the wizard window to display the Printing 1099-MISC And 1096 Forms dialog box.

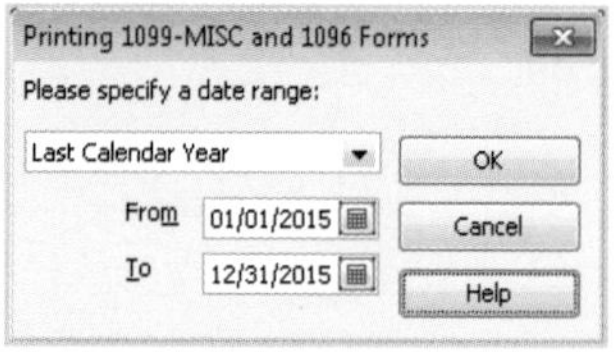

2. Select the date range, which is usually **Last Calendar Year**, since you have to send the forms out by the end of January.

3. Now, click **OK** to open the Select 1099s To Print dialog box seen in Figure 7-17. As you can see, QuickBooks displays the vendors that are selected to receive 1099s.

4. To see what the printed forms will look like, click the **Preview 1099** button. Use the **Zoom In** feature to take a closer look and ensure all the information is correct.

5. Click the **Close** button to shut the Print Preview window and to return to the Select 1099s To Print window.

6. Make sure your 1099 forms are in the printer, and click the **Print 1099** button to open the Print 1099s dialog box.

7. If you have multiple printers, choose the appropriate printer from the **Printer Name** drop-down list.

8. Click the **Print** button to print your forms. When the 1099s have printed, you're returned to the Select 1099s To Print dialog box.

TIP

For laser or inkjet printers, set the number of copies to three. If you're using a dot-matrix printer with three-part forms, you only need one copy.

Figure 7-16: *You can either print and mail your forms or file them electronically.*

9. Click the **Print 1096** button to open the 1096 Information dialog box.

1096 Information	
Form 1096 summarizes the 1099s.	OK
Please fill in the additional information below to complete your Form 1096.	Cancel
Contact Name Edward Smith	
☐ This is my final return.	

10. Enter the name of a contact person in your company who can answer questions about your 1099 forms (the contact name will be printed on the 1096 form).

Print two copies of the 1096 (one to send to the IRS and one for your files). Send each vendor a copy of the 1099 form by January 31, and send the IRS a copy of each 1099, along with the 1096 Transmittal Form, by the end of February. The third copy of the 1099 is for your files.

Repeat these steps for each box number of the 1099-MISC form you are required to print (most small businesses only use Box 7).

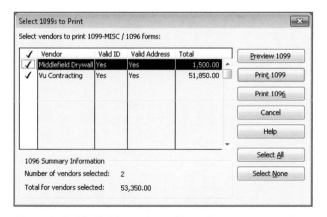

Figure 7-17: *All eligible vendors with total payments over the threshold amount are automatically selected for 1099 printing.*

How to...

- ⊘ *Understanding the Report Center Views*
- ⊘ *Selecting a Report Tab*
- ⊘ *Understanding Basic QuickBooks Reports*
- • *Filter Reports*
- • *Change Data Display*
- ⊙ *Setting Display Tab Options in Summary Reports*
- • *Change Header/Footer Settings*
- • *Configure Fonts & Numbers Tab Options*
- ⊙ *Memorizing Reports*
- ⊙ *Running Multiple Reports*

Chapter 8
Using QuickBooks Reports

Generating reports in QuickBooks is one of the main reasons for putting all that work and effort into the data entry and number crunching. QuickBooks reports provide insights into your finances that enable you to keep an eye on how you're doing, where your money is coming from, where it's going, and even how you can improve your business. Of course, there is that one caveat that keeps popping up throughout this book: the information you get out of QuickBooks (reports) is only as good as the information you put into QuickBooks. If the data you enter is inaccurate or incomplete, your reports are going to reflect that.

Navigate the Report Center

The Report Center is your headquarters for QuickBooks reporting. You can open it by selecting **Reports | Report Center** from the menu bar. As you can see in Figure 8-1, it offers a series of tabs as well as three different modes of viewing.

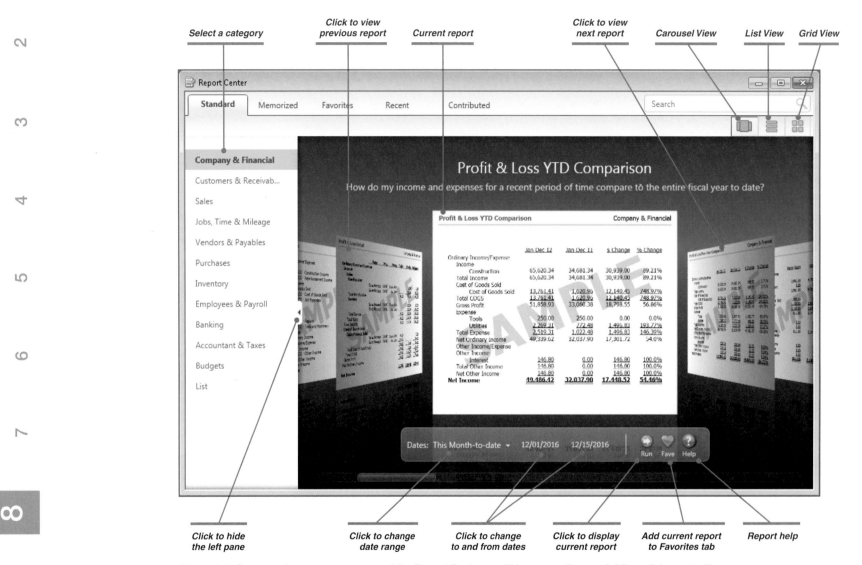

Select a category | Click to view previous report | Current report | Click to view next report | Carousel View | List View | Grid View

Click to hide the left pane | Click to change date range | Click to change to and from dates | Click to display current report | Add current report to Favorites tab | Report help

Figure 8-1: *Once you learn your way around the Report Center, you'll be generating useful financial reports like a pro.*

QUICK**FACTS**

UNDERSTANDING THE REPORT CENTER VIEWS

The first thing to note about the Report Center is that it offers three different viewing modes. You can change the mode by clicking one of the view buttons in the upper-right corner below the Search box (see Figure 8-1):

- **Carousel View** The default view is the Carousel View. It's a flashy, graphically oriented view, as you can see in Figure 8-1. It provides a rotating slide show of images of the different reports available for the category selected in the left pane. The image in the center is the currently selected report. You scroll through the reports using the images on either side as Previous (image to the left) and Next (image to the right) buttons. When the report you're looking for is in the center, you can use the buttons below the report image to manipulate the report. You can change the report dates, display the current report, add the current report to the Favorites tab, and even display help on the selected report. To save time, you can double-click the currently selected report image to open it.

- **List View** If you like things a little more neatly arranged, you'll probably like the List View. It's a straightforward listing of the reports available for the category selected in the left pane. Each report listing includes a brief description of the report, as well as icons for running the report (Run), displaying a preview (Info), adding it to the Favorites menu (Fave), and accessing help (Help). To the right of the icons are buttons for changing the date range or the To and From dates.

- **Grid View** The Grid View is a hybrid view that incorporates a little of each of the other two views. The reports are represented by images that appear
Continued . . .

Getting around in the Report Center is pretty easy once you figure out where the buttons are to change the view. If you take a look at Figure 8-1, you'll see that they're in the upper-right corner of the window. For more information on each view, check out the "Understanding the Report Center Views" QuickFacts.

Try each of the different views and decide which one you prefer. Regardless of the view you select, the category pane on the Standard tab remains the same (see the "Selecting a Report Tab" QuickFacts for more on Report Center tabs)—only the reports pane on the right changes.

Choose a category in the left pane to see the available reports of the type selected. The reports that appear in the right pane will be the same, regardless of the view you're in. However, the presentation will differ from one view to the next.

When you need to find a report quickly, there's always the reliable search box located to the right of the category tabs. Enter a search word or phrase in the text box, and click the magnifying glass icon to the right. A new tab, Search Results, appears displaying those reports matching your search criteria. When you're done, click the X on the Search Results tab to close it.

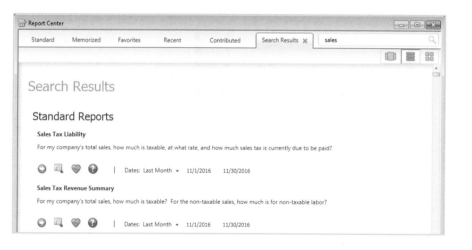

UNDERSTANDING THE REPORT CENTER VIEWS *(Continued)*

in an organized grid that you can scroll through like a list. Icons for running, previewing, adding to Favorites, and accessing help appear below the image, along with buttons for changing dates.

The view mode you select remains in effect for all the tabs in Report Center. Therefore, as you move through the tabs, the information will be displayed in the same format for each until you change the view mode.

SELECTING A REPORT TAB

Once you've chosen a view mode, you can take a tour of the five tabs available in the Report Center:

- **Standard** The Standard tab is where you'll find all the reports QuickBooks has to offer. Select a category in the left pane to display all the reports of that type in the right pane. Use the buttons below the report image or listing to manage the report. Click the Dates fields to change the date range or the To and From dates. Clicking the Run icon displays the selected report in a standard QuickBooks report window. The Info icon (available only in the List View and the Grid View) displays a preview of the report, while the Fave icon adds the selected report to the Favorites tab. Last, but not least, is the question mark icon, which is used to display a help topic on the currently selected report.

- **Memorized** The ability to modify reports and then save those changes by memorizing the report is a great time-saver. The Memorized tab is where you'll find all those reports you modified and memorized.

Continued . . .

Configure Report Preferences

Like most other features in QuickBooks, the reports feature has some basic settings that can be customized to make it work your way. Configuration options for reports include both company-wide options as well as individual user options.

1. Select **Edit I Preferences** to open the Preferences dialog.

2. Click the **Reports & Graphs** icon in the left pane to activate the preferences.

3. Click the **My Preferences** tab in the right pane, and configure the user preferences:

- **Prompt Me To Modify Report Options Before Opening A Report** If you invariably tweak every report you run, checking this option offers you the opportunity to make those changes even before the report opens. With this option enabled, the Modify Report dialog box opens on top of the report. You can either modify the settings or just close the dialog to run the report with the default settings.

- **Reports And Graphs** Your selection here tells QuickBooks how often to refresh reports and graphs so they reflect the most up-to-date information. If you want QuickBooks to tap you on the shoulder when data changes, select **Prompt Me To Refresh**. If you want QuickBooks to automatically keep the report current, choose **Refresh Automatically**. If you don't want QuickBooks to take any action, select **Don't Refresh**.

SELECTING A REPORT TAB (Continued)

It is, in reality, a Report Center view (Carousel, List, or Grid) of the Memorized Report List, which you can display by selecting **Reports | Memorized Reports | Memorized Report List**. As a matter of fact, if you want to make any changes, you have to make them in the Memorized Report List by clicking the **Edit Memorized List** button at the top of the Memorized tab to open the Memorized Report List window.

- **Favorites**   Whether or not you like them better than the other reports, this is where you'll put the reports you use most often. Obviously, this is the same concept found in web browsers for your favorite (most frequently accessed) webpages. The reports included here are organized into the same categories found on the Standard tab, but without a category pane on the left.

- **Recent**   The Recent tab keeps track of the reports you've opened. The left pane contains time periods such as Today, Last 1–7 Days, and so on. When you select a time period on the left, the reports opened during that time are displayed on the right.

- **Contributed**   Taking advantage of the fact that many users like to customize reports and share them, Intuit has added the Contributed tab. Here you'll find customized reports that you can download and use as you wish. You can search for reports by industry using the View Industry drop-down list at the top of the tab. You can also sort the reports by criterion you select from the Sort By drop-down list. To help others decide how useful the reports may be, you can even rate the reports by clicking the **Rate** icon that appears (along with several others) when you hover your mouse over the report image (Grid View) or listing (List View).

- **Graphs Only**   Obviously, these options only apply to graphs. The first, Draw Graphs In 2D (Faster), draws two-dimensional graphs instead of the default three-dimensional graphs. For graphs representing a large amount of data or for slower computers, this might speed things up. The second option, Use Patterns, is helpful if you plan to print the graphs in black and white. With this option enabled, QuickBooks replaces the different colors, used by default, with different patterns.

4. Click the **Company Preferences** tab, and set the company-wide options. Remember, only the QuickBooks administrator or an external accountant user can change company-wide preferences:

- **Summary Reports Basis**   Do you want your reports to show income and expenses when they are entered into QuickBooks as invoices and bills (accrual) or when the actual payments are received and paid (cash)?

- **Aging Reports**   Use this option to let QuickBooks know how you want to calculate overdue days on aging reports.

NOTE

If you're like me and prefer the quick and dirty method of getting the job done, you'll be glad to know that you can just as easily access QuickBooks reports through the menu system. Click **Reports** on the menu bar to view a list of the report categories. Click a category to display a submenu of available reports. Click the report name, and you're in business.

QUICKFACTS

UNDERSTANDING BASIC QUICKBOOKS REPORTS

While QuickBooks offers a large variety of reports for reviewing and analyzing your financial data, there are a few report types that are especially important to understand:

- **P&L reports** More commonly known as income statements or statements of income (or earnings), the P&L reports can tell you, at a glance, how you're doing. Are you making money, losing money, or just breaking even? They can even tell you why if you look closely. By calculating your income and expenses and seeing what's left over, they determine your profitability. You'll find them under the Company & Financial submenu of the Reports menu.

- **Balance sheet reports** Unlike the P&L reports, which cover a specific period (month, quarter, year, and so on), the balance sheet reports provide a picture of your financial situation at the moment you run the reports. They compare three things—your assets (the stuff you own), your liabilities (debts), and your equity (capital invested). The bottom line: your assets should

Continued . . .

- **Format** Click this button to open the Report Format Preferences dialog box in which you can set the defaults for headers and footers, as well as fonts and numbers.

- **Reports – Show Accounts By** This option is straightforward. Do you want accounts to appear in reports by name, description, or both? If you have account numbers enabled, they will appear as part of the name.

- **Statement Of Cash Flows** Click the **Classify Cash** button to open the Classify Cash dialog box where you can add and remove accounts that appear on the Statement of Cash Flows report. It is highly recommended that you consult with your accountant before making any changes here.

5. Click **OK** to save and apply the settings.

Customize Reports

Running the standard QuickBooks reports using the default settings is occasionally adequate. But, more often than not, you'll need to make some changes to display the data you want to see, the way you want to see it. The first place to look for customizing options is on the report toolbar shown in Figure 8-2.

As you can see in Figure 8-2, each report toolbar contains a series of buttons that provide access to customizations and related features. For example, all reports

Profit & Loss								
Customize Report	Share Template	Memorize	Print	E-mail ▾	Excel ▾	Hide Header	Collapse	Refresh
Dates	This Month-to-date	▾	From 12/01/2016	To 12/15/2016	Columns	Total only	▾	Sort By Default ▾

1:28 PM		Wode Construction		
12/15/16		**Profit & Loss**		
Accrual Basis		December 1 - 15, 2016		
			◇ Dec 1 - 15, 16 ◇	
	Ordinary Income/Expense			
	Income			
	40100 · Construction Income			
	40110 · Design Income	▶ 3,000.00	◀	
	40130 · Labor Income	20,515.50		
	40140 · Materials Income	12,161.91		
	40150 · Subcontracted Labor Income	15,461.25		
	Total 40100 · Construction Income		51,138.66	
	40200 · Sales		200.00	
	40500 · Reimbursement Income			
	40520 · Permit Reimbursement Income	0.00		
	Total 40500 · Reimbursement Income		0.00	
	Total Income		51,338.66	

Figure 8-2: *QuickBooks reports are easy to customize.*

UNDERSTANDING BASIC QUICKBOOKS REPORTS *(Continued)*

equal your liabilities and your equity combined (assets = liabilities + owners' (or shareholders') equity). Balance sheet reports are also located on the Company & Financial submenu of the Reports menu.

- **Statement of cash flows** While the Statement of Cash Flows report can't really show if your business is doing well, it can let potential creditors know if it's likely you'll be able to repay loans they're considering giving you. Do you consistently have enough cash on hand to service your obligations? As its name indicates, it's all about the flow of cash—cash coming into the business and cash going out of the business. Since it doesn't take things like accounts payable and accounts receivable into consideration, it's not a good gauge of your overall financial health. To access the Statement of Cash Flows report, head for the Company & Financial submenu.

- **Trial Balance report** The Trial Balance report, located on the Accountant & Taxes submenu, is of more interest to your accountant than to your banker. Rather than tell whether your company is making money, the Trial Balance report lets your accountant know if your accounts are in balance. In a double-entry accounting system such as QuickBooks, there is always a credit to balance a debit and vice versa. The Trial Balance report displays all your accounts to ensure that debits and credits are equal (in balance).

have a Customize Report button that opens the Modify Report dialog, where you can change everything from the data displayed to the font it's displayed in. You'll also find a Memorize button so you can save the report for future use after you change it to suit your needs. Buttons for sharing (including on the Popular Report tab of the Report Center), printing, e-mailing, exporting, and more are also available on the toolbar.

Filter Reports

One of the most useful customization options is the ability to display only the data you need. You can accomplish this by applying filters that limit the displayed data and by setting your own report criteria. Most QuickBooks reports offer two filtering avenues. The first is the row of fields located below the toolbar at the top of the report. The second is the Filters tab of the Modify Report dialog box.

USE THE FILTER FIELDS

If you look at the top of most reports, you'll see a row of fields positioned just below the toolbar. In almost every report, you'll find a Dates field that contains a drop-down list of predefined data ranges, such as Today, This Week, This Month, and so on. Usually, there are also From and To fields that allow you to enter your own custom date range.

TIP

One way to gain a little more viewing space on the opening screen of a report is to click the **Hide Header** button found at the top of the report. It temporarily conceals all the header information, such as company name, title, and so on. To reveal the header information, click the same button, now renamed **Show Header**.

When you select a predefined date range or create your own custom range, you are telling QuickBooks that you only want to see data from those dates. You are thus filtering out all other data. If you decide to create a custom date range, you'll note that the Dates field changes to Custom, indicating that the From and To fields now hold the filter criteria.

USE THE MODIFY REPORT FILTERS TAB

By far, the largest collection of customizing options is found in the Modify Report dialog. As you can see in Figure 8-3, it contains four tabs, one of which is the Filters tab.

1. To apply filters using the Filters tab, click the **Customize Report** button on the report toolbar to open the Modify Report dialog box.

2. Next, click the **Filters** tab to display the filters options. Most reports (but not all) contain the three elements seen in Figure 8-3—a Choose Filter column, one or more fields for entering criteria related to the filter choice, and a list of the current filter choices.

- **Choose Filter** This is a list of the available fields in the report by which you can filter data.

- **Filter Criteria Fields** Depending on your selection in the Choose Filter column, you will have one or more fields in which to enter or choose criteria for the selection. For example, if you select **Account** in the Choose Filter column, an Account drop-down list appears from which you can choose all accounts, multiple accounts, all accounts of a specific account type, or any individual account. In addition, you can elect to display split detail.

- **Current Filter Choices** Since you can apply multiple filters to reports, the Current Filter Choices section lists all the filters you've created. You can remove filters by selecting them and clicking the **Remove Selected Filter** button.

3. While it may seem unnatural (unless you regularly read Arabic, Hebrew, or any of the other many right-to-left written languages), the place to start in the Filter tab is on the right side, with the Current Filter Choices area. Here you'll see filters that are already applied to the report.

Figure 8-3: **Use filters to display only the data you need.**

4. Select the filter you want to remove from the report, and click the **Remove Selected Filter** button. If necessary, repeat until all the filters you want to eliminate are removed.

5. Now, jump back to the left side of the dialog box and select a field from the **Choose Filter** list to create a new filter.

6. As soon as you select a field, its available filter attributes appear to the right of the Filter list. Set the criteria for the filter here.

7. Using the steps outlined here, create as many filters as needed.

8. Click **OK** to save the filters and apply them to the report.

As you select different fields from the Choose Filter list, a brief description of the available filters appears below the list with a Tell Me More button that opens the help file when clicked. To set the filters back to their original state, click the **Revert** button.

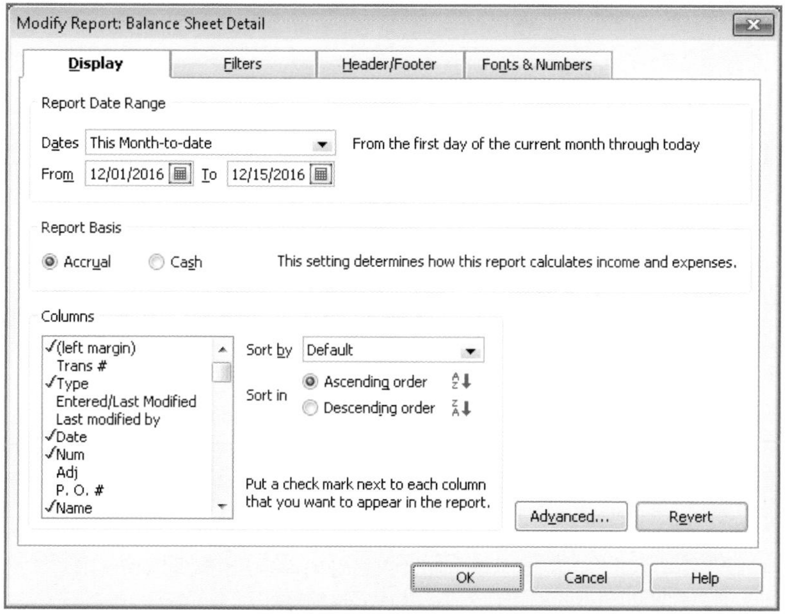

Change Data Display

While filters are great for isolating the data you want to view in a report, managing how that data appears requires a different set of options. You'll find all the settings you need to manipulate the report presentation on the Display tab of the Modify Report dialog box. Not all reports are the same. Therefore, not all reports offer the same options. The major differences are between detail reports and summary reports.

USE DISPLAY TAB OPTIONS IN DETAIL REPORTS

Detail reports include a wealth of information and therefore require a way to display as much of that information as possible. As you can see in Figure 8-4, the Display tab options are extensive.

1. Open a detail report using either the Report Center or the Reports menu.

2. In the open report, click the **Customize Report** button to open the Modify Report dialog box. By default, it opens to the Display tab.

Figure 8-4: **Detail reports let you add as many columns as you need.**

NOTE

Regardless of your accounting basis (cash or accrual), you can set some reports to display data using either method. Selecting Accrual means that the report will display income and expenses based on the dates invoices and bills are created. Using the Cash basis means that income and expenses appear on the report only when income is received in the form of customer payments and when expenses are paid in the form of vendor payments.

3. From the **Dates** field, select a date range for the report.

4. If you're running a financial report (P&L, balance sheet, and so on), you'll see a Report Basis section. Select either **Accrual** or **Cash** as the basis for the report.

5. In the **Columns** list, select (or deselect) columns that you want to appear in the report. Placing a check mark to the left of the column name adds the column to the report. Removing the check mark removes the column from the report.

6. To change the sort order of the report, use the **Sort By** drop-down list. You can sort by any of the columns that are selected in the Columns list (and, therefore, appearing in the report).

7. From the Sort In section, choose the direction of the sort. Your choices are Ascending Order, which sorts the data from A to Z, or Descending Order, which reverses that order and sorts from Z to A.

8. Click the **Advanced** button to view the Advanced Options dialog box.

9. Choose which accounts to include by making your selection in the Include column:

   - **All**   Choose All to include every account in your Chart of Accounts, even if there was no activity in the account for the date range selected.

   - **In Use**   When you select In Use, only those accounts with activity during the date range are included in the report.

10. In the Open Balance/Aging section, choose the calculation method used to determine the customer's open balance:

    - **Current (Faster)**   If you want to see precisely what each customer owes as of the date you're running the report, this is the choice to make.

    - **Report Date**   By choosing Report Date, you see customer balances as of specific dates. When you change the date range for the report, the open balances are recalculated.

SETTING DISPLAY TAB OPTIONS IN SUMMARY REPORTS

Summary reports, while just as powerful as detail reports, do not include the breadth of information, and therefore require different Display tab options.

Some have more options, and others fewer. For example, the Inventory Valuation Summary report has nothing but the date range fields, while the Purchase By Vendor Summary report has even more fields than the Balance Sheet Summary report.

1. Open a summary report using either the Reports menu or the Report Center.

2. Click the **Customize Report** button to view the Display tab of the Modify Report dialog box.

3. Use the **Dates** field and the **From** and **To** fields to set the date range of the report.

4. Set the basis of the report to either **Accrual** or **Cash**. Remember, regardless of your accounting basis, you can use either as a report basis.

5. From the **Display Columns By** drop-down list, choose the manner in which you want the report numbers shown. Summary reports usually display a single column of figures, which includes totals for the selected accounts (customers, vendors, and so on). By making a selection from the Display Columns By field, you can have those totals broken down by time periods, such as day, week, month, and others. Some reports let you break down the numbers by fields other than date fields also.

6. Set the sort order of the report by making a selection from the **Sort By** drop-down list. Summary reports generally have limited options for changing the sort order. *Continued . . .*

Modify Report: Summary Balance Sheet

Tabs: **Display** | Filters | Header/Footer | Fonts & Numbers

Report Date Range

Dates: This Fiscal Year-to-date — From the first day of the current fiscal year through today

From: 01/01/2016 To: 12/15/2016

Report Basis

◉ Accrual   ○ Cash   This setting determines how this report calculates income and expenses.

Columns

Display columns by: Total only ▼ across the top.   Sort by: Default ▼

Sort in: ◉ Ascending order ○ Descending order

Add subcolumns for

☐ Previous Period   ☐ Previous Year   ☐ % of Row   ☐ % of Column
   ☐ $ Change   ☐ $ Change
   ☐ % Change   ☐ % Change

[Advanced...] [Revert]

[OK] [Cancel] [Help]

11. If, after making a series of changes, you decide you want to put things back to the way they were, all you have to do is click the **Revert** button.

12. Click **OK** to save your changes and apply them to the open report.

Change Header/Footer Settings

In addition to customizing the data that appears in your reports, you can modify the way your report looks. The Header/Footer tab of the Modify Report dialog, as you might guess, lets you change the information that appears in the report header and in the report footer. Unlike options in the Display and Filters tabs, the options found in the Header/Footer tab (see Figure 8-5) are the same for (almost) all reports.

1. Open the desired report from the Report Center or the Reports menu.

2. Click the **Customize Report** button to open the Modify Report dialog box.

3. Select the **Header/Footer** tab to access the options for modifying the information found in the report headers and footers.

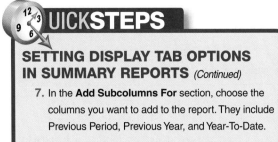

SETTING DISPLAY TAB OPTIONS IN SUMMARY REPORTS *(Continued)*

7. In the **Add Subcolumns For** section, choose the columns you want to add to the report. They include Previous Period, Previous Year, and Year-To-Date.

8. Click the **Advanced** button to display the Advanced Options dialog box.

Advanced Options

Display Rows	Display Columns	Reporting Calendar
○ Active	● Active	● Fiscal Year
○ All	○ All	○ Calendar Year
● Non-zero	○ Non-zero	○ Income Tax Year

OK   Cancel   Help

9. In the Display Rows column, select **Active** to show only active accounts (customers, vendors, and so on). To see both active and inactive accounts, choose **All**. To show only those accounts that have amounts (positive or negative), select **Non-Zero**.

10. Move to the **Display Columns** section and set the options, which are the same as those in the Display Rows column.

11. Choose the type of year to use for this report. If your fiscal year, calendar year, and tax year are the same, it makes no difference which you choose. If, however, your year types cover different time periods, changing this option will modify the report accordingly.

12. To put the Display tab options back to their original state, click the **Revert** button.

13. Click **OK** to save the changes and apply them to the report.

Modify Report: Summary Balance Sheet

Display	Filters	Header/Footer	Fonts & Numbers

Show Header Information

- ☑ Company Name — Wode Construction
- ☑ Report Title — Summary Balance Sheet
- ☑ Subtitle — As of December 15, 2016
- ☑ Date Prepared — 12/31/01
- ☑ Time Prepared
- ☑ Report Basis
- ☑ Print header on pages after first page

Show Footer Information

- ☑ Page Number — Page 1
- ☑ Extra Footer Line
- ☑ Print footer on first page

Page Layout

Alignment: Standard

OK   Cancel   Help

*Figure 8-5: **Header and footer data provide important information about each report.***

4. Set the Show Header Information options:

- **Company Name** Do you want your company name printed at the top of this report? If so, check the **Company Name** option, and enter the name as you want it to appear.

- **Report Title** If you don't like the default name of the report, you can change it in this field. As a matter of fact, if you don't want the report to have a title, you can remove the check mark from the option, and the title will be omitted.

Show Header Information

- ☑ Company Name — Wode Construction
- ☑ Report Title — Summary Balance Sheet
- ☑ Subtitle — As of December 15, 2016
- ☑ Date Prepared — 12/31/01
- ☑ Time Prepared
- ☑ Report Basis
- ☑ Print header on pages after first page

- **Subtitle** Especially useful for complex reports, a subtitle can help explain what the report is all about. Uncheck the option to run the report without a subtitle.

- **Date Prepared**   This is an important option, as it lets you know at a glance how current the report is. However, it's also a little confusing when you first encounter it. The default is 12/31/01, which might make you think that QuickBooks has lost its mind. The truth of the matter is this field is not for the actual date, but rather for the date format. Therefore, the 12/31/01 is really telling you that the date will appear in the DD/MM/YY format, nothing else. From the drop-down list, select the format to use.

- **Time Prepared**   If you run the report more than once a day, this is a good field to include. It lets you know exactly when the report was run.

- **Report Basis**   Actually, if you noticed, I qualified my earlier statement about the Header/Footer tab being the same for all reports. They're almost the same for all reports. Only those reports with Report Basis options in the Display tab include a Report Basis option in the Header/Footer tab. Check it to display the basis (accrual or cash). Uncheck it to hide the basis.

- **Print Header On Pages After First Page**   When you run a multipage report, do you want the header to appear on every page of the printed report or just on the first page? Check this option to print the header on every page. You won't see the effects of this option in the on-screen display of the report, only in the printed version.

5. Configure the Show Footer Information options:

   Show Footer Information

   ☑ Page Number   Page 1 ▾

   ☑ Extra Footer Line

   ☑ Print footer on first page

   - **Page Number**   A large multipage report without page numbers can prove to be very confusing when you remove the staple to run it through the copier and then drop it on the floor. Check this option to include page numbers, and then select the page number format from the drop-down list next to it.

   - **Extra Footer Line**   Use this option to include a line of information (i.e., an explanation, disclaimer, or "Prepared by:") in the report footer.

   - **Print Footer On First Page**   This option is the reverse of the Print Header On Pages After First Page option. Without this option checked, the footer appears on all pages of the printed report except the first. However, if you check the **Print Footer On First Page** option, the footer then appears on the first page as well. This option only applies to the printed report, not the on-screen version.

6. From the **Alignment** drop-down list, select the alignment setting for header and footer information. Your choices include Standard, Left, Right, and Centered. As you make your choice, you'll see the effect in the preview below the drop-down list.

7. Click the **Revert** button to reset the Header/Footer tab options to their original state.

8. Click **OK** to save the changes and return to the open report.

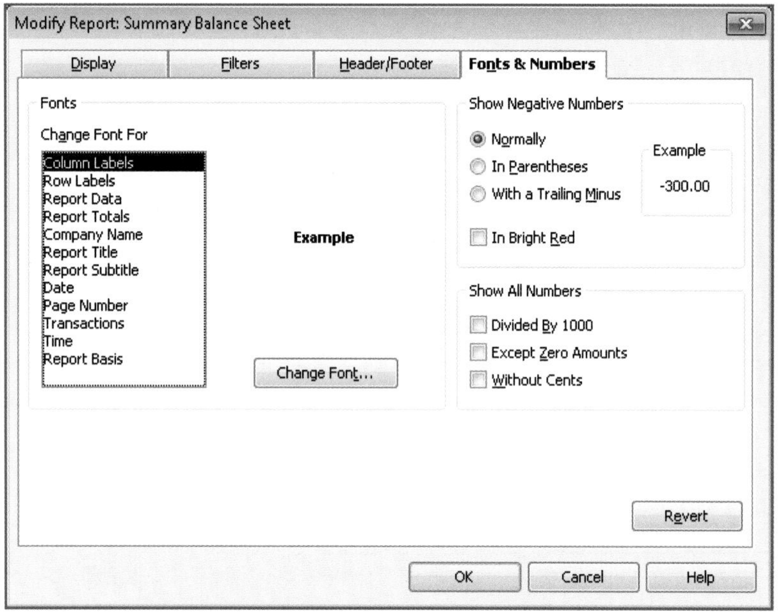

Configure Fonts & Numbers Tab Options

The Fonts & Numbers tab of the Modify Report dialog box is where you'll find options for changing the fonts used for individual report elements and for indicating how you want numbers displayed. If you're like me and want to see negative numbers in parentheses and in bright red so you don't miss them, head for the Fonts & Numbers tab seen in Figure 8-6.

1. Open the report you want to customize.

2. Click the **Customize Report** button to open the Modify Report dialog box.

3. Click the **Fonts & Numbers** tab to display the available options.

4. From the **Change Font For** list, select a report element for which you want to modify the font.

5. Click the **Change Font** button to display the font attributes dialog box. It is named for the element selected in the Change Font For list.

Figure 8-6: *Use the options in the Fonts & Numbers tab to dress up (or down) your report's appearance.*

TIP

You don't have to worry about remembering or recording the original font settings. If you decide later that you don't like the new settings, you can use the **Revert** button on the Fonts & Numbers tab to reset them to their original state.

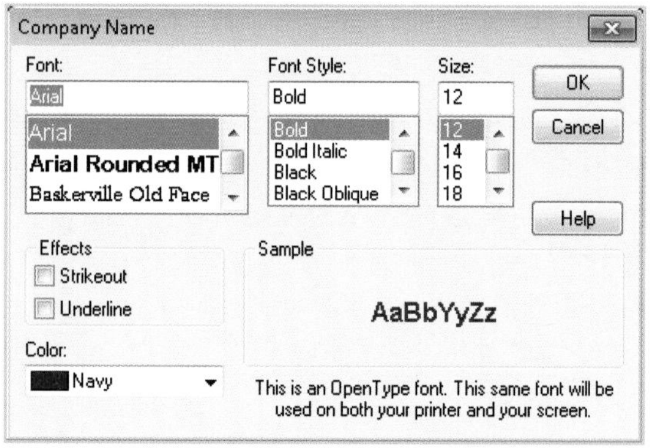

MEMORIZING REPORTS

With so many options for customizing reports, it's not unusual to make significant changes to one or more reports, which can be time-consuming. If you frequently run the same reports with the same changes, you'll quickly tire of recustomizing them each time. Fortunately, QuickBooks offers a much simpler and more elegant solution—the ability to memorize custom reports.

1. Open the report you want to save.

2. Click the **Customize Report** button, and make changes as needed.

3. Return to the customized report, and click the **Memorize** button to display the Memorize Report dialog box.

4. Give the report a unique name that will enable you to recognize it the next time you need it.

5. If you have a lot of memorized reports, you can check the **Save In Memorized Report Group** option and select a report group from the drop-down list.

6. If you want to share this report with others (and include it on the Popular Reports tab of the Report Center), check the **Share This Report Template With Others** option.

7. Click **OK** to save the memorized report.

Continued . . .

6. Change any of the font attributes you desire. You can change the font itself, its style, size, color, and/or effects.

7. After you make your font changes, click the **OK** button to return to the Fonts & Numbers tab. You can see the effect of your changes in the "Example" preview.

8. In the Show Negative Numbers section, tell QuickBooks how you want negative numbers to display in the report:

- **Normally**   By default, negative numbers are shown as regular numbers preceded by a minus sign.

- **In Parentheses**   If you prefer to see negative numbers surrounded by parentheses, choose this option. The minus sign is removed, and the negative number is encased in a pair of parentheses.

- **With A Trailing Minus**   For those who like to see the minus sign on the other side (the right side) of the negative number, this is the option for you.

- **In Bright Red**   Regardless of which of the first three options you choose for negative numbers, you can add this one for extra emphasis. Personally, I couldn't do without it. Check the **In Bright Red** option to change the font color of negative numbers to red.

9. Next, set the Show All Numbers options:

- **Divided By 1000**   Hopefully, you'll need this option. It's easier to keep track of those large six-, seven-, or more digit numbers when you divide them by 1,000. With this option selected, 25,000 becomes 25, while 250,000 becomes 250, and so on.

- **Except Zero Amounts**   This option, which is found on all reports except detail reports, hides zero amounts when selected.

- **Without Cents**   To make the report cleaner and easier to read, you can have QuickBooks automatically round every number to the nearest dollar by checking this option.

10. To restore changes made to the options in the Fonts & Numbers tab, click the **Revert** button.

11. Click **OK** to save the new settings and return to the open report.

QUICKSTEPS

MEMORIZING REPORTS (Continued)

The next time you want to run the memorized report, select **Reports | Memorized Reports** to display the submenu of memorized reports and report groups. Locate the report and click its listing to run it. The customized report opens, displaying current data, with all the modifications you made previously. You can also access memorized reports from the Memorized tab in the Report Center.

QUICKSTEPS

RUNNING MULTIPLE REPORTS

If you run a variety of reports each morning, you can simplify your life by using the Process Multiple Reports feature found in QuickBooks. It enables you to select and run individual memorized reports simultaneously or to choose entire groups of memorized reports to run with a single click.

1. From the menu bar, select **Reports | Process Multiple Reports** to open the Process Multiple Reports dialog box.

2. By default, the window opens with all memorized reports displayed. If you want to display a particular report group, or even all reports not belonging to a group, make your choice from the **Select Memorized Reports From** drop-down list.

3. Place a check mark in the leftmost column of each report you want to include. If you make a mistake, click the check mark to remove it.

Continued . . .

Export Report Data

As good as the QuickBooks reporting features are, there may be times when you need, or want, to share the data with other users. When you find yourself in this position, you can simply export the report data into a format that can be used by non-QuickBooks users.

1. Either using the Report Center or the Reports menu, open the report you want to export.

2. Click the **Customize Report** button, and make all necessary changes.

3. Return to the report, and click the **Excel** button, where you'll find two choices:

   ● **Create New Worksheet** Use this option to export your report data to a new or existing worksheet, or .csv file for the first time.

   ● **Update An Existing Worksheet** Once you've exported report data to an Excel worksheet, you can use this option to refresh the worksheet without overwriting

Process Multiple Reports				
Select Memorized Reports From	<All Reports>			
Choose the reports to process,	✓ <All Reports>			
	<Ungrouped Reports>			
	Accountant		From	To
✓ Report	Banking			
Accountant:Balance Shee	Company	e	01/01/2016	12/15/2016
Accountant:General Ledg	Customers		12/01/2016	12/15/2016
Accountant:Journal Entri	Employees		12/15/2016	12/15/2016
Accountant:Profit & Loss	Vendors	This Month-to-date	12/01/2016	12/15/2016
Accountant:Trial Balance		This Month-to-date	12/01/2016	12/15/2016
Banking:Check Detail		This Month-to-date	12/01/2016	12/15/2016
Banking:Deposit Detail		This Month-to-date	12/01/2016	12/15/2016
Company:Balance Sheet		This Fiscal Year-to-date	01/01/2016	12/15/2016
Company:Profit & Loss		This Month-to-date	12/01/2016	12/15/2016

Display   Print   Cancel   Help

RUNNING MULTIPLE REPORTS

(Continued)

4. Although the applied date range is shown in the Date Range column, you cannot change it. What you can change, however, that's almost as good, is the From and To dates. Click the calendar icon in each field to select the appropriate date period for the selected report.

5. Click the **Display** button for an on-screen version of the selected reports. QuickBooks opens each report and cascades the whole group so you can see the title bar of each one.

6. If you want to send all the reports to the printer, click the **Print** button instead. The Print Reports dialog box opens so you can select the printer and set printing options first. Be sure that you have selected the correct reports before tying up your printer with a long queue of reports.

7. The Process Multiple Reports dialog closes automatically when you finish displaying or printing the selected reports. If you decide to do neither, click the **Cancel** button to close the window.

TIP

If you run the same reports every morning (or afternoon), you should create a report group called Morning Reports (or Afternoon Reports) and include all those reports that get run at the same time. If you want to include a report in multiple groups, customize it and then memorize it to the first group. When you finish memorizing it, you're returned to the report. Click the **Memorize** button again, tell QuickBooks you want to create a new memorized report, give it a slightly different name (i.e., Custom Sales Report AM), and memorize it again.

certain changes you may have made to the file, such as headers, formatting, formulae, and more.

4. Choose the format to which you want to export the report information:

- **In New Workbook** To import into a new, empty Excel worksheet, choose this option. When you click **Export**, QuickBooks will launch Excel and insert the report data into a new worksheet.

- **In Existing Workbook** If you want to incorporate the report data into an existing Excel spreadsheet, use this option. After you make this selection, you have to locate and select the existing workbook and indicate which sheet in the workbook you want to use. This selection will add the report data to a new worksheet in the existing file.

- **Update An Existing Worksheet** When you only want to refresh the data in an existing worksheet, use this option. As soon as you locate the workbook to use, a second drop-down list appears so you can choose the worksheet to be updated. This is great for worksheets that you may have customized in Excel. Column and header changes are unaffected, as well as some formatting and changed formulae.

- **A Comma Separated Values (.csv) File** Use this format if you want to import the data into a word processing or spreadsheet program. This creates a text file in which the fields are separated by commas, alerting the importing software to the beginning and end of each field.

5. Click the **Advanced** tab to configure the formatting, features, and printing options for the exported report:

- **QuickBooks Options** If you want to keep the fonts, colors, row height, and/or space between columns the same in both the report and the worksheet, check the appropriate option(s).

- **Excel Options** These options are handy for setting useful features in Excel, such as freezing panes so the report header remains visible as you scroll through the report in Excel. Check the relevant option to turn on the Excel feature. If you want to include a worksheet with instructions in the export, make sure the **Include QuickBooks Export Guide Worksheet With Helpful Advice** option is checked.

- **Printing Options** To ensure the report prints properly once it's been exported to Excel, check the suitable option(s) in this section. If you want to see the report header in the Excel worksheet, select **On Printed Report And Screen**. Otherwise, the header is placed in the Header/Footer tab of the Page Setup dialog in Excel. The header will appear in printouts; you just won't see it on the spreadsheet as you're working. Including row labels on all pages of multiple page reports (Repeat Row Labels On Each Page) usually makes it easier to follow the report.

6. Click **OK** to close the Advanced Excel Options dialog box.

7. When all the settings are configured to your satisfaction, click **Export** to launch Excel and export the report data.

Of course, exporting to Excel is only going to work if you have a copy of Microsoft Excel installed on the computer you're currently working on. If not, export the report to a .csv file and move it to a computer with a copy of Excel installed.

TIP

While memorizing reports is generally reserved for customized reports, there's no reason you can't memorize an uncustomized report for the sole purpose of including it in the Process Multiple Reports dialog or in a memorized report group to use in the Process Multiple Reports dialog.

How to...

- Back Up Your Data
- Scheduling Regular Backups
- Verify Data
- Restoring a Backup
- Creating a Portable Company File
- Rebuild Data
- Getting Ready to Rebuild Data
- Condense Data
- Working with the Accountant's Copy
- Importing Your Accountant's Changes
- Use the File Import Utilities
- Exporting Addresses to Text Files
- Export List Files
- Understanding IIF Files
- Attach and Retrieve Documents
- Understanding Password Protection
- Configuring Credit Card Protection
- Add Users

Chapter 9
Performing QuickBooks Maintenance

QuickBooks is a powerful accounting tool, but it's also a sophisticated software tool that enables you to do more than just track your financial data. It provides everything you need for securing your data, sharing it with your accountant or other users, importing and exporting it, and even managing related documents. In this chapter we're going to cover those features and more.

Manage Housekeeping Chores

Unfortunately, some of the most mundane functions of QuickBooks are also the most important. All those hours of inputting and crunching financial information will be to no avail if your data is lost or corrupted. While we all like to think it won't happen to us, the sad truth is, sooner or later, it happens to everybody. Power surges occur, hard disks die, files get corrupted, and viruses sneak in.

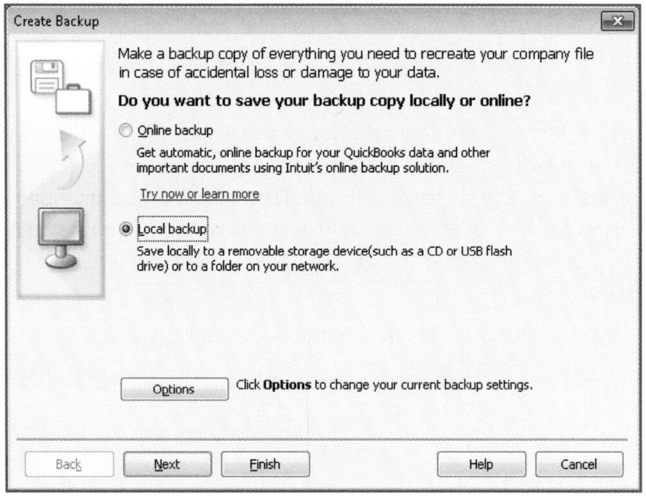

Figure 9-1: *You can make an online backup or a local backup.*

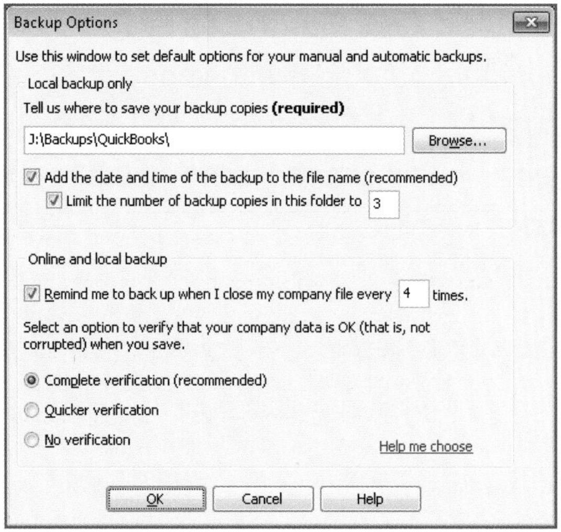

Figure 9-2: *Where and how do you want your backup file saved?*

Back Up Your Data

The first and most important line of defense is creating backups. If you make a backup copy of your QuickBooks file every day, you will only have a minimum amount of work to do when your data is lost.

1. Select **File I Create Backup** from the menu bar to open the Create Backup dialog box shown in Figure 9-1.

2. Choose **Local Backup** to save to a hard drive, CD, or flash drive. The Online Backup feature enables you (for a fee) to save your backup file to a remote computer.

3. Click the **Options** button to display the Backup Options dialog seen in Figure 9-2.

4. Set the backup options:

   ● **Backup Location** This is an important decision. You should never back up to your local hard disk, unless your hard disk is backed up to a remote location every night. You should back up to a remote computer, a CD-R, a CD-RW, a DVD, flash drive, or some other media that can be stored away from your computer. To ensure that you're covered in case of a corrupted backup file, you should have a minimum of two backup media that you alternate every day. For example, if you're using flash drives, have two (or more) that you alternate every day. Back up on flash drive A today, flash drive B tomorrow, flash drive A the following day, and so on. If one of them has a corrupt backup file, chances are the other will be okay. If you're security-conscious, you'll probably want to use seven media, one for each day of the week.

   ● **Date And Time** It's a good idea to have QuickBooks time/date stamp each file so you know exactly when it was created.

   ● **Number Of Backup Copies** If your backup media is rewritable and large enough to accommodate multiple backup copies, you can tell QuickBooks to create several copies before overwriting the older ones.

NOTE

Rewritable discs are usually identified by the letter W (for reWritable). For example, a regular "write once" CD is called a CD-R, while a rewritable is called a CD-RW. The same goes for a DVD (DVD-R or DVD-RW). For Blu-ray discs it's a little different; BD-R for write-once discs, and BD-RE for rewritable.

Burn a Disc

How do you want to use this disc?

Disc title: Dec 18 2016

○ **Like a USB flash drive**
Save, edit, and delete files on the disc anytime. The disc will work on computers running Windows XP or later. (Live File System)

○ **With a CD/DVD player**
Burn files in groups and individual files can't be edited or removed after burning. The disc will also work on most computers. (Mastered)

Which one should I choose?

[Next] [Cancel]

*Figure 9-3: **If you have a rewritable disc and Windows XP or higher, choose the first option.***

NOTE

As of this writing, the dialog box shown in Figure 9-3 only appears the first time you make a backup to a CD/DVD drive. After the first time, it no longer appears. Hopefully, the bug will be fixed by the time you read this.

- **Backup Reminder** Unless you're religious about backing up, it's easy to forget. Setting a backup reminder for every three or four times you close your company file is a good idea.

- **Backup Verification** While it's true that verifying your backup data takes longer, especially if you have a large QuickBooks file, it's also true that a quick but corrupted backup file is completely useless to you. Therefore, it's recommended that you turn on verification. Another reason to use complete verification is that it resets your transaction log file, which can grow to an enormous size and slow down QuickBooks' performance.

5. Click **OK** to save the backup options and return to the Save Backup dialog.

6. Click **Next** and select **Save It Now.** We'll cover scheduled backups in the next section.

7. Now, click **Next** to open the Save Backup Copy dialog box.

8. If necessary, you can change the filename and location (which are determined by the settings you configured in the Backup Options dialog box). Then click **Save** to create the backup file.

9. If you elected to save the file to a flash or remote drive, QuickBooks writes the file to the selected media and displays a confirmation message. However, if you chose to save to a CD/DVD or Blu-ray drive, QuickBooks displays the Burn A Disc dialog box shown in Figure 9-3 asking how you want to use the selected drive. While the QuickBooks help file goes into a lot of detail explaining the differences, the choices are really very simple:

    - **Like A USB Flash Drive** This option only works if you have a rewritable disc in the selected drive. It allows you to not only write files to the disc, but also to erase them and write over them if you so choose. If you insert a write-once disc (not rewritable), QuickBooks will attempt to format the disc and save the backup, but will fail.

    - **With A CD/DVD Player** If the disk in the selected drive is not a rewritable disc, choose this option. The files will be written to a temporary backup disc on your hard drive and QuickBooks will display a dialog box offering you the choice to Burn Now or Burn Later. Choose Burn Now to make the backup immediately using the Windows CD-Burning Wizard. If you want to use your own burning software, choose Burn Later.

QUICKSTEPS

SCHEDULING REGULAR BACKUPS

It's a good idea to set up a schedule for creating backups automatically so you don't have to worry about it when your memory fails, or when you're not available to make the backup.

1. Select **File | Create Backup** to open the Save Backup dialog.

2. Choose **Local Backup** and click **Next** to display the options for when to save.

3. Select the **Only Schedule Future Backups** option, and click **Next** to display the scheduling options, as seen in Figure 9-4.

4. If you want to create an automatic backup each time you close QuickBooks, check the **Save Backup Copy Automatically When I Close My Company File Every** *<number>* **Times** option, and enter the number of closings between automatic saves.

5. Click the **New** button in the Back Up On A Schedule section to open the Schedule Backup dialog.

6. Enter a unique description that will enable you to easily identify this schedule (i.e., Daily, Nightly, Every Other Day, and so on).

7. Click the **Browse** button, and select a location to which you want the backup saved.

   Since backing up to a CD is a multistep process that QuickBooks cannot complete without user interaction, you cannot schedule a backup to a CD drive. Although QuickBooks will initially accept a CD drive entered in the Location field, it will reject it when you attempt to save the schedule.

Continued . . .

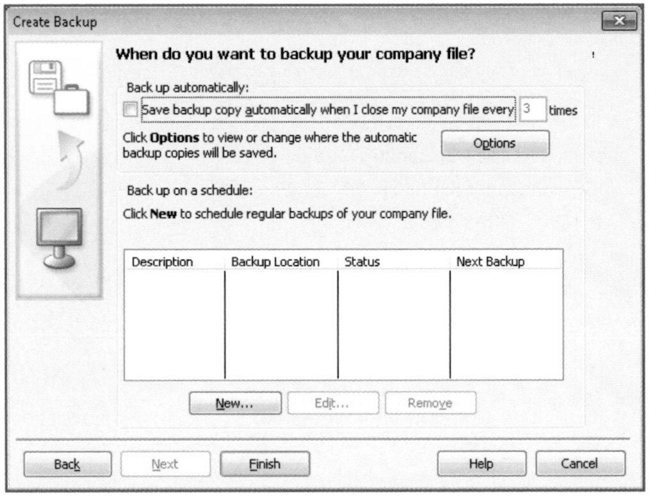

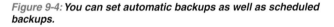

Figure 9-4: *You can set automatic backups as well as scheduled backups.*

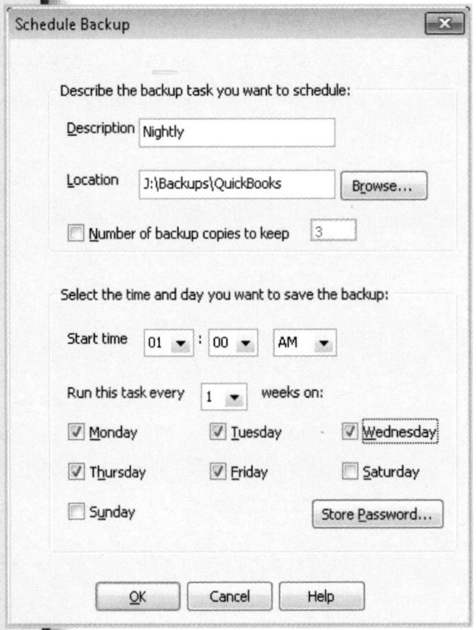

Remember to keep your backups in a safe place. If your computer gets stolen and your backup is a flash drive still sitting in the USB port, it's not going to do you much good. It's also a good idea to keep periodic backups off-site to ensure that in the event of a major catastrophe, like a fire, you still have access to most of your financial data.

8. To keep multiple copies of backups on the same media, check the **Number Of Backup Copies To Keep** option, and enter the maximum number of backups to retain on the media. When the maximum number is reached, QuickBooks overwrites the oldest backup on the media to retain the indicated number of copies.

9. In the **Start Time** fields, enter the time you want the backup to start.

10. Select the number of weeks. Select **1** if you want the backup to run every week, **2** if you want it to run every other week, and so on.

11. Select the days that you want the backup to run. If you want it to run every day, check all the days. If you want it to run only during the week, check Monday through Friday.

12. Click **Store Password** and enter your Windows (not QuickBooks) user name and password. Without them, the scheduled backup(s) will not run.

13. Click **OK** to save your new schedule. If you forgot to set your Windows password, the Store Windows Password dialog box appears, since you cannot save a scheduled backup without your Windows user name and password.

14. Create as many scheduled backups as needed, and then click **Finish** to close the Save Backup window.

Now you're all set. The only thing you must remember to do is leave the computer running with QuickBooks shut down to ensure all files are closed and available for backup.

Use QuickBooks Data Utilities

QuickBooks offers three data-related utilities that enable you to verify, rebuild, and condense and archive your financial data. Each of them is accessible from the Utilities submenu of the File menu.

Verify Data

If QuickBooks displays error messages, or you find that names or transactions seem to be missing, or you discover other inexplicable discrepancies, you may have a data integrity problem. Most (but not all) data problems are encountered when QuickBooks is used in a networked environment and either the server or the client crashes while the company file is open. The first thing to do is run the data verification utility to see if the problem is with your company file.

1. Select **File | Utilities | Verify Data**.

2. QuickBooks displays a message that it must close all windows before proceeding. Click **OK** to continue with the data verification. A Working dialog appears, informing you of the progress of the data verification process.

3. Once the verification process is complete, QuickBooks displays a message informing you of the results. If you're lucky, everything is okay. If you're not, it will let you know that errors were found. Click **OK** to continue.

If no errors were found, you can breathe a sigh of relief and continue working. If, on the other hand, the utility encountered errors, the next step is to run the Rebuild Data utility (see the section "Rebuild Data" later in this chapter).

RESTORING A BACKUP

When the inevitable happens and you have to utilize one of those backups you've been making regularly, you'll need to use the Restore function in QuickBooks.

1. Select **Open Or Restore Company** from the File menu to display the Open Or Restore Company dialog box shown in Figure 9-5.

2. Select **Restore A Backup Copy**, and click **Next**.

3. Select **Local Backup** and click **Next** to display the Open Backup Copy dialog box. If you subscribe to the QuickBooks Online Backup service, choose **Online Backup** and follow the on-screen instructions.

4. Locate and select the backup file you want to use, and then click **Open**. QuickBooks displays an advisory dialog suggesting that you rename the file so that your existing company file is not overwritten.

5. Click **Next** to open the Save Company File As dialog box. If you're restoring because your existing company file is corrupted beyond salvation, you can accept the default (to overwrite your existing company file) and click **Save**. However, if there is any doubt, you might want to follow the advice in the preceding message and enter a new filename to retain your original company file. Just remember to use the new company file and not the old one from this point forward.

6. Click **Save** to restore the backup copy and open the new company file.

As soon as QuickBooks opens the new company file, a confirmation dialog box displays alerting you that the restore has been successful. If you have to log in to QuickBooks, the dialog box appears after you log in.

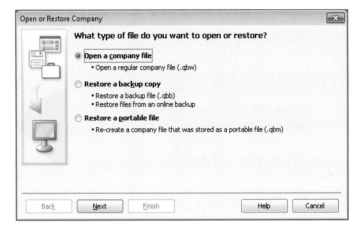

Figure 9-5: *Data loss doesn't have to be a disaster if you have a good backup to restore.*

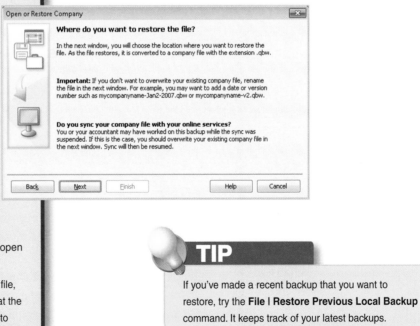

TIP

If you've made a recent backup that you want to restore, try the **File | Restore Previous Local Backup** command. It keeps track of your latest backups.

CREATING A PORTABLE COMPANY FILE

For those times when you need to send or transport a slimmed-down version of your company file, QuickBooks offers the portable company file. This file type contains only your financial data. It does not contain logos, letters, templates, graphics, or the transaction log file. This makes it small enough to send via e-mail or limited removable media.

1. Select **File | Create Copy** from the menu bar to open the Save Copy Or Backup dialog.

2. Choose **Portable Company File**, and click **Next** to open the Save Portable Company File dialog.

3. Select a location, enter a filename (or use the default), and click **Save** to create the portable file. Remember where you saved it so you can retrieve it without an exhaustive search.

4. QuickBooks displays an informational dialog to let you know it must close and reopen the company file first. Click **OK** to proceed.

5. QuickBooks creates the portable file and notifies you of its location (your second, and last, chance to note where you saved it).

6. Click **OK** to close the informational dialog box and return to work in QuickBooks.

Now you can attach the file, which has a .qbm extension, to an e-mail (depending on the file size and your e-mail account restrictions), or save it to removable media to transport to another computer.

Rebuild Data

When the Verify Data utility informs you that errors were found, it's time to rebuild your data. Running the Rebuild Data utility is easy. However, before you run the utility, you should perform some important maintenance chores that will ensure the process works as effectively as possible (see the "Getting Ready To Rebuild Data" QuickSteps).

1. When you're ready to run the utility, select **File | Utilities | Rebuild Data**.

2. QuickBooks insists that you make a backup copy first and advises against using an existing backup to ensure you don't overwrite a good backup in case this one turns out to be a bad one. Click **OK** to begin the backup.

> **QuickBooks Information**
> Before rebuilding the data file, a backup must be made.
> Do not use existing backup disks! If you do so, you may replace your one good backup with a bad backup.
> [OK]

3. Select the appropriate backup location (online or local), and click the **Options** button to configure the backup options. Again, make sure you don't overwrite existing backups.

4. Click **Next** to open the Save Backup Copy dialog box (basically a Windows "Save" dialog), where you can modify the filename and location if so desired.

5. Click **Save** to create the backup.

6. Once the backup is created, the data rebuilding process begins automatically without any input from you. Once it's finished, QuickBooks informs you of the fact. Click **OK** to return to work in QuickBooks.

> **QuickBooks Information**
> Rebuild has completed.
> [OK]

CAUTION

If your company file is not properly prepared before running the Rebuild Data utility, the process can cause further damage to your company file. Therefore, before proceeding with the Rebuild Data utility, read the "Getting Ready to Rebuild Data" QuickSteps.

GETTING READY TO REBUILD DATA

While the rebuilding process itself is pretty simple, you need to prepare for it properly to ensure that you get a complete and accurate rebuild. Consequently, there are several things you should do before running the utility.

First, if the file you want to rebuild is on a network computer, copy it to your local hard disk and then run the Rebuild Data utility.

Second, make sure that all inactive list items are visible and that the lists are reset to their original sort order:

- **Chart of Accounts**   Open the Chart of Accounts (**CTRL+A**) and make sure the **Include Inactive** option at the bottom of the window is checked (if you have inactive accounts) to display all accounts, including those marked inactive. Now click the **Account** button and select **Re-sort List** to return the list to its original sort order. Click **OK** to confirm.

- **Item List**   Select **Lists | Item List** to open the Item List. At the bottom of the window, check the **Include Inactive** option to display both active and inactive items. Then click the **Item** button, and select **Re-sort List** to return the list to its original sort order. Click **OK** to confirm.

- **Name List**   This is not one of the standard lists you'll find on the Lists menu. It's a compilation of the customer list, vendor list, Employee list, and Other Names List. To open it, you must first open the Write Checks window by pressing **CTRL+W**. Then place your cursor in the **Pay To The Order Of** field, and press **CTRL+L** to open the Name List. The process is the same here. Check the **Include Inactive** option, and re-sort the list (click the **Name** button, and select **Re-sort List**).

Hopefully, the Rebuild Data utility will fix all the problems found by the Verify Data utility. Begin working in your company file, and try to repeat the actions that alerted you to problems in the first place. If you find everything is working smoothly, you should be okay to go back to work in QuickBooks with peace of mind. If the problems are still present, contact Intuit Technical Support. To visit the Intuit support site online, choose **Help | Support** from the menu bar.

Condense Data

This utility is not about data integrity, but about removing old and unused data from your company file. Unless you actively eliminate data that you no longer need, it continues to build up year after year, increasing the size of your file and slowing QuickBooks' performance. Unless you need every detail of every transaction you've ever created, you should periodically run the Condense Data wizard. It removes the details, but leaves summary information. It also removes unused list items.

1. Choose **File | Utilities | Condense Data** from the menu bar to start the wizard seen in Figure 9-6.

2. Select **Transactions Before A Specific Date** to clean up old (closed) transactions.

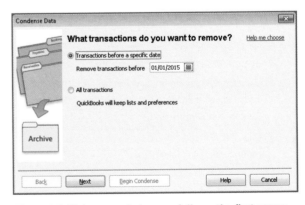

*Figure 9-6: **Make your choice carefully on the first screen of the wizard.***

TIP

If you find it handy having all your names in a single list, you can add a Name List icon to the Icon Bar by selecting **View I Add "Name List" To Icon Bar** while the Name List window is open (and the active window).

NOTE

If you have any existing budgets, QuickBooks warns you that you may lose some of that budget data during the cleanup process. If you don't care, click **Yes**. If you want to save your budget data first (export it to Excel), click **No**, export your budgets, and then return to the Condense Data wizard.

CAUTION

Be sure to choose the first option in step 1, Transactions Before A Specific Date, and not the second, All Transactions, unless you want to remove *every* transaction in your company file. The second option is useful if you want to make a copy of your company file but without transactions—perhaps to use as the basis for a different company file. As you walk through the wizard, read each step carefully and make the appropriate choices.

3. Set the cutoff date for removing transactions. Only closed transactions dated on or before the date you set here will be removed.

4. If you have inventory enabled, the next screen asks how inventory transactions should be handled. Your choices are to summarize or keep. Summarize removes transactions and replaces them with inventory adjustments. The second option is a little misleading. It doesn't actually keep your inventory transactions. It condenses them until it hits an open transaction in the date range and then stops, leaving the rest untouched.

5. Click **Next** and choose additional criteria for deleting transactions (see Figure 9-7).

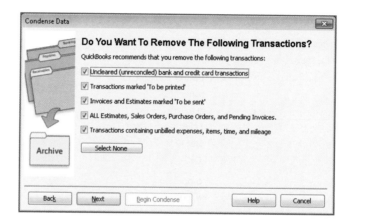

Figure 9-7: **There are some closed transactions QuickBooks won't delete unless you give it the okay.**

6. After you select your additional criteria, click **Next** to view the unused list entries screen.

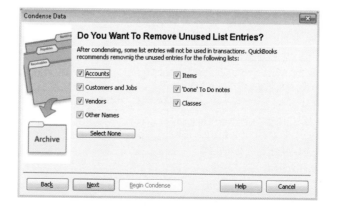

TIP

Depending on the date you set in the opening screen, you may or may not want to eliminate transactions that conform to one or more of the criteria listed here. If you're deleting transactions from a year or more ago, you probably aren't going to print, send, or submit an invoice for them now. If you've been reconciling your bank and credit card accounts and there are any uncleared transactions, you probably don't want to start all over. However, if you're removing more recent transactions, you might want to consider keeping some of the transactions that fit in these categories.

TIP

Since the dividing date determines exactly what you can work on while the Accountant's Copy is outstanding, you should not set the date lightly. If you're giving the accountant a copy for a specific purpose (to create a report, to make special adjustments, and so on), set the date to include only the data needed for the accountant to perform those operations. See the "Working with the Accountant's Copy" QuickFacts for more information.

7. Select those item types that you want to remove. This is another area in which the cutoff date you set will probably determine the choices you make.

8. Click **Next** to view the final screen of the wizard. It's an informational screen that explains the actions that will be taken.

9. If you have any doubts, use the **Back** button to review your choices. When you're satisfied, click the **Begin Condense** button.

10. Part of the cleanup process is the creation of an archive file. When the cleanup is finished, a message appears letting you know that your old data has been removed and an archive file has been created. Note the location and name of the archive file, and click **OK** to return to work in QuickBooks.

If, at some time in the future, you need to access the details of those transactions you removed, you can open the archive file and see all the transactions as they were prior to the cleanup.

Create an Accountant's Copy

When the accountant needs to work on your company file, all you have to do is create an Accountant's Copy and send it off.

1. From the menu bar, select **File | Accountant's Copy | Save File** to open the Save Accountant's Copy dialog box.

2. Select **Accountant's Copy** and click **Next** to set the dividing date (see Figure 9-8).

3. From the **Dividing Date** drop-down list, select a preconfigured date (i.e., End Of Last Month), or select **Custom** to set a specific dividing date.

WORKING WITH THE ACCOUNTANT'S COPY

If you do the bookkeeping in QuickBooks and your accountant takes care of the more complex accounting functions, you'll appreciate the Accountant's Copy feature. It enables you to create a copy of your company file that your accountant can work on, while you continue to work in your copy of the company file. The trick is, each copy is limited to certain functions until the Accountant's Copy changes are integrated into your copy of the file:

- **Original company file limitations** The first limitation you're faced with is the dividing date. You cannot change any transactions before the dividing date. Those are available to your accountant only. In your Chart of Accounts, you can add new accounts, but you cannot edit, merge, or make existing accounts inactive. Nor can you create subaccounts for existing accounts. You cannot edit or merge list items; otherwise, you can perform all other functions. You can perform account reconciliations, but any done with transactions dated before the dividing date will be undone when you import the changes from your accountant.

- **Accountant's Copy limitations** Your accountant also has limitations. To begin with, your accountant can only work on transactions prior to the dividing date. Payroll, non-posting transactions, funds transfers, and sales tax payments cannot be added, edited, voided, or deleted. Inventory adjustments and credit card bill payments can be added and deleted, but not edited or voided. List items created before the dividing date can only be viewed. In addition, some fields can be changed to facilitate the accountant's work, but will not be retained when the changes are imported into

Continued . . .

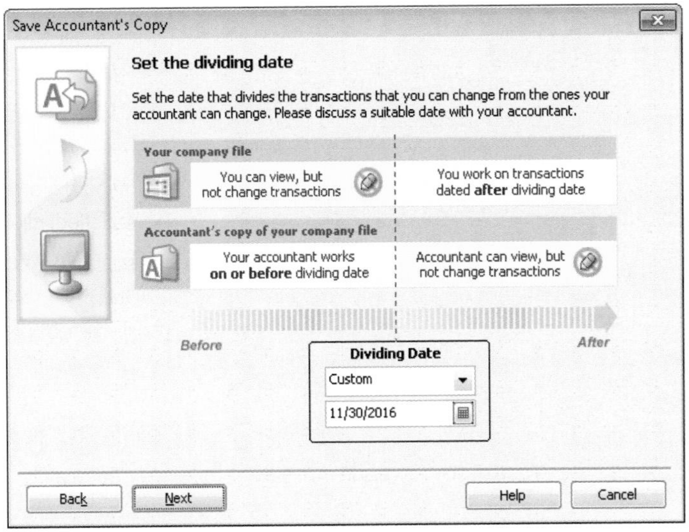

Figure 9-8: *It's important to choose the right dividing date.*

4. Click **Next** to start the creation process.

5. QuickBooks displays a dialog informing you that it must close all windows. Click **OK** to proceed to the Save Accountant's Copy dialog box.

6. Select a location and filename for the copy, and click **Save** to create the Accountant's Copy.

7. QuickBooks displays a confirmation that the file was successfully created. Click **OK** to return to QuickBooks.

Now you can attach the file to an e-mail (depending on file size and your e-mail account limitations), or copy it to a CD or flash drive and deliver it to your accountant. When you look for it, remember that it has a .qbx extension. Also, remember that you are limited in what you can do until the accountant's changes have been returned to you and imported into your company file.

WORKING WITH THE ACCOUNTANT'S COPY *(Continued)*

the original file. Fields that can be changed and retained are highlighted, while fields that can be changed but not retained are not highlighted. Until the accountant's changes are incorporated into your company file, QuickBooks alerts you to the fact that you're working in a limited version of your company file. First of all, each time you open the company file a dialog appears, informing you that an Accountant's Copy is outstanding. After you open the file, the QuickBooks title bar includes the following text: "(Accountant's Changes Pending)."

QUICKSTEPS

IMPORTING YOUR ACCOUNTANT'S CHANGES

Once your accountant has finished working on the Accountant's Copy and returns it to you, the next step is to import the changes.

1. Select **File | Accountant's Copy | Import Accountant's Changes From File** to open the Import Accountant's Changes dialog box. If your accountant has saved the changes to the Web, use the **Import Accountant's Changes From Web** command instead. As long as you're connected to the Internet, the changes are downloaded automatically. Then skip to step 3.

2. Locate the Accountant's Changes file (which has a .qby extension), select it, and click **Open** to display the Incorporate Accountant's Changes dialog box, which lists all the changes made by the

Continued . . .

You may have also noticed the Send To Accountant command on the Accountant's Copy menu (**File | Accountant's Copy | Send To Accountant**). If you have a broadband Internet connection and a company file under 200MB, you can use this free (to you) service to upload the Accountant's Copy to an Intuit server, where your accountant can then download it (if he or she has a subscription to the service). When you upload it, Intuit automatically sends your accountant an e-mail notification that the file is available for download. Since your accountant cannot download the file without a subscription to the service, you might want to check before sending the file.

Import and Export

QuickBooks provides the ability to exchange information with other users through its import and export features. You can import Excel files, IIF files, Web Connect files, timer files from the QuickBooks Timer program, and documents into the Document Center. On the export side, you can pour QuickBooks lists into IIF files, dump your addresses into text files, and export QuickBooks timer lists into IIF files. You can also export your QuickBooks report data into an Excel spreadsheet. You'll find more about exporting report information in Chapter 8.

Use the File Import Utilities

QuickBooks offers four utilities for importing data quickly and easily. Each is designed to handle a specific file type.

IMPORT EXCEL FILES

First there is the Excel Import utility. As you might suspect, you use this utility to import Microsoft Excel files into QuickBooks. The one thing to remember is that it won't work unless you have a copy of Microsoft Excel installed on your computer.

1. Select **File | Utilities | Import | Excel Files** to launch the Add Your Excel Data To QuickBooks wizard. As you can see in Figure 9-9, the wizard offers three types of Excel imports—customer information, vendor information, and inventory information.

QUICKSTEPS

IMPORTING YOUR ACCOUNTANT'S CHANGES *(Continued)*

accountant and a note from your accountant, if one was included.

3. If you want to create a list of the changes before you import them, click the **Save As PDF** button or the **Print** button.

4. To import the changes, click the **Incorporate Accountant's Changes** button.

5. QuickBooks displays a dialog box informing you that it must close all windows. Click **OK** to proceed.

6. Before QuickBooks will complete the import, it insists on creating a backup copy of your existing data. Click **OK** to open the Save Backup Copy dialog box.

7. Select a location and filename for the backup, and click **Save**.

8. QuickBooks creates the backup file and displays a confirmation dialog. Click **OK** to import the accountant's changes. If you elected to create a PDF file or to print a hard copy, that is also done.

When the import is complete, QuickBooks redisplays the Incorporate Accountant's Changes dialog with a confirmation that all changes have been imported successfully. Click **Close** to shut the dialog. QuickBooks then advises you to change your closing date to prevent anyone from making changes that would affect the data just imported from your accountant. Click **Yes** to change the closing date, or click **No** to leave it as is.

One final note. If you used the Import Accountant's Changes From Web command, QuickBooks automatically sends a notification to your accountant that you have imported the changes. A dialog displays, alerting you to this fact.

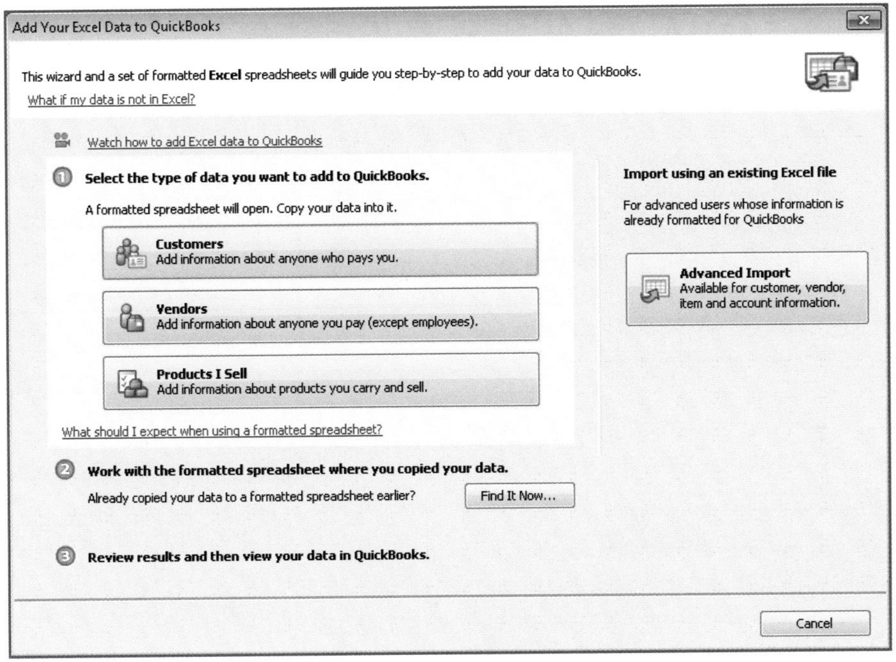

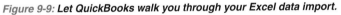

Figure 9-9: **Let QuickBooks walk you through your Excel data import.**

2. Select the type of data to import. As soon as you click one of the buttons—Customers, Vendors, Products I Sell (inventory)—QuickBooks launches Excel and opens a preformatted spreadsheet ready for your input (see Figure 9-10).

3. Copy and paste data into the worksheet.

4. Fix any errors that appear.

5. Press **CTRL+S** to open the Save As dialog box.

6. Choose the location and filename for the worksheet, and click **Save**.

7. Click the **Add My Data Now** button to import the new information and return to the wizard.

8. You can either use the **View The** *<list name>* **List** button to close the wizard and view the list or just click the **Close** button.

CAUTION

Since you can't undo an import, you're stuck with the data you bring in. Therefore, it's a good idea to make a backup of your company file in case you change your mind after the import is finished. The first time you run the Excel Import utility, QuickBooks asks if you want to continue working or create a backup copy. Click **No** to stop the import wizard so you can return to QuickBooks and make a backup copy before proceeding.

NOTE

You cannot import data into QuickBooks unless the Excel file has been saved. If you attempt to import the data without first saving the worksheet, QuickBooks balks and gives you the chance to save the worksheet.

NOTE

The Intuit support site also offers a QuickBooks Import Excel & CSV toolkit to assist in importing Excel files (http://support.quickbooks.intuit.com/support/pages/Executable/QuickBooks_Import_Excel_and_CSV.exe).

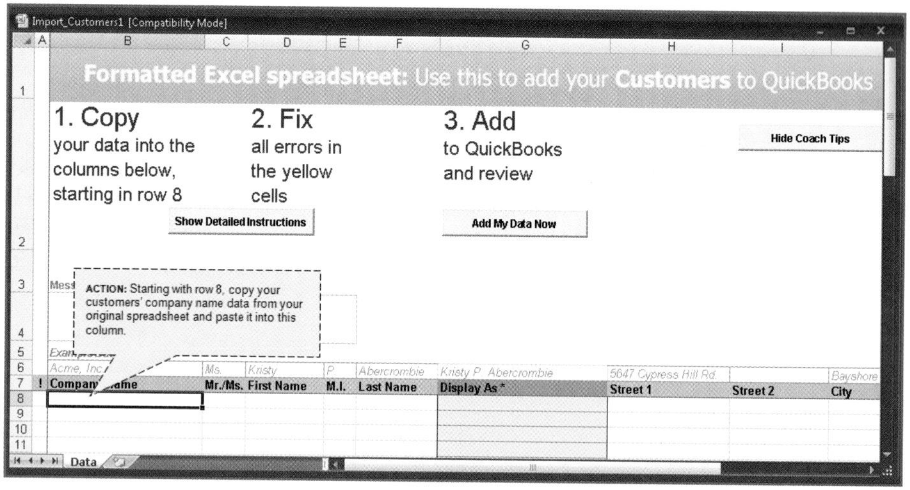

Figure 9-10: *All you have to do is enter the data you want to import.*

IMPORT IIF FILES

If you've exported lists from another company file, or if you've created a custom IIF file, you can import the resulting IIF file directly into QuickBooks. This is an easy way to exchange data with other QuickBooks users.

1. Select **File | Utilities | Import | IIF Files** to open the Import dialog box.
2. Locate the IIF file you want to import, and click **Open**. That's all there is to it. QuickBooks automatically imports the file and displays a confirmation dialog when it's done.
3. Click **OK** to close the confirmation dialog box and return to work in QuickBooks.

IMPORT WEB CONNECT FILES

Web Connect files are specialized IIF files used for downloading online banking transactions from your bank. See Chapter 2 for more information on Web Connect files.

IMPORT TIMER ACTIVITIES

Timer activity files are another specialized type of IIF file created by the QuickBooks Timer utility found on the QuickBooks CD. The Timer enables QuickBooks users to track the amount of time spent on individual tasks and

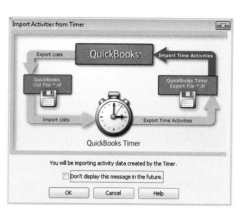

QUICKSTEPS

EXPORTING ADDRESSES TO TEXT FILES

For sharing contact information about customers and jobs, vendors, employees, and/or other names, this export utility is ideal. You can export any or all names to a tab-delimited text file that can be imported into any contact management application that accepts tab-delimited text files. You can also open it in Word or Excel and print a hard copy if needed.

1. Select **File | Utilities | Export | Addresses To Text File** to open the Select Names For Export Addresses dialog box.

2. From the drop-down list, select a single name, multiple names, all names from a specific list, or **All Names** to export every name in the four names lists included (Customers:Jobs, Vendors, Employees, Other Names).

3. If you have customer jobs with address data that is different from that of the customer, check the **Include Jobs** option.

4. Click **OK** to open the Save Address Data File dialog box.

5. Select a location and filename for the new text file, and click **Save**. QuickBooks may display a warning message alerting you that not all fields contain data. Click **OK** to continue, and then recheck the data if need be.

6. QuickBooks exports the name information and confirms that the file has been successfully created. Click **OK** to return to work in QuickBooks.

Just remember where you saved the file so you can access it later and share it with others or import it into another application.

record it. The activity files can then be imported to QuickBooks to automatically fill out timesheets for the users.

1. Select **File | Utilities | Import | Timer Activities** to launch the Import Activities From Timer dialog.

2. Click **OK** to display the Import dialog.

3. After you've located the timer file to import, click **Open**, and QuickBooks does the rest.

Although timer files are .iif files, they are a different breed from the ones used in the Import IIF Files utility. Therefore, if you select a non-timer .iif file, it will not work. QuickBooks will let you know, in no uncertain terms, that the file you're trying to import is not a timer file.

Export List Files

When you have information you want to share with others, you can use the Export utilities to transform the data into a format that can be imported by QuickBooks or other applications.

EXPORT LISTS TO IIF FILES

When you want to share list data with other QuickBooks users, the list export utility comes in quite handy.

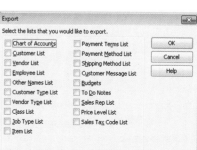

1. Select **File | Utilities | Export | Lists To IIF Files** to open the Export dialog box.

2. Check each list you want to include in the export. You can export a single list, multiple lists, or all the lists at once.

CAUTION

Do not attempt to use the **File | Utilities | Export | Lists To IIF Files** command for timer files. While you can export basically the same information into an IIF file, it will not create the specific format needed by the QuickBooks Timer to import the data.

QUICKFACTS

UNDERSTANDING IIF FILES

IIF (Intuit Interchange Format) files are used for importing and exporting lists and transactions in QuickBooks. They are tab-delimited text files that can be created, opened, and edited in spreadsheet programs such as Microsoft Excel.

IIF files are great for transferring lists between QuickBooks users since QuickBooks incorporates an easy-to-use list export utility. You can also use them to transfer information from other programs into QuickBooks. Unfortunately, unless you have a lot of data to transfer and spend time learning how to create precisely structured IIF files, it may be easier to enter the data by hand.

There are a number of things to be aware of when using IIF files:

- QuickBooks will allow you to import the same IIF file multiple times without warning you. As a result, it will re-create all the items on the list each time you import it.

- There is no way to automatically remove lists or transactions after you import them, so be sure to create a backup before you start the import process. If you change your mind, you can restore the backup to eliminate the imported items.

Continued . . .

3. Click **OK** to open another Export dialog box (this one is really a Windows Save dialog box, renamed Export).

4. In the Export dialog box that appears, select a location and filename for the list file, and click **Save**.

You can now send the file to another QuickBooks user, who can then import it into QuickBooks. You can also use it to import into another company file yourself. It's a great way to share a customized inventory or other list.

EXPORT QUICKBOOKS TIMER LISTS

To use the QuickBooks Timer to record time spent on individual activities, the Timer must first have a list of customers and jobs, employees, vendors, other names, service items, and classes (if you use classes).

1. Select **File | Utilities | Export | Timer Lists** to display the Export Lists For Timer dialog box.

2. Click **OK** to open the Export dialog.

3. Select a location and filename for the export file, and click **Save** to create and save the list file.

Understand Document Management

Document Management is a handy storage feature for retaining copies of documents that you may want, or need, to have quick access to in connection with your business. It provides a centralized location for storing business-related documents within QuickBooks. For example, you can store contracts, pricing agreements, collection letters, brochures, product photos, e-mails, and a variety of other documents. If you use Microsoft Outlook for your e-mail and information management, you can easily store Outlook documents by dragging and dropping them into the Doc Center. Any time you need to refer to a document, select **Company | Documents | Doc Center** to open the Doc Center (see Figure 9-11) and access it.

QUICKFACTS

UNDERSTANDING IIF FILES (Continued)

- When you import lists of items that contain balances, only the items are imported; the balances are left behind.

- Payroll data is off limits to IIF files. You can neither import nor export payroll data in an IIF file.

- You can import transactions, but you cannot export them.

- Not all lists can be exported and imported. Among those not available for import and export are the Fixed Asset Item List, the Payroll Item List, the Currency List (if you enable multiple currencies), the Memorized Transaction List, and the Vehicle List.

If you decide that you want to learn more about IIF files, especially creating them to import transactions, you should download the QuickBooks IIF Import Kit from the Intuit support site (http://support.quickbooks.intuit.com/support/Articles/HOW12778).

NOTE

In previous versions, the Document Management service had an online component that enabled you to store attached documents on Intuit's servers for a fee. While the online service has been discontinued for new users, customers with existing subscriptions can still access and use it.

TIP

Double-clicking in an Attach column next to a name or list item opens the Attachments dialog for the name or item selected.

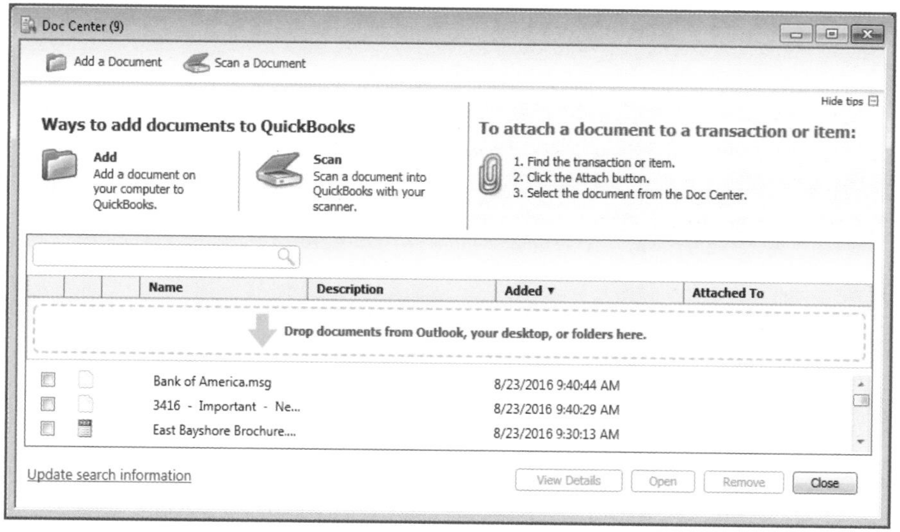

Figure 9-11: *The Doc Center provides easy access to business-related documents.*

You can add documents directly to the Doc Center using one of the following methods:

- **Add** Click the **Add A Document** button to open the Select Documents To Add To Inbox dialog box. Locate and select the document(s), and click **Open**.

- **Scan a document** Clicking the **Scan A Document** button launches the QuickBooks Scan Manager, which enables you to scan a document into the Doc Center from any compatible scanner installed on your system.

- **Drag and drop** From Windows Explorer or My Computer, locate the document(s) you want to add, and simply drag them into the Doc Center window and drop them in the indicated area. You can also drag and drop Outlook items including e-mail messages, contacts, tasks, and so on.

Attach and Retrieve Documents

The Document Management feature is more than just a storage service. It also allows you to link (attach) a file to a particular customer, vendor, transaction, or even list item. Simply click an **Attach** button or an **Attach** command (found in many list and form windows), and QuickBooks opens the Attachments dialog so you can select a stored document to link to.

The Attachments dialog contains three buttons—Computer, Scanner, and Doc Center:

- **Computer**   When you click the **Computer** button, a Select Documents To Add To Inbox dialog opens. It's a typical Windows "Open" dialog that allows you to locate files and folders on your local, remote, or removable disks. Locate the document(s) you want to attach, and click **Open**. To select multiple documents, hold down the CTRL key and left-click each document to add.

- **Scanner**   If the document you want to attach is not on an accessible hard disk (or other media type), you can scan it directly into QuickBooks by clicking the **Scanner** button, which opens the QuickBooks Scan Manager dialog. Of course, you must have a compatible scanner installed to utilize this function. If you have multiple scanners, choose the one to use. Select a scan profile, set the other options, and click **Scan**. The document is scanned into QuickBooks and automatically attached.

UNDERSTANDING PASSWORD PROTECTION

Passwords are an important, but often poorly implemented, security tool. While passwords are not a 100 percent guarantee against unauthorized access, when used properly, they are a strong deterrent to most would-be intruders. The problem with passwords, more often than not, is their implementation. Using a strong password, storing it properly, and changing it frequently, which are the basics of good password protection, are not always easy. Therefore, all too many users opt for an easy-to-remember (and therefore, easy-to-break) password, and never change it unless they're forced to. Creating and adhering to good password policies will ensure that your QuickBooks data is as safe as it can be:

- **Use strong passwords**   Most users want a password that's easy to remember, so they opt for addresses, phone numbers, birth dates, and so on. Of course, the reason they're easy to remember is that they are common knowledge. This means that anyone who is familiar with the user can probably figure out those passwords. Strong passwords, on the other hand, are passwords that incorporate a combination of upper- and lowercase letters along with numbers, and have no direct connection with the user. Everyone in your company should use a password that is at least seven characters long and incorporates a combination of upper- and lowercase letters and numbers.

- **Store passwords in a safe place**   Since strong passwords are usually not easy to remember, they need to be written down and stored. Putting them on a Post-it Note stuck to your monitor is not the solution. Neither is a slip of paper thrown in your top drawer. A locked drawer or cabinet

Continued . . .

- **Doc Center**   If you've already added documents to the Doc Center and want to attach one of them to a record, transaction, or other item, click the **Doc Center** button. The Select Doc Center Documents dialog opens, where you can choose any of the documents currently stored in the Doc Center. Select one (or more), and click the **Attach** button.

Although documents you attach to a QuickBooks item (record, transaction, item, and so on) appear in the Doc Center, they are not available in the Select Doc Center Documents dialog box for attaching to other records or items. This also applies to documents you've added to the Doc Center. Once you attach them to a record or item, they are no longer available in the Select Doc Center Documents dialog. What this means is that you can only link each document to one record or item.

Once a document is linked to a list name, item, or transaction in QuickBooks, the paperclip icon on the Attach button changes to green. When viewed in a list, a name or item with an attachment displays a paperclip icon in the Attach column.

To open the document after you've attached it, click the **View** button. Keep in mind that you must have the application associated with the file type installed on your computer. In other words, trying to open a PDF document without having Adobe Acrobat Reader (or Adobe Acrobat) installed is going to result in an error message, not a viewable document.

These are just the basics of Document Management. Spend a little time perusing and using the Document Management commands on the Company menu to learn how you can make the most of this handy feature.

Maintain Security

Financial information, whether yours or your customers', is extremely sensitive and should be guarded from unauthorized access. Fortunately, QuickBooks offers some tools to ensure that all financial information is locked away from prying eyes.

UNDERSTANDING PASSWORD PROTECTION (Continued)

should be your first choice. If you can't put it in a locked place, at least put it somewhere where your average snooper isn't going to find it.

- **Change passwords regularly**   To avoid having someone either figure it out accidentally or break it, you should change your password every few months.

Since most users will only grudgingly follow good password procedures, the QuickBooks administrator, who has control over passwords, should create and enforce good password policies.

QUICKSTEPS

CONFIGURING CREDIT CARD PROTECTION

If you accept credit card payments from your customers, you should be careful about how you retain and protect that information. Not only is it important from a confidence standpoint, but a legal one as well. The credit card industry has a set of standards called the Payment Card Industry Data Security Standard (PCI DSS) that is issued to provide merchants with guidelines on protecting customer credit card data. To stay on the good side of both your customers and the credit card companies (and to avoid fines and lawsuits), you should make strict compliance with the PCI DSS standard operating procedure.

1. Log on as the QuickBooks administrator, since only the administrator can enable credit card protection.

2. Select **Company | Customer Credit Card Protection** to display the Enable QuickBooks Customer Credit Card Protection dialog box.

Continued . . .

Add Users

The first line of defense in data security is restricting access. QuickBooks allows you to add individual users, who are given as little or as much access to sensitive data as needed.

1. Choose **Company | Set Up Users And Passwords | Set Up Users** to open the User List dialog box.

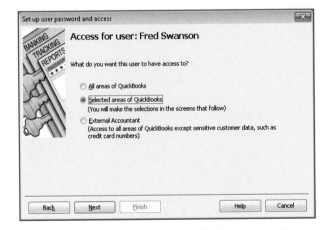

2. Click the **Add User** button to start the Set Up User Password And Access wizard.

3. Enter a user name, a password, and a password confirmation; and click **Next** to view the access options (see Figure 9-12). If you don't assign a password, QuickBooks reminds you that this is not recommended.

*Figure 9-12: **QuickBooks offers three basic access options.***

CONFIGURING CREDIT CARD PROTECTION *(Continued)*

3. Read the list of things enabling protection will do, and click the **Enable Protection** button to set up a complex password.

4. Enter a new password consisting of no fewer than seven characters, with a combination of uppercase letters, lowercase letters, and numbers.

5. Select a challenge question and enter the answer so you can reset your password in the event you forget it.

6. Click **OK** to save the password. QuickBooks displays a dialog recommending steps to take to maintain good credit card data protection.

7. Click **OK** to close the dialog box.

Make sure that only users who require access to customer credit card information have permission to access it. In addition, have those users with access to customer credit card information create complex passwords, and change them every few months.

4. Select the appropriate access option for this user:

- **All Areas Of QuickBooks**   This option gives the user unlimited access to everything you store in QuickBooks, and should be assigned only to those trusted employees who require such access.

- **Selected Areas Of QuickBooks**   This is the most common access assigned. You can give different employees access to only those areas that they need.

- **External Accountant**   If you have an outside accountant or bookkeeper come in and work on your company file, you'll want to create an External Accountant user. This provides the user with access to everything except sensitive customer information.

5. Click **Next** to proceed.

If you selected All Areas Of QuickBooks or External Accountant, QuickBooks asks if you're sure you want to assign this user such expansive access. After that, you're done. Just click **Finish**.

If, however, you chose Selected Areas Of QuickBooks, you now have to let QuickBooks know exactly which areas, if any, you want to make available to the user. The screens are self-explanatory. Read each screen, make your choice(s), and click **Next** until you reach the final screen, and then click **Finish**.

How to...

- *Understanding QuickBooks Preferences*
- *Using Multiple Currencies*
- *Setting E-mail Defaults*
- *Configuring Web Mail*
- • *Perform Basic Customization*
- • *Use Additional Customization*
- *Understanding Form Elements*
- • *Customize Templates*
- *Using Form Actions*

Chapter 10
Customizing QuickBooks

QuickBooks installed out of the box is configured to operate the way the Intuit programmers think the average user works. Since there's probably no such thing as the "average" user, you'll be glad to know that you can do a lot to change the way QuickBooks works so that it works your way. In this chapter we'll cover the various options you have for customizing QuickBooks and making it more user-friendly for you.

Add the Favorites Menu

The Favorites menu comes in handy for performing routine tasks in QuickBooks. As you might expect, it functions somewhat like the Favorites menu in your web browser. However, instead of holding bookmarks to your favorite websites, it holds your favorite (most frequently used) menu commands.

1. The Favorites menu should appear automatically on your menu bar. However, if you don't see it, select **View I Favorites Menu** to add it to the menu bar.

QUICKFACTS

UNDERSTANDING QUICKBOOKS PREFERENCES

Probably the most important customization tool in QuickBooks is the Preferences dialog box, which contains configuration options for 23 different areas of QuickBooks. The options included range from turning on account numbering, to setting colors for the QuickBooks Desktop, to tracking multiple currencies, and a whole lot more.

The Preferences dialog box, shown in Figure 10-1, can be accessed by selecting **Edit | Preferences** from the menu bar. As you can see, it contains 23 icons on the left, as well as two tabs: My Preferences and Company Preferences on the right.

Before you start changing any settings, it's important to understand the difference between the two tabs on the right.

- **My Preferences** Any options found on the My Preferences tab apply only to the user who is logged on at the time the settings are configured. If you have three users accessing QuickBooks on the same computer but logging on individually, they can all have their own custom settings on the My Preferences tab. For example, one user could set the Desktop View options so that QuickBooks appeared using the Desert Isle color scheme, while another user could select Rose Ribbon, and the third Sky Blue. As each user logs on, the color scheme would switch to the one set by the user in the My Preferences tab of the Desktop View preferences.

- **Company Preferences** Company Preferences, on the other hand, are not individual preferences, but preferences that apply to the company file, regardless of who's logged on. In addition,

Continued . . .

2. Select **Favorites | Customize Favorites** to open the Customize Your Menus dialog box shown in Figure 10-2. The left pane contains all available menu commands, while the right pane displays those selected to appear on the Favorites menu.

3. Select a command in the **Available Menu Items** column, and click the **Add** button to include it on the Favorites menu.

4. To remove an item from the Favorites menu, select it in the **Chosen Menu Items** column and click the **Remove** button.

5. Use the **Move Up** and **Move Down** buttons to reposition menu items on the Favorites menu.

6. When you're done, click **OK** to save the menu changes and close the dialog box.

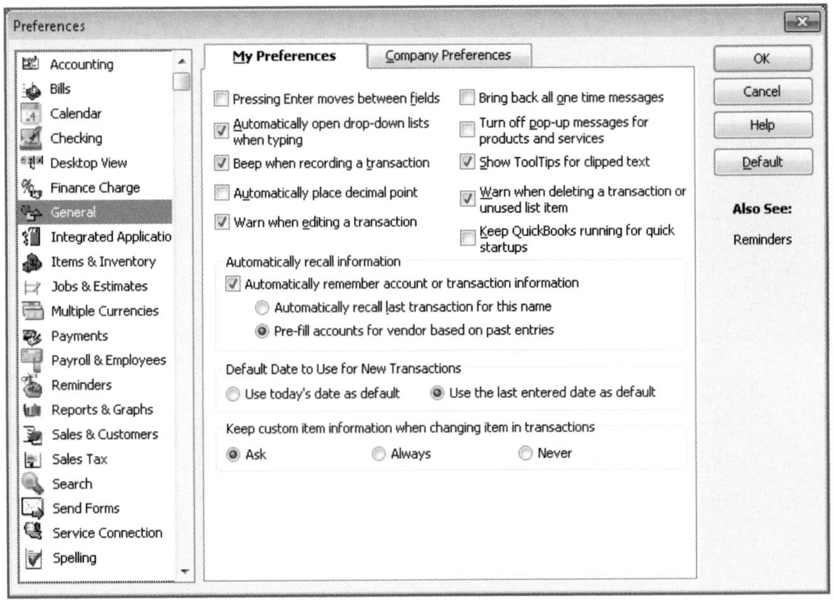

Figure 10-1: QuickBooks offers a lot of options that put you in control.

QUICK**FACTS**

UNDERSTANDING QUICKBOOKS PREFERENCES *(Continued)*

only the QuickBooks administrator can change Company Preferences. Once an option is set on the Company Preferences tab, all users will have to work with that option. For example, if the QuickBooks administrator checks the Always Show Years As 4 Digits (1999) option on the Company Preferences tab of the General Preferences area, every user who logs into QuickBooks will see the year displayed with all four digits.

Since most of the preferences are covered in the chapters on those features associated with the preferences, there's no need to go over them here. Review each chapter for details on setting the necessary options.

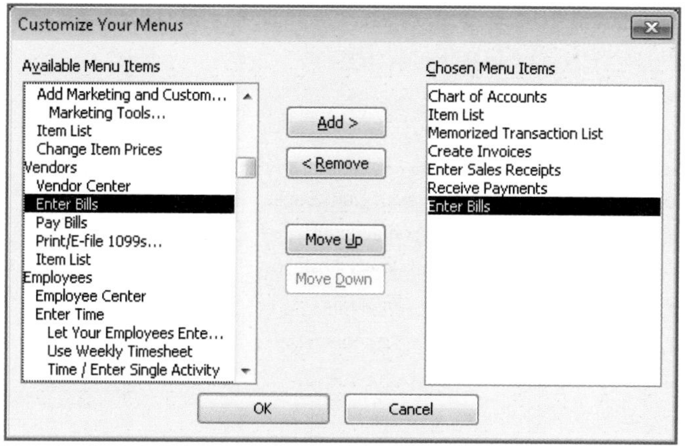

Figure 10-2: Create your own customized menu.

Use the Favorites menu as you would any other menu. Open the menu and select the desired command to activate the feature associated with it. As you can see in Figure 10-3, you can even add entire menus and submenus to the Favorites menu.

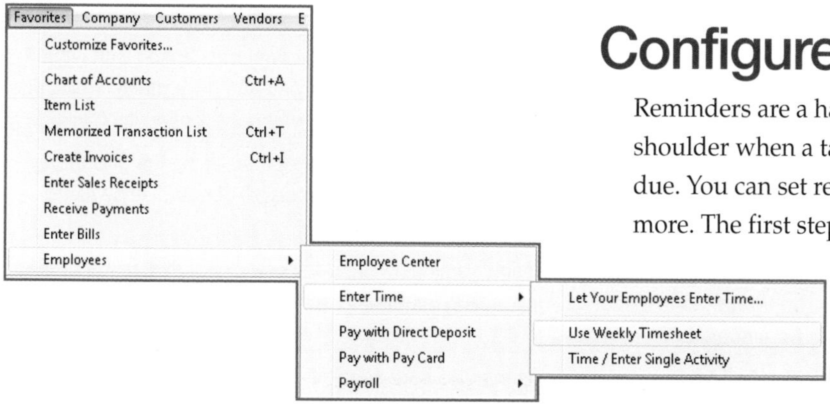

Figure 10-3: You can add individual commands or entire menus of commands.

Configure Reminders

Reminders are a handy QuickBooks feature that you can use to tap you on the shoulder when a task or transaction that is scheduled to be executed comes due. You can set reminders for items to print, bills to pay, money to deposit, and more. The first step in using reminders is to set the preferences for them.

1. Select **Edit | Preferences** to open the Preferences dialog box.

2. Choose the **Reminders** icon in the left pane, click the **My Preferences** tab, and check the **Show Reminders List When Opening A Company File** option to ensure that you see the list of reminders each time you open your company file.

QUICKSTEPS

USING MULTIPLE CURRENCIES

If you happen to conduct business in currencies other than the U.S. dollar, you'll be glad to know that QuickBooks is capable of handling multiple currencies. To turn the feature on, open the Preferences dialog box (**Edit | Preferences**), select the **Multiple Currencies** icon, and choose the **Yes, I Use More Than One Currency** option on the Company Preferences tab. Then make the appropriate selection from the **Select The Home Currency You Use In Transactions** drop-down list.

After you enable multiple currencies tracking, the Currency List is created (**Lists | Currency List**) and six new commands are added to the Company | Manage Currency menu:

- **Download Latest Exchange Rates**   If you open the Currency List, you'll see that it contains a listing of the world's major currencies. Initially, most are inactive. You can activate the currencies you use by removing the X in the Active Status column of the Currency List. Once you've activated the currencies you use, select **Company | Manage Currency | Download Latest Exchange Rates** to connect to the Internet and download the current exchange rates for the active currencies.

- **Currency Calculator**   This command launches a Currency Calculator that enables you to perform calculations using the foreign currency exchange rate to calculate totals in either your home currency or the foreign currency.

- **Home Currency Adjustment** · If you need to make adjustments to currency values for reporting purposes, use this command to open the Home Currency Adjustment dialog box. Keep in mind that

Continued . . .

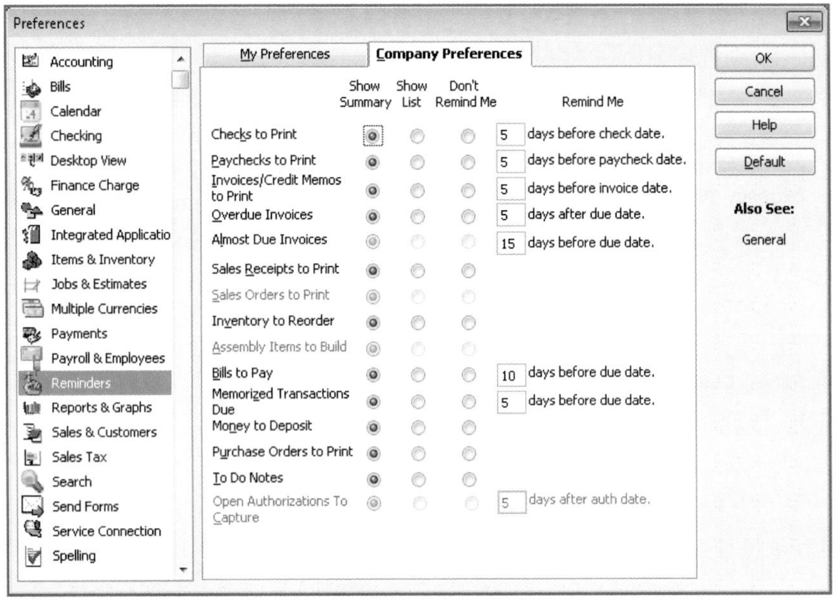

Figure 10-4: Fine-tuning QuickBooks reminders is easy.

3. Click the **Company Preferences** tab, and set the options for how and when the reminders appear (see Figure 10-4):

- **Show Summary**   Check this option to display only a brief description with limited details. For example, if you set a reminder for bills to pay and have multiple bills due at the same time, only the total amount due displays when this option is checked.

- **Show List**   When you want more details, check this option. Using the bills to pay example, checking the Show List option will cause each bill due to display along with the amount due.

- **Don't Remind Me**   If you enable reminders but don't use or need all features that generate them, select this option to eliminate the activity from appearing on the Reminders List.

- **Remind Me**   For those items that are date-sensitive, you can use this option to tell QuickBooks how far in advance to alert you to the fact that an activity is due.

4. Click **OK** to save the changes and close the Preferences dialog.

Once reminders options are set, items will appear on the Reminders List as dictated by the choices you made when setting these options.

(Continued)

currencies do fluctuate. Therefore, it is important to ensure your reports are accurate by keeping currency rates up to date.

- **Currency List**   Select this command to display the Currency List that contains most of the world currencies. You can add, modify, and delete currencies, as well as update their exchange rates.

- **Learn About Multicurrency**   To display the QuickBooks help file overview of the multicurrency feature, click this command.

- **Multicurrency Resource Center**   Use this online resource to learn more about doing business on a global scale.

Once you've enabled multiple currencies, you'll find that the total fields on transaction forms display the three-letter code for your home currency. In addition, they include an Exchange Rate field.

NOTE

Multiple currencies can be activated only by the QuickBooks administrator. Also, keep in mind that once you turn multiple currencies tracking on, you cannot turn it off. Therefore, be sure to make a backup of your company file before turning the feature on.

Set Spell-Checking Options

Nothing undermines your professionalism like spelling errors in your printed or e-mailed transaction forms. To help eliminate them, QuickBooks has a built-in spell-checker that you can either use manually or set to check forms automatically. To manually check the spelling in transaction forms, simply click the **Spelling** button found in invoices, sales receipts, estimates, purchase orders, and credit memos. If you want QuickBooks to automatically check your forms, you must turn the feature on.

1. Select **Edit | Preferences** to open the Preferences dialog box.

2. Click the **Spelling** icon in the left pane, and then click the **My Preferences** tab in the right pane to display the spell-checker options.

3. Check the **Always Check Spelling Before Printing, Saving, Or Sending Supported Forms** option to turn on the auto-spell-check feature.

SETTING E-MAIL DEFAULTS

If you send your forms using e-mail, you'll probably want to customize the way the accompanying e-mail message is configured and sent.

1. Select **Edit | Preferences** to open the Preferences dialog, choose the **Send Forms** icon, and select the **My Preferences** tab.

2. Check the **Auto-check The "To Be E-mailed" Checkbox If Customer's Preferred Send Method Is E-mail** option. If a customer's default send method is set for e-mail, this setting automatically checks the To Be E-mailed option on transaction forms for the customer so you don't have to remember each time.

3. Select your preferred method for sending e-mail. You can either use Outlook if it's installed; a web mail account such as Gmail, Hotmail, or Yahoo!; or QuickBooks E-mail if you have an active subscription. See the "Configuring Web Mail" QuickSteps for details on setting up your web mail account to work with QuickBooks.

4. Click the **Company Preferences** tab to customize the e-mail message that accompanies each form.

5. Start by choosing the form to customize from the **Change Default For** drop-down list.

6. If you want to modify the salutation, make the appropriate selections from the next two drop-down lists for title and name.

7. If you want to send a blind copy to anyone, include the e-mail address in the Bcc field. Bcc addresses are not visible to the original recipient or to anyone copied (Cc) on the e-mail. In other words, the original recipients will be unaware that this person also received a copy.

Continued . . .

4. Tell QuickBooks which type of words the spell-checker should not bother to check. For example, Internet URLs frequently contain proper names, partial names, unusual spellings, and so on. This being the case, it would not be very effective to have the spell-checker bring it to your attention each time it encountered a "misspelled" URL.

5. Click **OK** to save your settings and close the Preferences dialog.

If you enable auto-spell-checking, QuickBooks will scan each supported form before you save it, print it, or send it. If it encounters any spelling errors in the description, memo, notes, or message fields, it displays the Check Spelling On Form dialog.

When it encounters an error, the spell-checker searches its database for a possible correction:

- If it finds the right one, select it from the **Suggestions** box, and click **Replace**.
- If you know this error is repeated in the form, select **Replace All** to take care of all the errors in one fell swoop.
- If the error really isn't an error, click the **Ignore** or the **Ignore All** button to let the spell-checker know the word is okay as-is.
- If the word is spelled correctly (or the way you want it to be), click **Add** to enter it in the spell-checker database so it doesn't flag it again in the future.
- If you want to change any of the options, click the **Options** button to display the same settings found in the Preferences dialog.

8. You can change the text that appears in the Subject field. Try to make the subject as concise and clear as possible. If the recipient does not immediately recognize that this is an important piece of e-mail, it may end up in the trash or the junk folder.

9. The message body is yours to fill in as you want.

10. If you want to spell-check the message body and subject line, click the **Spelling** button.

11. Click **OK** to save the changes and close the Preferences dialog box.

Now, whenever you send a form of the type just customized, it will contain all the changes made here.

QUICKSTEPS

CONFIGURING WEB MAIL

A handy QuickBooks feature is the ability to use web mail accounts to e-mail QuickBooks forms such as invoices, statements, and others. If you decide to use your Hotmail, Gmail, or Yahoo! account, you'll first have to set it up.

1. Select **Edit I Preferences** from the menu bar to open the Preferences dialog box.

2. In the left pane choose the **Send Forms** icon, and then click the **My Preferences** tab.

3. Select **Web Mail** in the Send E-mail Using option.

4. Next, click the **Add** button to display the Add Email Info dialog box.

Continued . . .

Customize Templates

While QuickBooks provides a basic group of transaction forms to use, you may find that it does not include exactly the right form for your needs. When this happens, don't panic—customize!

That's right; you can make small changes to original templates, or make a copy of any existing form and tweak it until it suits your needs. If the template has Intuit in the name (i.e., Intuit Product Invoice), you can only make minor changes without first creating a copy. Other templates without Intuit in the name (i.e., Custom Credit Memo) can be modified extensively. However, it's not a bad idea to make a copy of any template you plan to change significantly. That way, if you decide you don't like your changes, you can always revert to the original.

Perform Basic Customization

To ensure that you don't change a QuickBooks template beyond recognition, only small changes are allowed to the original templates with Intuit in the name (i.e., Intuit Product Invoice).

1. Select **Lists I Templates** from the menu bar to open the Templates window.

Name	Type
Attorney's Invoice	Invoice
Fixed Fee Invoice	Invoice
Intuit Packing Slip	Invoice
Intuit Product Invoice	Invoice
Intuit Professional Invoice	Invoice
Intuit Service Invoice	Invoice
Invoice from Proposal	Invoice
Time & Expense Invoice	Invoice
Custom Credit Memo	Credit Memo
Return Receipt	Credit Memo
Custom Sales Receipt	Sales Receipt
Daily Sales Summary	Sales Receipt

10

UICKSTEPS

CONFIGURING WEB MAIL *(Continued)*

5. Enter your web mail ID (usually your e-mail address) in the Email Id field.

6. From the Email Provider drop-down list, select the type of web mail account you use.

7. If you selected one of the named providers, the Simple Mail Transfer Protocol (SMTP) information is automatically entered and you can click **OK** to close the dialog box. However, if you selected Others, you must fill in the SMTP information yourself before clicking OK.

If you find that you have to modify any of the information for an account, highlight it in the table and click the **Edit** button.

Add Email Info

Email Id: wodeconstruction@hotmail.com

Email Provider: Hotmail/Live

SMTP Server Details
These default settings are usually correct. However, if you need to edit these settings click OK and click Edit in the next window.

Server Name: smtp.live.com

Port: 587

☑ SSL

OK   Cancel

NOTE

QuickBooks also offers the ability to create a "New" template by opening the Templates List (**Lists | Templates**), right-clicking anywhere, and selecting **New** from the shortcut menu. In reality you're not creating a new template, but rather customizing a copy of a basic template of the type you choose.

NOTE

The logo appears on printed forms and in previews, but does not appear in the on-screen transaction forms you fill out in QuickBooks.

2. Double-click the template you want to customize to display the Basic Customization dialog shown in Figure 10-5.

3. To add your logo to the form, check the **Use Logo** option and select your logo image file. When you return to the Basic Customization dialog, you'll see that the Select Logo button is now enabled so you can change the image.

4. To change the color used on the form, choose a new color from the **Select Color Scheme** drop-down list, and click the **Apply Color Scheme** button to review the change.

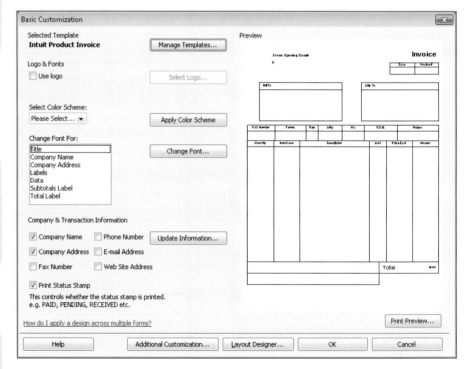

Figure 10-5: The left pane contains template options, and the right pane shows the effects of your choices.

Example

Font:
Arial

Font Style:
Bold

Size:
21

OK

Arial
Arial Rounded MT
Baskerville Old Face

Bold
Bold Italic
Black
Black Oblique

8
9
10
11

Cancel

Help

Effects
☐ Strikeout
☐ Underline

Sample

AaBbYyZz

Color:
Black

This is an OpenType font. This same font will be
used on both your printer and your screen.

5. If you want to use a different font for any part of the template, choose the section in the **Change Font For** column, and click the **Change Font** button to display the font dialog box (it's called Example for some reason).

6. To include or exclude company or transaction information, check the appropriate boxes in the **Company & Transaction Information** section.

7. If you realize that you want to make a change to your company information profile, click the **Update Information** button to open the Company Information dialog box.

8. If you want the status stamp (PENDING, RECEIVED, PAID, and so on) to appear on the printed form, check the **Print Status Stamp** option.

9. Click **OK** to save the changes and close the Basic Customization dialog box.

That's the extent of the customization you can do on the Intuit forms. Fortunately, there's a lot more you can do when you use the Additional Customization feature.

Use Additional Customization

If you need to make more changes to a template than the Basic Customization feature allows, the answer is simple. Use the Additional Customization feature. If you are modifying an Intuit template (it has "Intuit" in the template name), you must first make a copy of the template to work on. Otherwise, you can go straight to the Additional Customization window.

1. Open the Templates List (**List | Templates**), and double-click the template you want to modify.

2. Click the **Additional Customization** button located at the bottom of the window. If the template is a non-Intuit template, the Additional Customization window shown in Figure 10-6 displays. If the template is an Intuit template, the Locked Template dialog appears, informing you that you must first make a copy. Click the **Make A Copy** button to do so.

3. As you can see in Figure 10-6, the Additional Customization window contains five tabs (if progress invoicing is turned off, only four tabs will be present). Select a tab to configure the related options:

- **Header** The header of the form is everything above the body (actual transaction information). In the case of the Intuit Product Invoice shown in Figure 10-6, the header includes the row of fields starting with the P.O. Number and everything above that row.

TIP

To change the name of the template, or to make a copy of a non-Intuit (or Intuit) template, click the **Manage Templates** button in the Basic Customization window to open the Manage Templates dialog. The right pane contains the Template Name field, which you can change to suit your needs. To create a copy, click the **Copy** button. Intuit also provides an online forms collection, which you can access by clicking the **Download Templates** button at the bottom of the window.

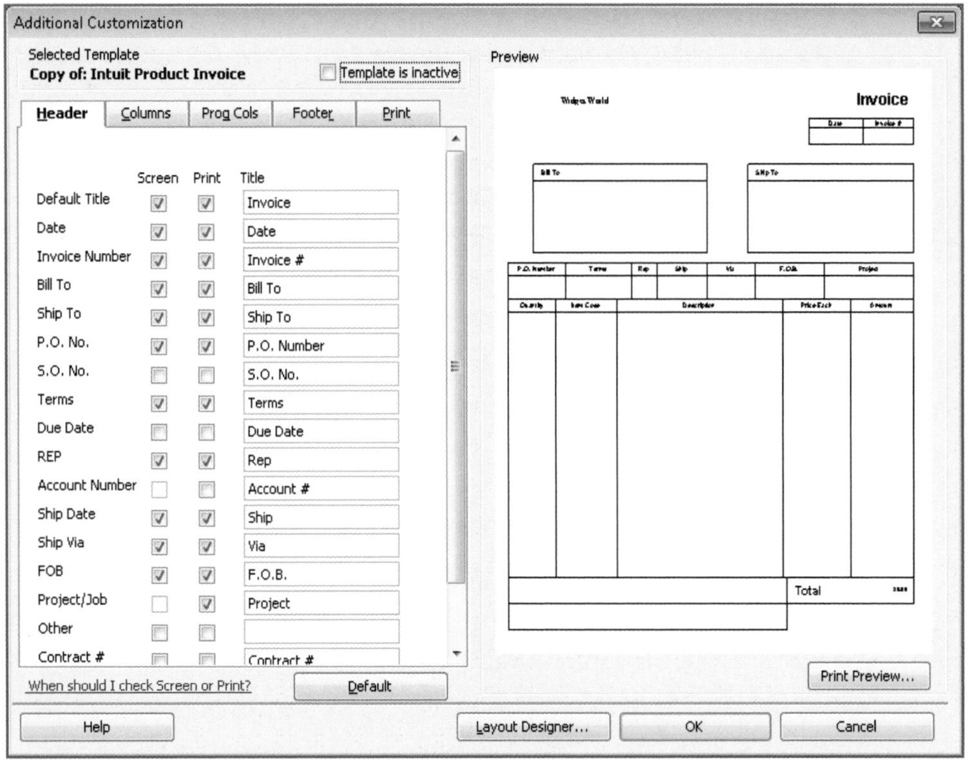

Figure 10-6: Additional Customization offers extensive options for fine-tuning your forms.

NOTE

When you change the Screen status of a field, it does not show in the Preview pane image. Changing the Print status, however, is reflected in the Preview pane. One more thing: as you change either the Screen or Print status, QuickBooks may display a dialog box informing you that you can use the Layout Designer (covered in the next section) to reposition fields overlapping due to the status change.

- **Columns** These are the columns (fields) that contain the transaction details such as item, quantity, price, and so on.

- **Prog Cols** If you've enabled progress invoicing (**Edit I Preferences I Jobs & Estimates I Company Preferences**), the Prog Cols tab appears, enabling you to select estimate columns to display in the transaction form.

- **Footer** The footer includes the subtotals, taxes, totals, messages, and other such items.

- **Print** Here you can set basic printing options. You can opt to use the default settings for this type of template, or create custom settings for this specific template.

4. Set the appropriate options on the Header, Columns, Prog Cols, and Footer tabs:

- **Field** The actual QuickBooks field name appears on the left. You cannot change the field name.

- **Screen** Check this box to make the field appear when you view the form on-screen. This is very handy for fields that you want to see and use for internal use but don't want included on the printed form.

- **Print** When the box in the Print column is checked, it means the field will appear on printed versions of the form. Make sure that only those fields you want visible to customers and others who may see the form (warehouse personnel, for example) are checked.

- **Order** In the Columns and Prog Cols tabs, you'll find another option you can set: Order. This enables you to assign a number to each column indicating its position on the form from left to right. For example, the column with order #1 is the first column on the left, followed by #2, and so on.

- **Title** While you cannot change the field name, you can change the title for it that appears on the form. Edit the Title field to reflect your own company terminology.

10

TIP

A quick way to customize forms is to use the Additional Customizations window first and then fine-tune your changes using the Layout Designer. As a matter of fact, the only way you can add or remove fields (columns) from the body of the template is to do so in the Columns tab of the Additional Customization window.

QUICK**FACTS**

UNDERSTANDING FORM ELEMENTS

A grasp of the underlying fundamentals will go a long way in helping you harness the power of the Layout Designer:

- **Form elements**   Everything you see on a QuickBooks template is an individual object. For example, the form title is a special type of text box called a label field. Fields that hold QuickBooks data, such as the Invoice # field, are actually two objects: a data field that holds the QuickBooks information, and a label field that holds the field title. The Layout Designer utilizes three field types:

  - **Data field**   To incorporate information that QuickBooks stores in its database, you use a data field. Customer name information, item descriptions, quantities, and prices are all examples of data fields.

  - **Text box**   The Layout Designer utilizes two types of text box fields: a regular text box and a label field text box. You can add a regular text box anywhere you want. A label field is created automatically when you add a data field. The only real difference between a text box and a label field (aside from the way they're created) is that the text box can hold multiple lines of text while the label field is limited to a single line.

Continued . . .

5. Click the **Print** tab to modify the print settings for this form. If you don't want to create custom print settings for this template, leave the **Use** *<form type>* **Printer Settings From Printer Setup** option selected. To create special print settings for this form only, select the **Use Specified Printer Settings Below For This <form type>** option. The custom settings are self-explanatory.

6. If at any time you change your mind about the changes you've made so far, click the **Default** button to return the form to its original state.

7. If you want a larger preview of the form, click the **Print Preview** button to see how the printed version will appear.

8. When you're satisfied with the changes, click **OK** to save the new template and close the Additional Customization window.

When you want to use the form, simply select it from the **Template** drop-down list in the appropriate transaction form window.

Use the Layout Designer

The Layout Designer is a powerful design tool that lets you take an existing template and add, remove, reposition, and resize fields to make your transaction forms look and act the way you want them to. While not everyone will need (or want) to create highly customized templates, many users who make minor changes in the Additional Customization window will find it necessary to adjust overlapping fields resulting from those changes. The only way to accomplish this is by using the Layout Designer.

Customize Templates

Now that you have the Layout Designer basics under your belt, you should take it out for a spin. A little practice will go a long way in familiarizing yourself with how the Layout Designer operates. For this exercise we'll use a copy of the Intuit Product Invoice.

1. Open the Templates List, right-click, and select **New** from the shortcut menu.

2. Select **Invoice** from the Select Template Type dialog box, and click **OK** to open the form in the Basic Customization window.

QUICKFACTS

UNDERSTANDING FORM ELEMENTS

(Continued)

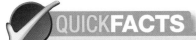

- **Image field** This field type is used primarily to hold your company logo image. However, you can add any graphic image you choose by placing an image field in the appropriate place.
- **Property dialogs** All objects on the template form have certain properties that define their appearance. The text box and data field have a large number of properties, which can be changed to suit your needs, while the image field is limited to selecting another image to replace it. The text box and data field properties include options for changing the text, adding or removing borders, and including a background fill color. Double-clicking an object opens its Properties dialog.
- **Form settings** There are a couple of basic settings that enable you to modify the form page itself. At the bottom of the Layout Designer window you'll find a Margins button and a Grid button. Click the Margins button to change the position of the margins, which are depicted on the form as a dotted rectangle representing the useable outer limits of the form. The Grid button allows you to change the size of the grid (the dotted background), as well as the snap settings, which help align objects automatically.

3. Click the **Manage Templates** button, and rename the template Custom Invoice Template. Click **OK** to save the name and return to the Basic Customization window.
4. Click the **Additional Customization** button to display the Additional Customization window.
5. Click the **Columns** tab, and check the **Print** box for the Item field. Don't worry if you get a warning that you may have overlapping fields.
6. Click the **Layout Designer** button to open the template in the Layout Designer as shown in Figure 10-7.

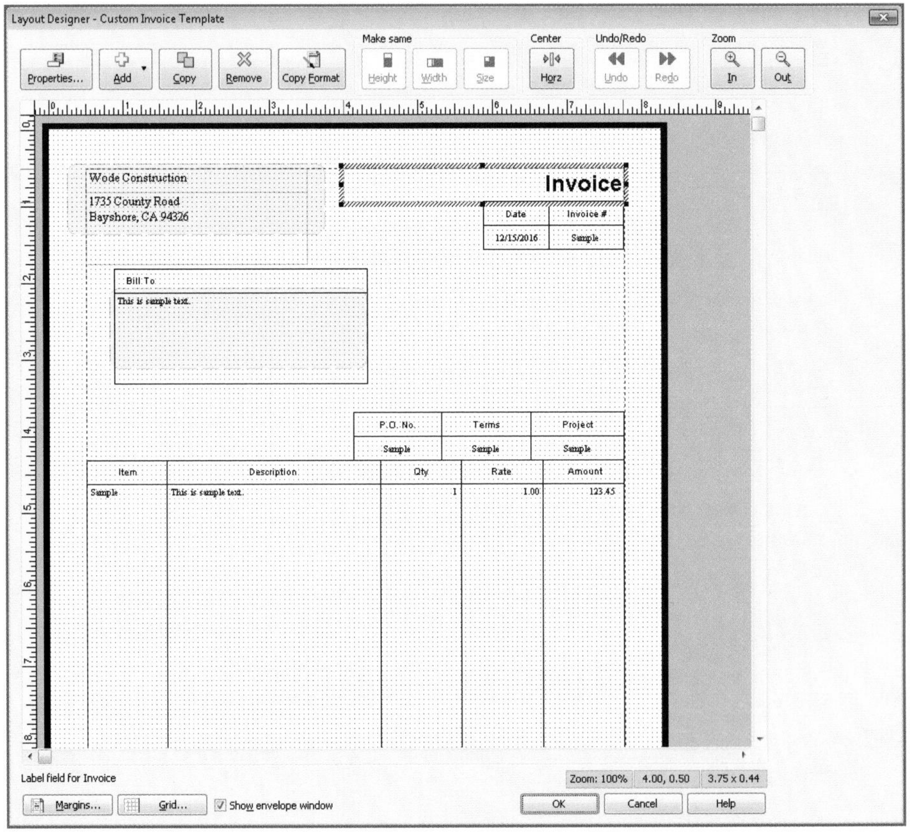

Figure 10-7: The Layout Designer offers a lot of tools for customizing templates.

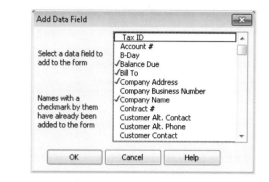

UICKSTEPS

USING FORM ACTIONS

To use the Layout Designer effectively, it's important to understand how basic actions such as selecting and moving objects are achieved:

- **Selecting objects** There are several ways to select objects on the form. The first is to simply click a single object to select it. To select multiple objects, you can use your mouse cursor to draw a rectangle around the objects you want to select. When using this method, you must surround almost the entire field to include it in the group. The second method for multiple selections is to hold down the **SHIFT** key and click each object you want included.

- **Moving objects** Objects can be moved all over the form by selecting them first and then using the mouse to drag them to a new location. You can also move objects incrementally by selecting them and using the arrow keys on your keyboard.

- **Opening Properties dialogs** You can open an object's Properties dialog by double-clicking the object, or by right-clicking the object and selecting **Properties** from the shortcut menu that appears.

- **Resizing objects** If you need a field to hold more (or less) information, you can change its size. Simply grab one of the sizing handles (the solid black squares on the field edges that appear when you select the object) and drag it right, left, up, or down as required. You can also make objects match the height, width, or both by selecting both objects (the first object selected is modified to match the last object selected) and clicking the **Height**, **Width**, or **Size** button.

7. Click the **Add** button on the toolbar, and select **Data Field** to open the Add Data Field dialog box.

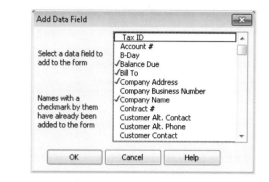

8. Scroll down and double-click **Rep** to add the Rep field to the template. As you can see, the new field is dropped in the middle of the template.

9. Place your cursor in the middle of either of the two fields (remember, data fields consist of the data field and a label field), and drag the fields to the left of the P.O. No. field. If need be, use the arrow keys to get the fields in position.

10. Double-click the **Bill To** label field (the one that says "Bill To") to open the Properties dialog box.

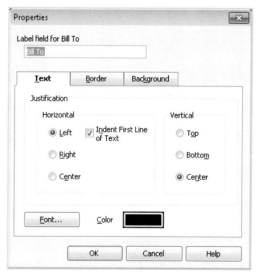

11. Click the **Font** button, and increase the font size to **10**. Click **OK** to close the Example dialog box.

12. Click the **Border** tab, and change the thickness to **2 pt**.

13. Click the **Background** tab, and check the **Fill Background** box. Then click the **Background Color** box and choose a light color for the background fill.

14. Click **OK** until the Properties dialog is closed.

15. Now, hold down the SHIFT key and click the **Rep** label field, then the **Rep** data field, and finally the **P.O. No.** label field.

16. Now click the **Width** button on the toolbar to make the first two fields match the width of the third. You'll notice that the Rep label and data fields now overlap the P.O. No. field.

17. Click anywhere on the template to deselect the three fields currently selected.

18. Select the **Rep** label field and the **Rep** data field, and use the arrow keys to move them to the left.

19. Spend a few minutes familiarizing yourself with the various commands. Create and delete objects, move them around, change their properties, and, above all, don't worry about the template. It's only a test form that can be safely deleted when you're finished.

When you're done experimenting, click **OK** to save the changes and return to the Basic Customization window. Click the **Print Preview** button to see how the form looks with all its changes. When you're all done, you can keep the form or return to the Templates List and delete it.

How to...

- ✒ *Preparing for a Budget*
- *Set Up Budgets Window Basics*
- *Handy Set Up Budgets Window Tools*
- ⚙ *Creating Profit and Loss Budgets with Additional Criteria*
- *Budget Overview Report*
- ⚙ *Exporting Your Budgets*
- ⚙ *Importing Budgets into QuickBooks*

Appendix
Budgeting and Planning

It's hard to meet your objectives unless you know what they are, which is where budgeting comes in. Whether it's monitoring costs, anticipating sales, or making sure you keep enough cash on hand to meet your obligations, budgets are, or should be, an integral part of your business. Fortunately, QuickBooks offers a powerful budget creation tool, along with a number of budget reports, that will allow you to construct useful budgets and stick to them.

Understand QuickBooks Budgets

QuickBooks offers two basic types of budgets, one with a couple of variations, and one without:

- **Profit And Loss** The more useful of the two, and the one with the variations, the Profit And Loss budget uses your income and expense accounts. You can create Profit And Loss budgets based on accounts for specific customers and jobs as well as for classes.

QUICK**FACTS**

PREPARING FOR A BUDGET

It's a lot easier to create a budget if you don't have to stop in the middle and add new accounts or activate inactive accounts (or deactivate active accounts). Therefore, before you jump into creating a budget, you should take care of the following:

- **Add new accounts**   Since the budget tool does not refresh itself unless you close and reopen it, new accounts created during the process do not appear in the budget tool. Adding new accounts before you start the budgeting process will save you the trouble of having to restart the budget tool to see them.

- **Activate (or deactivate) existing accounts**   The budget tool displays only those accounts marked "Active." Therefore, make sure that any currently inactive accounts that you want to use in the budget are marked "Active" and any active accounts you want to exclude are marked "Inactive."

- **First month**   The budget tool uses the first month of your fiscal year as its starting month. Therefore, you should make sure that you've set the correct first month of your fiscal year in the Company Information dialog box (**Company | Company Information**).

- **Balance Sheet**   You've probably already guessed that this one uses your balance sheet accounts (assets, liabilities, and equity). However, since it's hard to forecast and control those amounts, the Balance Sheet budget has limited uses.

With the Profit And Loss budget you have the choice of creating the budget either by entering all the data manually or by basing it on data from the previous year.

As good as the budget tool is, it's not perfect. While it helps you to create detailed budgets, it only allows you to create one budget of each type for each year. For example, if you want to create a Profit And Loss budget by accounts only (no customer, job, or class links) for next year, that's the only one you get for next year. You can modify it or create the same type for the year after, but you cannot create a second Profit And Loss budget by accounts only for next year. Therefore, if you want to try a few "what if?" scenarios, you're out of luck (well, not really, because you can export it to Microsoft Excel and manipulate it there).

The same goes for Balance Sheet budgets and Profit And Loss budgets by customer, job, or class. Fortunately, you can create one budget per year for each customer, job, or class.

Build a Profit And Loss Budget

Regardless of what budget type you want to create, the basic steps are similar. Since the Profit And Loss budget is the more complex of the two (it offers more options), let's use a Profit And Loss budget as our example.

1. From the menu bar, select **Company | Planning & Budgeting | Set Up Budgets** to open the Create New Budget wizard (if this is your first budget) or the last

used budget. If an existing budget opens, click the **Create New Budget** button to launch the wizard.

2. Enter the year for the budget.

3. Choose the **Profit And Loss** option, and click **Next** to proceed to the Additional Profit And Loss Budget Criteria screen.

4. Select the additional criteria for your Profit And Loss budget. We're going to select **No Additional Criteria** to keep it simple. Later sections in this appendix will cover the other options:

- **No Additional Criteria**   If you want to see a Profit And Loss budget with accounts only (no customer, job, or class link), this is the choice for you.

- **Customer:Job**   Choose this option if you want to see the income and expense accounts for a particular customer or job.

- **Class**   To create a budget with income and expense accounts linked to a specific class, select this option.

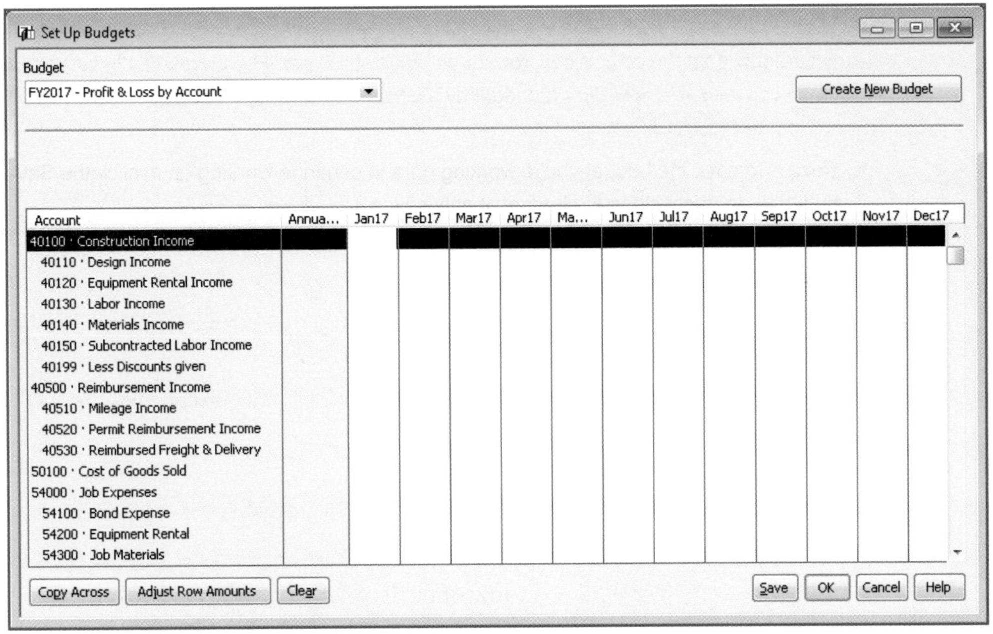

Figure A-1: *The Profit And Loss budget contains all your income and expense accounts.*

5. Click **Next** and decide how you want to create the budget. For those of you just starting out with QuickBooks (and, therefore, with no previous year's data), we're going to select Create Budget From Scratch:

- **Create Budget From Scratch** Select this method if you want to enter the numbers manually for each account.

- **Create Budget From Previous Year's Actual Data** If you have data from last year in QuickBooks, you can use this method to populate the income and expense fields with that data. It saves a lot of time and work, but be sure the numbers are good before using them.

6. Click **Finish** to open a blank Set Up Budgets window, as shown in Figure A-1.

7. Enter amounts in each column for each account you plan to budget for.

Set Up Budgets Window Basics

As you can see in Figure A-1, the Set Up Budgets window contains one field and a number of buttons, along with the account rows and columns. A quick overview of the basic window elements will make creating this or any other budget much easier:

- **Budget** If you've created multiple budgets, use this drop-down list to select the existing budget you want to view or edit.

- **Create New Budget** After you create your first budget, the budget tool opens with the last budget you worked on. If you don't want to work on any of your existing budgets, click this button to launch the Create New Budget wizard.

- **Account Listing** This one's pretty self-explanatory. All your accounts are listed in the rows and the months of the budget year in the columns. Enter your numbers in the appropriate cells to create your budget.

- **Clear** Don't get confused about this button. It clears the entire worksheet. If you think you're only going to clear a cell, row, or column with it, you'll be unpleasantly surprised when you click it. If you clear a budget by mistake, click the **Cancel** button to exit without saving your changes.

- **Save** To save the budget you're working on and continue working on it, click the **Save** button. It does not close the budget; it only saves it.

- **OK** If you're done working on the current budget, click **OK** to save it and close the budget tool.

- **Cancel** Clicking the **Cancel** button closes the Set Up Budgets window without saving any changes (and without asking) made since the last save.

- **Help** When in doubt, click the **Help** button. Unfortunately, the help available for budgets is a bit thin.

Handy Set Up Budgets Window Tools

In addition to the normal fields and buttons you need to open, save, and clear budgets, the Set Up Budgets window offers two timesaving features that will make your budgeting life a lot more pleasant once you get the hang of them.

The first is the Copy Across button located in the lower-left corner of the window. It's well named, because that's what it does—copies data across a row. If you're projecting income of $5,000 a month for the year, you could start in the first month and enter 5000, press TAB to move to the second month and enter 5000 again, and so on for all 12 months; or you could use the Copy Across button. Enter the first amount and then click the **Copy Across** button to let QuickBooks do the work for you. One click, and 5000 is entered into every cell to the right of the one you started in.

The next handy-dandy tool is the Adjust Row Amounts button. It lets you increase or decrease row amounts, either by a percentage or by a fixed amount. Place your cursor in the cell you want to begin with, and click the **Adjust Row Amounts** button to open the Adjust Row Amounts dialog box.

TIP

If you have a lot of accounts and therefore a lot of rows to fill, you might want to use a keyboard shortcut to activate the Copy Across feature instead of having to locate and click the Copy Across button each time. Just place your cursor in the starting cell and press **ALT+P**. You can then use the arrow keys to move through the accounts, adding and copying monthly amounts as you go.

CAUTION

If you have data in any cell to the right of the one you're starting in, it will be overwritten.

NOTE

The Adjust Row Amounts button does not copy data across; it only increments or decrements existing amounts. Therefore, if you use it on a row that only contains one amount, it will make the adjustment on that amount and leave the remaining cells at zero (if you use a percentage), or increment/decrement them with the amount of change only (if you use a dollar amount).

TIP

Since the Enable Compounding option is only available when you choose Currently Selected Month, you may be thinking that you can't use compounding for an entire year. If so, you'd be wrong. All you have to do is make sure your cursor is in the first month before clicking the **Adjust Row Amounts** button, and then select **Currently Selected Month** from the Start At drop-down list.

The Adjust Row Amounts dialog offers several different options. Keep in mind that where your cursor is in the budget when you click the Adjust Row Amounts button will have an effect on at least one of your options.

- **Start At** This tells QuickBooks which monthly amount cell to use as the starting point for the adjustment. You have two choices here: 1st Month or Currently Selected Month:

  - **1st Month** Choose this option to start the adjustment in the first monthly amount cell, regardless of where in the row your cursor was when you clicked the Adjust Row Amounts button. For example, if your first month is January and your cursor was in August, selecting this option automatically makes January the starting point for the adjustment.

  - **Currently Selected Month** This is just what you might think. Using the previous example, if your first month is January and your cursor was in August, selecting this option makes August the starting point for the adjustment.

- **Increase** The basic idea is obvious. You use this field to make a positive adjustment to the amount in each field, beginning with the starting month. You can enter either a dollar amount or a percentage. However, if you enter a percentage, you must remember to enter the % sign or QuickBooks interprets the number as a dollar amount. While you can enter a minus or plus sign before the number you enter, QuickBooks ignores it and increases the amount by the number or percentage entered.

- **Decrease** This one's identical to the previous option; it just decreases each monthly amount, starting with the Start At month.

- **Enable Compounding** This option only appears when you choose Currently Selected Month. Instead of simply adding (or subtracting) the dollar amount (or percentage) to each cell, this feature compounds it by a factor of one in each cell. In other words, if you tell it to increase the monthly amounts by $100 and enable compounding, it leaves the starting month untouched and adds $100 to the first month, $200 to the second month, $300 to the third, and so on. Take a look at Table A-1 for a more graphical display of the effects of compounding.

CURRENT MONTH ORIGINAL AMOUNT	INCREASE AMOUNT	COMPOUNDING	CURRENT MONTH NEW AMOUNT	NEXT MONTH	NEXT MONTH	NEXT MONTH
1,000.00	100.00	Enabled	1,000.00	1,100.00	1,200.00	1,300.00
1,000.00	100.00	Not Enabled	1,100.00	1,100.00	1,100.00	1,100.00

Table A-1: Compounding for Incremental Adjustments Up or Down

QUICKSTEPS

CREATING PROFIT AND LOSS BUDGETS WITH ADDITIONAL CRITERIA

Perhaps you've got a big job coming up for a customer and want to plan ahead and make sure the project stays on budget. Or maybe you're tracking your different locations by class and want to set different profit targets for each one. Whatever the reason, there's an easy way to tackle the problem: create a Profit And Loss budget using the additional criteria options.

1. Select **Company | Planning & Budgeting | Set Up Budgets** to start the Create New Budget wizard.

2. If you've already created a budget, the Set Up Budgets window opens with the last used budget displayed. Just click the **Create New Budget** button in the upper-right corner to launch the wizard.

3. Set the year for the new budget.

4. Choose **Profit And Loss (Reflects All Activity For The Year)**, and click **Next** to view the additional criteria screen.

5. Depending on your needs, select either **Customer:Job** to create a budget based on the income and expense accounts tied to a particular customer, or **Class** to generate a budget based on accounts linked to a specific class. For this example we're going to choose **Customer:Job**.

6. Click **Next** to view the creation method options.

Continued . . .

Even though I mentioned it in the earlier description of compounding, it bears repeating. Without compounding enabled, adjustments are made beginning with the starting month. However, when you enable compounding, the adjustment starts with the month after the Start At month. The reason is fairly simple. Since it's compounding, it must start out with a base number (the first month) and work its way up. Basically, it starts with zero added to the first month, one factor to the second, two factors to the third, and so on.

Run Budget Reports

It's not enough just to create budgets; you've got to keep an eye on how well you're sticking to those numbers. Fortunately, QuickBooks has a number of reports designed to do just that:

- Budget Overview
- Budget vs. Actual
- Profit & Loss Budget Performance
- Budget vs. Actual Graph

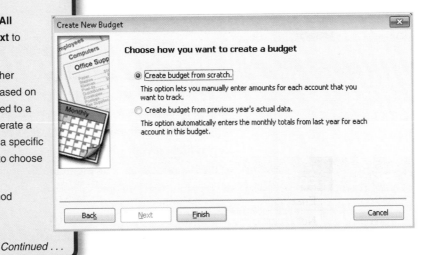

CREATING PROFIT AND LOSS BUDGETS WITH ADDITIONAL CRITERIA (Continued)

7. If you have data from the previous year that you want to use, select **Create Budget From Previous Year's Actual Data**; otherwise, leave the default selection of **Create Budget From Scratch**. For this exercise we're going to create the budget from scratch.

8. Click **Finish** to open the Set Up Budgets window with a blank Profit And Loss By Account And Customer:Job budget for the fiscal year you set (see Figure A-2).

9. From the **Current Customer:Job** drop-down list, select the customer or job for whom you want to create the budget.

10. Enter the monthly amounts for the appropriate accounts and months.

As you can see in Figure A-2, the only difference between a plain Profit And Loss budget and a Customer:Job Profit And Loss budget is the addition of the Current Customer:Job field. Everything else is identical. While you can still only create one Profit And Loss budget per year, it's now one per year, per customer or job. You can create one after the other without restarting the Create New Budget wizard. When you're done with one, save it and select another customer or job from the Current Customer:Job drop-down list.

If you want to create a Profit And Loss budget by class, use the steps in this section and select **Class** from the additional criteria options. Everything else is the same.

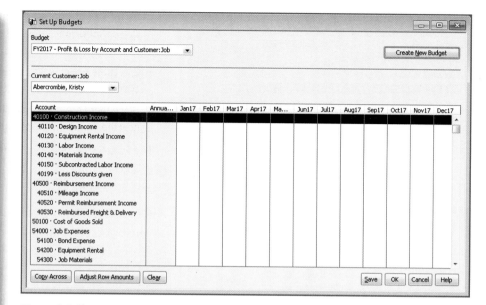

Figure A-2: *You can create a separate Profit And Loss budget for each customer or job.*

In the following sections we'll go over each report to see how it functions and the various options it offers.

Budget Overview Report

I can't say it much plainer than the title. It's an overview of your existing budget. After you create a budget and want to take a look at what you've projected for the period budgeted, run this report. Exactly how it displays those numbers depends on the choices you make when you run the report. Depending on your preference, you can run reports either from the menu bar or the Report Center. The menu bar is quick and easy, but doesn't offer the descriptions and preview samples you'll find in the Report Center. For this example we'll use the menu bar.

The options you see when you run the Budget Overview report vary, depending on the type of budget you're running it for.

NOTE

If you try to open any of the budget reports without first creating at least one budget, QuickBooks lets you know you have to create one before you can run a report.

No Budgets Exist

⚠ You have not created any budgets to run reports on. Click Create New to create a new budget.

[Create New]   [Cancel]

BUDGET OVERVIEW REPORTS FOR BALANCE SHEET BUDGETS

1. Select **Reports | Budgets | Budget Overview** to open the Budget Report dialog box shown in Figure A-3.

2. Select the Balance Sheet budget you want to run the Budget Overview report for, and click **Next**.

3. Since there are no more options, the next screen merely provides a small example of how the report will be laid out. Click **Finish** to generate the report.

The Balance Sheet report has the fewest of any options for running the report. However, you can customize the report by using the **Customize Report** button at the top of the report.

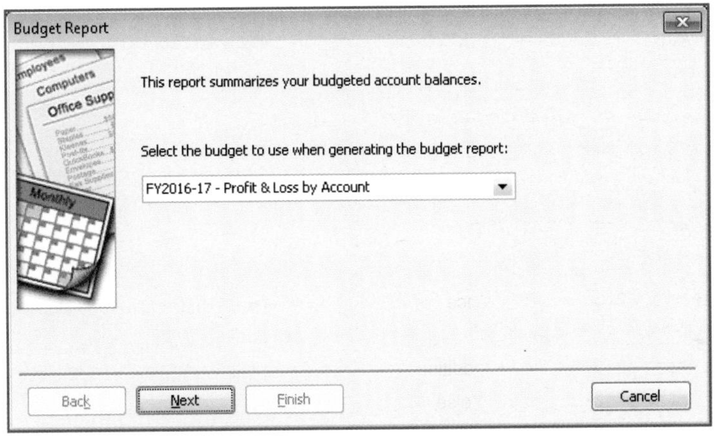

Budget Report

This report summarizes your budgeted account balances.

Select the budget to use when generating the budget report:

FY2016-17 - Profit & Loss by Account ▼

[Back] [Next] [Finish]   [Cancel]

Figure A-3: *Opening budget reports is a little more complex than opening other report types.*

BUDGET OVERVIEW REPORT FOR PROFIT & LOSS BUDGETS BY ACCOUNT ONLY

In reality, creating an overview report for Profit And Loss budgets by account is not much different from creating a Balance Sheet Overview report. There's an added step, but since it offers only one option, it's not of much use.

1. Select **Reports | Budgets | Budget Overview** from the menu bar to launch the Budget Report wizard.

2. From the drop-down list, choose the Profit & Loss By Account budget that you want to report on.

3. Click **Next** to view the layout options. Unfortunately, the layout options for the Profit & Loss Budget Overview report are limited to one layout, so you don't have a choice to make.

4. Since there's only one option on the drop-down list, you might as well click **Next**. Look if you must, but then click **Next**.

5. On the last screen, click **Finish** to generate the Budget Overview report for the Profit And Loss By Account budget.

If you created a budget using last year's figures and don't see some numbers you expected to see, it might be because the accounts are marked "Inactive." To see both "Active" and "Inactive" accounts, open the Modify Report dialog box (click the **Customize Report** button in the top-left corner), and click the **Advanced** button to open the Advanced Options dialog box.

In the Display Rows section, select **All**. You can select **All** in the Display Columns section also, but it's not really necessary. While you're here, you might also want to check the **Show Only Rows And Columns With Budgets** option to eliminate accounts on the report for which no amounts were entered.

RUN THE BUDGET OVERVIEW REPORT FOR PROFIT & LOSS BY CUSTOMER:JOB BUDGETS

When planning for an upcoming customer project, the Budget Overview report can be used to make sure the project is staying on budget. To make it even more useful, you have the option of choosing among several different layouts.

1. Use the **Budget Overview** command from the Reports I Budgets submenu to open the Budget Report wizard.

UICKSTEPS

EXPORTING YOUR BUDGETS

Whether you want to share your budgets, play "what if?" by manipulating the numbers, or create multiple budgets for the same year, the solution is simple: export the numbers. You can export budget information in one of two ways:

- Export the Budget Overview report to Microsoft Excel or a comma-delimited file (.csv). Most spreadsheet, database, and word-processing programs will import comma-delimited files. This is ideal for exporting a single budget.

- Export all your budgets to an IIF file using the QuickBooks export utility. IIF files are tab-delimited files that can be imported into most spreadsheet, database, and word-processing applications. However, the most common use for this method is sharing budgets with other QuickBooks users.

Exporting the Budget Overview report is simple enough. Select **Reports | Budgets | Budget Overview** to start the Budget Report wizard. Make the appropriate selections to run the report of your choice. Then click the **Customize Report** button, and make any necessary changes using the Modify Report dialog box. When you're satisfied with the report, click the **Excel** button at the top of the report and decide whether you want to export the report to a new Excel worksheet or an existing Excel worksheet. Choose the options for the export, and click the **Export** button to launch Microsoft Excel with the exported figures or to create the comma-delimited file.

When you want to export all of your existing budgets at one time, use the export utility. Select **File | Utilities | Export | Lists To IIF Files** to display the Export dialog box. Check the **Budgets** listing, and click **OK** to open a different Export dialog box. Indicate where you want the .iif file to be saved. After you give the file a name and click **Save**, QuickBooks informs you that the export has been successful. You can now import all the budgets into another application or use the QuickBooks import utility to bring them back into QuickBooks.

2. Select the Profit And Loss By Account And Customer:Job budget for which you want to create the report.

3. Click **Next** to view the layout options.

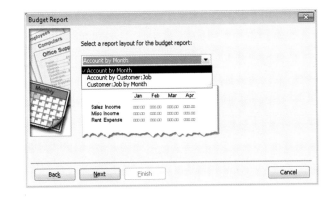

4. Choose a layout from the Select A Report Layout For The Budget Report drop-down list:

- **Account By Month**   This is the standard layout in which each account appears with budget totals for every month. No customer data is presented.

- **Account By Customer:Job**   Use this layout to view a listing of all accounts with totals for each customer. The accounts are the rows, and customer totals are the columns.

- **Customer:Job By Month**   To view the totals by customer, choose this layout. The customers appear in the rows, and the totals appear in the columns.

You'll notice that the layout name is actually an explanation of how each layout is organized. The first word represents the rows, and the word following the "By" represents the columns.

GENERATE THE BUDGET OVERVIEW REPORT FOR PROFIT & LOSS BY CLASS BUDGETS

To run the Budget Overview Report for Profit & Loss By Class Budgets, return to the previous section, and substitute "Class" for "Customer:Job." The layouts work exactly the same for both budget types.

QUICKSTEPS

IMPORTING BUDGETS INTO QUICKBOOKS

Whether you're importing a budget that you sent to Excel and modified, or you're importing an entire series of budgets exported by another QuickBooks user, the process is almost the same. The only difference is in the preparation of the import file. To import a file from Excel, you must first save it in Excel as a tab-delimited file and then change the .txt extension to .iif.

Importing an .iif file into QuickBooks is easy.

1. Select **File | Utilities | Import | IIF Files** to display the Import dialog box.

2. Locate the .iif file that you want to import.

3. Click **Open** to import the data. QuickBooks displays a dialog confirming that your data has been imported.

4. Click **OK** to return to work in QuickBooks.

You can now view the budget information either in the budget tool or in a budget report.

NOTE

While QuickBooks does offer an Excel import utility, it cannot be used for budgets. It is only for importing customer, vendor, and inventory item records. Therefore, do not attempt to use the import Excel utility found on the Utilities submenu for importing budgets from Microsoft Excel.

RUN MORE BUDGET REPORTS

In addition to the Budget Overview report, QuickBooks provides several more budget-related reports you can run:

- **Budget vs. Actual**   When you want to see how good your budgeting skills are, run this report. As the name says, it compares your budget numbers to the real numbers. For each account it displays the amount posted, the amount budgeted, and the difference in dollars and in percent. The layout choices for the Budget vs. Actual report are the same as those for the Budget Overview reports for Customer:Job and Class.

- **Profit & Loss Budget Performance**   This is another report comparing the budget to reality. However, it only uses the current month and the year-to-date numbers.

- **Budget vs. Actual Graph**   For those times when a graphical representation is needed, the Budget vs. Actual Graph is ideal. It opens automatically and offers a number of options for choosing the date range, budget type, and group to use.

Numbers

1096 Information dialog box, 155
1099 Contractors option, choosing, 9
1099 e-file service, using, 153
1099 forms, 151–155
1099 Reports, 109, 150–155
1099 tracking, configuring, 151
1099 vendors, configuring, 151
1099 Wizard, running, 151–153

A

access, restricting, 194–195
account numbering, turning on, 46–48
account register, 30–32. *See also* bank accounts
Account Type field, 47
accountants
    importing changes from, 186–187
    talking to, 2–3
Accountant's Copy, 184–186
accounting basis, accrual vs. cash, 166
accounts, creating and managing, 47–49
Accounts Payable Graph report, 108
Accounts Receivable Graph report, 90
Accrual option, selecting, 166
Add/Edit Multiple List Entries, 50–52, 117–118
addresses, exporting to text files, 189
Advanced Setup, using, 4–10
Aging Reports option, 161
alias, assigning to transactions, 42–43
A/P Aging Reports, 108
A/R Aging Detail report, 88
A/R Aging Summary report, 88
As Of item fields, 55
Asset Account items, 55
assets, tracking, 57–58
Average Days To Pay report, 90
award compensation, entering in payroll, 133

B

backing up data, 176–179
Balance Sheet budget, 212, 219. *See also* budgets
balance sheets report, 162–163

bank accounts. *See also* account register
    adding, 14–15, 30–31
    opening balance, 31
    reconciling, 33–37
    routing numbers, 30
    saving, 31
    Tax-Line Mapping field, 30
banking reports, running, 43–44
Banking section, Home page, 17–18
batch invoicing, 77–80
benefits, paying, 9
Bill Due field, calculating, 99
Bill Pay online banking, 38
bill tracking screen, displaying, 8
billable items, unpaid, 71
billing statements, turning on, 7–8
bills. *See also* invoices
    adding reminders to, 103
    applying credits to, 98
    applying discounts to, 98, 104
    assigning to accounts, 99
    avoiding duplicate numbers, 98
    displaying, 104
    entering, 98–99, 101
    entering for received items, 101
    entering notes about, 98
    entering recurring, 103–104
    Memo field, 98
    paying upon arrival, 105–107
    paying with credit cards, 106–107
    reviewing and paying, 103–105
    selecting for payment, 105
    setting preferences for, 98
    sorting, 104
    Write Checks window, 105
bonus compensation, entering in payroll, 133
bounced check item, creating, 32
Budget Overview reports, 218–221
budget reports, running, 217–222
Budget vs. Actual Graph reports, 222
budgets
    activating accounts, 212
    adding accounts, 212
    Balance Sheet, 212
    exporting, 221
    first month, 212

importing, 222
Profit and Loss, 211

C

Calendar, 21–23
Cash option, selecting, 166
CDs, using to back up data, 177
charitable organizations, giveaways for, 126
Chart of Accounts, 9–10, 46–47
Check Detail reports, running, 43
check numbers, adding for bank accounts, 31
checkbook. *See* account register
checks
    ordering, 31
    printing, 106
    writing for bills, 105
classes
    creating, 55–56
    enabling, 53–54
    subclasses, 55–56
COGS accounts, 54, 113
Collections Center, 86–87
Collections Report, 90
commands, adding, 199
commission, entering in payroll, 133
Community links, accessing, 23
companies
    creating, 3
    fiscal year, 5
company file
    copying prior to importing, 188
    creating, 6, 181
    removing transactions from, 183
Company Preferences tab, 43
Company section, Home page, 17–18
Company Snapshot, 19–21
compensation, entering in payroll, 133
Condense Data utility, 182–184
conversion utility, accessing, 16
Copy Across feature, using with budgets, 215
Cost items, 54
Create Invoices window, 74–76
credit, selling on, 56–57
Credit Card Charges window, opening, 106
credit card information, retaining, 67

credit cards
    paying bills with, 106–107
    protecting, 194–195
credit memos, 81–83
credits
    applying to bills, 98
    applying to payments, 87
    creating for damaged inventory, 128
    entering, 101–102
CTRL key. *See* keyboard shortcuts
Currency List, 62, 200–201
Customer & Vendor Profile Lists, 56–57
Customer Balance reports, 89
Customer Center, 64–66
Customer Contact List report, 90
Customer Message List, 57
Customer Phone List report, 90
Customer Type List, 56
customers. *See also* Sales & Customers preferences
    adding, 11–14, 16, 65–66
    adding notes for, 64
    avoiding multiple entries, 66
    batch invoicing, 77–80
    credit card information, 67
    editing, 16
    making inactive, 66
    merging, 65–66
    modifying notes for, 64
    naming, 65
    removing, 66
    selecting, 64
    sorting names of, 67
    viewing transactions, 16
Customers & Jobs list, 64–65
Customers & Receivables reports, viewing, 88–90
Customers section, Home page, 17–18
Customize Columns dialog box, 117–118

D

data
    backing up, 176–178
    condensing, 182–184
    preparing for rebuilding of, 182
    rebuilding, 181–182

data security, 194–195
data verification utility, running, 179
decimal point, setting preferences for, 26
deduction items, entering for employees, 137
deleting employees, 140–141
Deposit Detail reports, running, 43
deposit slips, printing, 32
deposits, making, 32–33
Description On Purchase Transactions items, 54
Description on Sales Transactions items, 54
Desktop View options, setting, 27–28
Direct Connect, 38–40
Discount items, 53
discounts
    applying to bills, 98, 104
    applying to invoices, 76
    discounts, 87
Discrepancy Report, 34–37
discs, rewritable, 177
Doc Center, 190–193
drop-down lists, setting preferences for, 25
DVDs, using to back up data, 177

E

EasySaver feature, 115–116
EasyStep Interview, using, 4–10
editing records, 118
e-mail defaults, setting, 202–203
Employee Center, 135, 139, 140
employee types, 135, 143–144
employees
    adding, 11–14, 140–141
    addition items, 137
    assigning to payroll schedules, 147
    columns, 142
    deduction items, 137
    default information, 143–144
    deleting, 140–141
    editing, 140–141
    payroll schedules, 137
    preferences, 141
    setting up, 135–138
    sorting transactions for, 141

    viewing transactions for, 141–142
    wage items, 137
Employees section, Home page, 17–18
Enter Bills window, opening, 103
ENTER key, setting preferences for, 25
estimates screen, viewing, 7
Excel, pasting from, 14
Excel files, importing, 186–188
exchange rates, downloading, 62
expenses, tracking, 98–99
Expenses tab, using with bills, 99–100
exporting
    addresses to text files, 189
    budgets, 221
    lists to IIF files, 189–190
    report data, 172–174
    Timer lists, 190
Express installation, performing, 3
Express Start wizard, using, 3–4

F

F1 key, pressing, 23. *See also* keyboard shortcuts
Favorites menu, adding, 197–199
fields
    changing titles of, 206
    customizing, 116–118
    hiding in Preview pane, 206
    printing on forms, 206
    Screen status, 206
file names. *See* Renaming Rules
finance charges, assessing, 82–83
financial info, gathering, 2
Find field, searching with, 64
fiscal year, choosing, 5, 10
Fixed Asset Item List, 57–58
Flat view, 64
FOB: Free On Board, 72
Form 1099. *See* 1099 forms
form actions, 209
form elements, 207–208
forms
    adding logos to, 204
    customizing, 207
    printing fields on, 206

G

Getting Started section, Home page, 17–18
giveaways, tracking, 125–127
GJE (General Journal Entry), using with
    giveaways, 126
Gmail, configuring, 14, 203–204
Group items, 52

H

help system 23–24
Help tab, 132
Hierarchical View, 64
Home page, 17–18
Hotmail, configuring, 203–204
hourly wage, entering in payroll, 133
How To links, accessing, 23

I

Icon Bar
    accessing help from, 24
    Add Separator button, 20
    adding icons to, 19
    adding Name List icon to, 183
    customizing, 19–20, 24
    fitting icons on, 20
    grouping icons, 20
    modifying icons, 19
    moving icons, 20
    removing icons from, 19
    Search box in, 20
    using, 18
IIF (Intuit Interchange Format) files
    exporting lists to, 189–190
    importing, 188
    using, 190–191
.iif files, importing, 222
importing
    budgets, 222
    Excel files, 186–188
    IIF files, 188
    Timer activities, 188–189
    Web Connect files, 188

Income Account items, 55
income tax year, choosing, 5
indented view, returning to, 64
industry type, choosing, 5
installing QuickBooks, 3
Intuit Community, accessing, 23–24
inventory. *See also* Physical Inventory Worksheet
    accounts, 114
    adjusting quantity, 123–124
    adjusting value, 124–125
    adjustments, 114–115
    EasySaver feature, 115–116
    managing damaged, 127–128
    parts, 114–115
    Pending Builds report, 128
    preferences, 112–113
    reports, 127–128
    Stock Status reports, 127
    tracking, 112, 114–116
    tracking giveaways, 125–127
    Valuation Detail report, 127
    Valuation Summary report, 127
inventory count, preparing for, 121
inventory items
    adding, 112–114
    calculating sales prices, 115
    COGS accounts, 113
    customizing fields for, 116–117
    Markup function, 115
    purchase orders, 115
    removing, 128
    subitems, 114–115
inventory loss, reason for, 123
Inventory Part items, 52, 113
inventory tracking screen, displaying, 8–9
inventory worksheet, accessing, 119
invoice numbers, avoiding duplicates, 72
invoice packing slips, template for, 72
invoices. *See also* bills; Open Invoices report
    changing customer information, 76
    creating, 16
    discounts, 76
    generating, 74–76
    memorizing, 76–77
    preparing batches of, 77–80

receiving payments for, 85
using credit memos with, 81
viewing for payments, 87
zero-based, 125
invoicing, enabling, 8
item fields, 54–55
Item List, 52–54, 112
Item Price List report, 90
item types, 52–54
items
    adding, 54–55
    receiving, 100–101

J

Job options, 68–69
Job Type List, 56
jobs, creating, 67–70
journal entry window, opening, 126

K

keyboard shortcuts
    account register, 30
    bank accounts, 30
    Chart of Accounts, 47
    Choose Account Type, 30
    Collections Center, 86
    Customer Center, 64–65
    F1 key, 23
    Help tab, 132
    inventory, 112
    invoices, 74
    Memorize Transaction dialog box, 77
    New Class dialog box, 55
    New Currency dialog box, 62
    New Customer dialog box, 65
    New Item dialog box, 32, 54
    New Price Level dialog box, 59
    Save As dialog box, 187
    transaction journals, 126
    Use Register dialog box, 31, 37
    vendors, 96
    Write Checks window, 105

L

Layout Designer, 207–210. *See also* templates
list data, entering quickly, 49–52
list items
    deleting, 56–57
    entering, 49, 55
    modifying, 56–57
lists, exporting to IIF files, 189–190
logos, adding to forms, 204

M

Make Deposits window, using, 33–34
Memorize Report dialog box, 122
Memorize Transaction dialog box, 77
memorizing
    invoices, 76–77
    reports, 171–173
menus of commands, adding, 199
messages, setting preferences for, 26
Missing Checks reports, running, 43
Multiple Currencies feature, 62
My Preferences tab, 43–44, 198

N

name information, configuring, 27
Name List icon, adding to Icon Bar, 183
New Item dialog box, opening, 32
Non-inventory Part items, 52
non-inventory parts, 114
notes
    adding for customers, 64
    including on bills, 98
    modifying for customers, 64
numbered accounts, using, 46–47

O

objects. *See* form actions
On Hand field, 116
Online Banking Center, 38–40
online preferences, setting, 43–44
Open Invoices report, 90. *See also* invoices

Open Window List, displaying, 19
opening balances
    adding, 13, 31
    determining, 49
Other Charge items, 52
Outlook, importing from, 12–13
overtime, entering in payroll, 133

P

P&L report, 162
packing slips, receiving, 100–101
passwords, 6, 193–195
Pay Bills window, opening, 103
Pay Stub & Voucher Printing preference, 139
paychecks, 146, 148–149
Payment items, 53
Payment Method List, 57
Payment Toolbar, showing and hiding, 71
payments
    calculating, 71
    credits, 87
    discounts, 87
    invoicing, 72
    receiving, 71–72, 85–87
    sales orders, 72
    types, 86–87
    undeposited funds, 72
    viewing invoices, 87
Payments To Deposit window, 33
payroll, 130–131
    activating manually, 132
    employee types, 135
    liabilities payment options, 149–150
    running, 147–149
    salary information, 133–134
    termination checks, 148
    wage information, 133–134
Payroll Item List, 60–61
payroll items
    creating, 61, 133–134
    managing, 131
payroll preferences, 138–140
payroll preparation, 130–131
payroll reports, running, 150
payroll schedules, 137, 146–147

payroll services, 129–130
Payroll Setup wizard
    limitations, 138
    running, 131–132
PCI DSS (Payment Card Industry Data Security Standard), 194
Pending Builds report, 128
Physical Inventory Worksheet, 119–123, 127. *See also* inventory
piecework, entering in payroll, 133–134
preferences
    Company Preferences tab, 198–199
    configuring, 25–27
    date for transactions, 26
    decimal point, 26
    drop-down lists, 25
    ENTER key, 25
    General category, 25–27
    messages, 26
    My Preferences tab, 198
    name information, 27
    online features, 43–44
    recalling information, 26
    Time Format option, 27
    ToolTips, 26
    transactions, 25–27
    year format, 27
Preferences dialog box, 24
Previous Reconciliation reports, running, 44
price levels, 58–60
prices, saving on, 115–116
printing
    1099 forms, 154–155
    checks, 106
    deposit slips, 32
products, adding, 14–15
Profit And Loss budgets
    Adjust Row Amounts button, 215–216
    Budget Overview reports for, 219–221
    Copy Across feature, 215
    creating, 212–214, 217–218
    Enable Compounding option, 216
    explained, 211
    Set Up Budgets window, 214–215
purchase orders, 115, 119–120
purchase reports, running, 109

Q

Quick Start Center, 15–16
QuickBooks
    Enterprise version, 2
    Home page, 17–18
    installing, 3
    interface, 16
    Premier version, 2
    Pro version, 2
    Setup dialog box, 3–4
    versions, 2
QuickBooks Setup wizard
    bank accounts, 14–15
    customers, 11–14
    employees, 11–14
    importing from Outlook, 12–13
    importing from Web mail, 14
    launching, 11
    pasting from Excel, 14
    products, 14–15
    services, 14–15
    vendors, 11–14

R

Rebuild Data utility, 181–182
receivables. *See* Customers & Receivables reports
Reconcile Adjustment window, displaying, 36
Reconcile window, displaying, 35
Reconciliation Discrepancy feature, 37, 44
reconciliations, undoing, 37
reconciling bank accounts, 33–37
records, editing, 118
register. *See* account register
reminders
    adding to bills, 103
    configuring, 199–200
Renaming Rules, 42–43
Reorder Point items, 55
Report Center, 88–89
    Accounts Receivable Graph report, 90
    A/R Aging Detail report, 88
    A/R Aging Summary report, 88
    Average Days To Pay report, 90
    Carousel View, 159

categories, 158–159
Collections Report, 90
Contributed tab, 161
Customer Balance Detail report, 89
Customer Balance Summary report, 89
Customer Contact List report, 90
Customer Phone List report, 90
date ranges, 158
Favorites tab, 158, 161
Grid View, 158–160
help, 158
hiding panes, 158
Item Price List report, 90
List View, 159
listing reports in, 158
Memorized tab, 160–161
Open Invoices report, 90
opening, 157
Recent tab, 161
search box, 159
Standard tab, 160
Transaction List by Customer report, 90
Unbilled Costs by Job report, 90
viewing reports in, 158
report data, exporting, 172–174
reports
    Aging Reports, 161
    balance sheets, 162–163
    banking, 43–44
    Customers & Receivables, 88–90
    data display, 165–167
    detail, 165–167
    discrepancies, 34
    filtering, 163–165
    Fonts & Numbers tab, 170–171
    Graphs Only option, 161
    Header/Footer tab, 167–169
    Hide Header button, 164
    increasing viewing space, 164
    inventory, 127–128
    memorizing, 171–173
    Modify Report dialog box, 164–165
    P&L, 162
    preferences, 160–162
    purchases, 109
    Revert button, 170–171

    running multiple, 172–173
    sales, 91–92
    statement of cash flows, 163
    summary, 167–168
    Summary Reports Basis, 161
    Trial Balance, 163
    Vendors & Payables, 108–109
Reports menu, 162
restoring backups, 180
routing numbers, adding, 30

S

Sales & Customers preferences, 71–72. *See also* customers
Sales Price items, 54
sales receipts
    creating, 16
    entering, 80
    using, 79–81
    zero-based, 125
Sales Rep List, 56
sales reports, 88, 91–92
Sales Tax Code List, 58–61
sales tax, configuring, 73–74
Sales Tax items, 53
Sales Tax Liability report, 109
Sales Tax Revenue Summary, 109
Sales Tax screen, displaying, 7
sales tax vs. use tax, 107–108
Save As dialog box, 187
searches
    amount filter, 25
    date range filters, 25
    with Find field, 64
    narrowing, 24
    viewing results, 25
security, 194–195
service charges, defined, 35
Service items, 52
services, adding, 14–15
Setup dialog box, displaying, 3–4
Ship Via List, 57
Sick and Vacation preference, 139
software, converting from, 16
spell-checking options, setting, 201–202

Splits button, 31
start date, choosing, 3
statement of cash flows report, 163
statements
    adding charges, 81–82
    assessed finance charges, 85
    customers, 84
    E-mail button, 85
    finance charges, 82–83
    PDF (Portable Document Format), 85
    printing options, 84
    reviewing, 85
    sending, 81–85
    sending to printer, 85
    templates, 84
    transactions, 84
    turning on, 7–8
subaccounts, 47–49
subclasses, creating, 55–56
subitems
    creating, 53
    inventory items, 114–115
Subtotal items, 52
summary reports, 167–168

T

Tax Code items, 55
tax lines, determining, 49
taxes, withholding, 9. *See also* sales tax; use tax
Tax-Line Mapping field, 30, 48
templates. *See also* Layout Designer
    copying, 205
    creating, 204
    customizing, 203–207
    fonts, 205
    managing, 205
    renaming, 205
termination checks, creating, 148
Terms List, 56
time data, using for paychecks, 146
Time Format option, accessing, 27
time tracking, turning on, 9, 143

Timer activities, importing, 188–189
Timer lists, exporting, 190
timesheets
    batch, 146
    recording single activities, 144–145
    using, 143–145
    weekly, 145
tips, entering in payroll, 133
to-do items, adding to Calendar, 23
toolbar. *See* Icon Bar
ToolTips, setting preferences for, 26
Total Value items, 55
transaction journal, viewing, 71, 126
transactions
    displaying status of, 21–22
    downloaded, 40–42
    editing, 71
    entering in account register, 30–32
    matched, 40–41
    matching, 42–43
    removing from company file, 183
    Renaming Rules, 42–43
    saving before printing, 27
    setting preferences for, 25–27
    splitting, 31
    unmatched, 41–42
    viewing for employees, 141–142
    zero-based, 126
transactions lists, 64, 90, 109
Transactions tab, 70–71
Trial Balance report, 163
Troubleshooting links, accessing, 23

U

Unbilled Costs by Job report, 90
Undo Last Reconciliation feature, 37
Unpaid Bills Detail report, 108
USB flash drive, using to back up data, 177
Use Register dialog box, 37
use tax, 107–109
User List dialog box, opening, 194

V

vacation preference, 139
Vehicle List, 57
Vendor Balance Reports, 108
Vendor Center, 93, 95
Vendor Lists report, 109
Vendor Type List, 56
vendors. *See also* Customer & Vendor Profile Lists
    adding, 11–14, 96–98
    adding columns, 96
    displaying columns, 96
    filtering lists of, 94
    moving columns, 96
    removing columns, 96
    sorting listings of, 96
    tracking for 1099s, 150–155
    viewing transactions for, 95
Vendors & Payables reports, 108–109
Vendors section, Home page, 17–18
Vendors tab, expanding, 96
ViewMyPaycheck preference, 139
views
    Flat, 64
    Hierarchical, 64
    indented, 64

W

W-2 employees option, choosing, 9
wage items, entering for employees, 137
Web Connect, 38–40, 188
Web mail, 14, 203–204
weekly timesheet, using, 145
windows, displaying, 19
workers. *See* employees
Workers' Compensation preference, 139
worksheets, accessing, 119
Write Checks window, opening, 105

Y

Yahoo! mail, 14, 203–204
year format, configuring, 27